NATIONAL GEOGRAPHIC LEARNING | CENGAGE Learning

Exploring Science

Focus on the ▶ NEXT GENERATION SCIENCE STANDARDS
For States, By States

Program Authors

Randy L. Bell, Ph.D.
Malcolm B. Butler, Ph.D.
Kathy Cabe Trundle, Ph.D.
Judith S. Lederman, Ph.D.

Program Consultants

Gina Cervetti, Ph.D.
Nell K. Duke, Ed.D.
Philip E. Molebash, Ph.D.

W9-BFR-117

Contents

Physical Science

Life Science

Interdependent Relationships in Ecosystems

Earth Science

Master the Next Generation Science Standards

Exploring Science provides expert instruction for the Next Generation Science Standards (NGSS). Implement the NGSS with confidence and ensure that your students master 21st century science skills. Combine instruction in Science and Engineering Practices, Disciplinary Core Ideas, and Crosscutting Concepts to meet the rigor of the Performance Expectations within the NGSS.

- Focus on 100% of the NGSS for grades K–5
- Introduce real-world science research with National Geographic Explorers, scientists, and photographers
- Connect NGSS content with investigations, engineering practices, and case studies for complete NGSS immersion

Grade K

Grade 1

Grade 2

Engage with print or eBook formats; both are available in English and Spanish to meet dual language needs.

Exploring Science for Kindergarten has three Big Books for Life, Earth, and Physical Science for whole class instruction of 100% of the NGSS. For grades 1-5, target 100% of the NGSS for Life, Earth, Physical Science, and Engineering Practices in one student book.

Grade 3

Grade 4

Grade 5

Student Support

Students receive all of the resources needed to gain a thorough understanding of NGSS concepts and practices. National Geographic visuals and engaging content capture student interest while reinforcing their understanding of the NGSS.

Print books and eBooks are available in English and Spanish.

Grade 2 Student Book

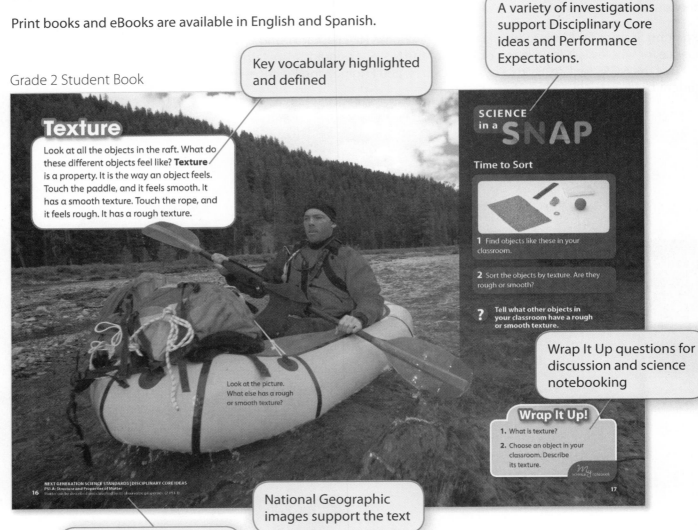

Key vocabulary highlighted and defined

A variety of investigations support Disciplinary Core ideas and Performance Expectations.

Wrap It Up questions for discussion and science notebooking

National Geographic images support the text

NGSS printed on the page

Support Disciplinary Core Ideas and Meet Performance Expectations

Hands-on activities provide support for Disciplinary Core Ideas and Performance Expectations within the NGSS. Investigate and Science in a Snap features offer opportunities for hands-on experiences to reinforce science concepts.

In the program, students are introduced to National Geographic Explorers and scientists who solve real-world problems. In Think Like a Scientist and Think Like an Engineer features, students meet Performance Expectations in ways such as making observations, designing solutions, planning and conducting investigations, making and using models, analyzing and interpreting data, and constructing arguments.

Teacher Support

Disciplinary Core Ideas and Performance Expectations are addressed thoroughly and concisely within the student books. The standard being taught is displayed on the page for clarity and simplicity

Teacher's Guides for each grade provide the support needed to implement and assess the NGSS. Master the NGSS Performance Expectations with lessons that are based on the 5E model of Engage, Explore, Explain, Elaborate and Evaluate.

Grade 1 Teacher's Guide

NGSS and Objectives

Student Science Notebook opportunities

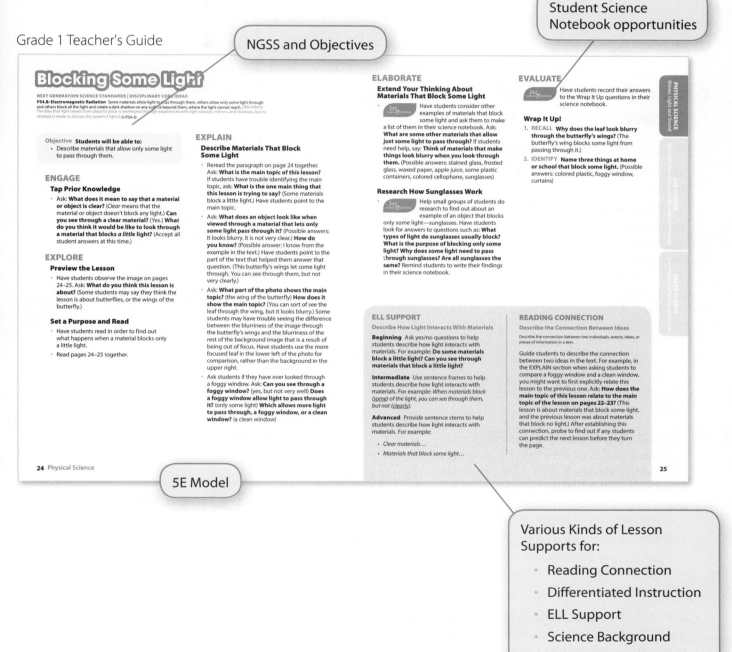

Blocking Some Light

NEXT GENERATION SCIENCE STANDARDS | DISCIPLINARY CORE IDEAS

PS4.B: Electromagnetic Radiation Some materials allow light to pass through them, others allow only some light through and others block all the light and create a dark shadow on any surface beyond them, where the light cannot reach. [(Boundary: The idea that light travels from place to place is developed through experiences with light sources, mirrors, and shadows, but no attempt is made to discuss the speed of light.)] (1-PS4-3)

Objective Students will be able to:
• Describe materials that allow only some light to pass through them.

ENGAGE

Tap Prior Knowledge
• Ask: **What does it mean to say that a material or object is clear?** (*Clear* means that the material or object doesn't block any light.) **Can you see through a clear material?** (Yes.) **What do you think it would be like to look through a material that blocks *a little* light?** (Accept all student answers at this time.)

EXPLORE

Preview the Lesson
• Have students observe the image on pages 24–25. Ask: **What do you think this lesson is about?** (Some students may say they think the lesson is about butterflies, or the wings of the butterfly.)

Set a Purpose and Read
• Have students read in order to find out what happens when a material blocks only a little light.
• Read pages 24–25 together.

EXPLAIN

Describe Materials That Block Some Light
• Reread the paragraph on page 24 together. Ask: **What is the main topic of this lesson?** If students have trouble identifying the main topic, ask: **What is the one main thing that this lesson is trying to say?** (Some materials block a little light.) Have students point to the main topic.
• Ask: **What does an object look like when viewed through a material that lets only some light pass through it?** (Possible answers: It looks blurry. It is not very clear.) **How do you know?** (Possible answer: I know from the example in the text.) Have students point to the part of the text that helped them answer that question. (This butterfly's wings let some light through. You can see through them, but not very clearly.)
• Ask: **What part of the photo shows the main topic?** (the wing of the butterfly) **How does it show the main topic?** (You can sort of see the leaf through the wing, but it looks blurry.) Some students may have trouble seeing the difference between the blurriness of the image through the butterfly's wings and the blurriness of the rest of the background image that is a result of being out of focus. Have students use the more focused leaf in the lower left of the photo for comparison, rather than the background in the upper right.
• Ask students if they have ever looked through a foggy window. Ask: **Can you see through a foggy window?** (yes, but not very well) **Does a foggy window allow light to pass through it?** (only some light) **Which allows more light to pass through, a foggy window, or a clean window?** (a clean window)

ELABORATE

Extend Your Thinking About Materials That Block Some Light
• Have students consider other examples of materials that block some light and ask them to make a list of them in their science notebook. Ask: **What are some other materials that allow just some light to pass through?** If students need help, say: **Think of materials that make things look blurry when you look through them.** (Possible answers: stained glass, frosted glass, waxed paper, apple juice, some plastic containers, colored cellophane, sunglasses)

Research How Sunglasses Work
• Help small groups of students do research to find out about an example of an object that blocks only some light—sunglasses. Have students look for answers to questions such as: **What types of light do sunglasses usually block? What is the purpose of blocking only some light? Why does some light need to pass through sunglasses? Are all sunglasses the same?** Remind students to write their findings in their science notebook.

EVALUATE

Have students record their answers to the Wrap It Up questions in their science notebook.

Wrap It Up!
1. RECALL **Why does the leaf look blurry through the butterfly's wings?** (The butterfly's wing blocks some light from passing through it.)
2. IDENTIFY **Name three things at home or school that block some light.** (Possible answers: colored plastic, foggy window, curtains)

ELL SUPPORT
Describe How Light Interacts With Materials

Beginning Ask yes/no questions to help students describe how light interacts with materials. For example: **Do some materials block a little light? Can you see through materials that block a little light?**

Intermediate Use sentence frames to help students describe how light interacts with materials. For example: *When materials block (some) of the light, you can see through them, but not (clearly).*

Advanced Provide sentence stems to help students describe how light interacts with materials. For example:
• *Clear materials…*
• *Materials that block some light…*

READING CONNECTION
Describe the Connection Between Ideas

Describe the connection between two individuals, events, ideas, or pieces of information in a text.

Guide students to describe the connection between two ideas in the text. For example, in the EXPLAIN section when asking students to compare a foggy window and a clean window, you might want to first explicitly relate this lesson to the previous one. Ask: **How does the main topic of this lesson relate to the main topic of the lesson on pages 22–23?** (This lesson is about materials that block some light, and the previous lesson was about materials that block no light.) After establishing this connection, probe to find out if any students can predict the next lesson before they turn the page.

PHYSICAL SCIENCE
Waves: Light and Sound

24 Physical Science

25

5E Model

Various Kinds of Lesson Supports for:
• Reading Connection
• Differentiated Instruction
• ELL Support
• Science Background
• Teach with Technology

Physical Science

Grade 3. Forces and Interactions

Performance Expectations

Students who demonstrate understanding can:

3-PS2-1. Plan and conduct an investigation to provide evidence of the effects of balanced and unbalanced forces on the motion of an object. [Clarification Statement: Examples could include an unbalanced force on one side of a ball can make it start moving; and, balanced forces pushing on a box from both sides will not produce any motion at all.] [*Assessment Boundary: Assessment is limited to one variable at a time: number, size, or direction of forces. Assessment does not include quantitative force size, only qualitative and relative. Assessment is limited to gravity being addressed as a force that pulls objects down.*]

3-PS2-2. Make observations and/or measurements of an object's motion to provide evidence that a pattern can be used to predict future motion. [Clarification Statement: Examples of motion with a predictable pattern could include a child swinging in a swing, a ball rolling back and forth in a bowl, and two children on a see-saw.] [*Assessment Boundary: Assessment does not include technical terms such as period and frequency.*]

3-PS2-3. Ask questions to determine cause and effect relationships of electric or magnetic interactions between two objects not in contact with each other. [Clarification Statement: Examples of an electric force could include the force on hair from an electrically charged balloon and the electrical forces between a charged rod and pieces of paper; examples of a magnetic force could include the force between two permanent magnets, the force between an electromagnet and steel paperclips, and the force exerted by one magnet versus the force exerted by two magnets. Examples of cause and effect relationships could include how the distance between objects affects strength of the force and how the orientation of magnets affects the direction of the magnetic force.] [*Assessment Boundary: Assessment is limited to forces produced by objects that can be manipulated by students, and electrical interactions are limited to static electricity.*]

3-PS2-4. Define a simple design problem that can be solved by applying scientific ideas about magnets. [Clarification Statement: Examples of problems could include constructing a latch to keep a door shut and creating a device to keep two moving objects from touching each other.]

Disciplinary Core Ideas

PS2.A: Forces and Motion

- Each force acts on one particular object and has both strength and a direction. An object at rest typically has multiple forces acting on it, but they add to give zero net force on the object. Forces that do not sum to zero can cause changes in the object's speed or direction of motion. (Boundary: Qualitative and conceptual, but not quantitative addition of forces are used at this level.) (3-PS2-1)

- The patterns of an object's motion in various situations can be observed and measured; when that past motion exhibits a regular pattern, future motion can be predicted from it. (Boundary: Technical terms, such as magnitude, velocity, momentum, and vector quantity, are not introduced at this level, but the concept that some quantities need both size and direction to be described is developed.) (3-PS2-2)

PS2.B: Types of Interactions
- Objects in contact exert forces on each other. (3-PS2-1)
- Electric and magnetic forces between a pair of objects do not require that the objects be in contact. The sizes of the forces in each situation depend on the properties of the objects and their distances apart and, for forces between two magnets, on their orientation relative to each other. (3-PS2-3), (3-PS2-4)

Science and Engineering Practices
Planning and Carrying Out Investigations
Planning and carrying out investigations to answer questions or test solutions to problems in 3–5 builds on K–2 experiences and progresses to include investigations that control variables and provide evidence to support explanations or design solutions.
- Plan and conduct an investigation collaboratively to produce data to serve as the basis for evidence, using fair tests in which variables are controlled and the number of trials considered. (3-PS2-1)
- Make observations and/or measurements to produce data to serve as the basis for evidence for an explanation of a phenomenon or test a design solution. (3-PS2-2)

Asking Questions and Defining Problems
Asking questions and defining problems in grades 3–5 builds on grades K–2 experiences and progresses to specifying qualitative relationships.
- Ask questions that can be investigated based on patterns such as cause and effect relationships. (3-PS2-3)

- Define a simple problem that can be solved through the development of a new or improved object or tool. (3-PS2-4)

Connections to Nature of Science
Scientific Investigations Use a Variety of Methods
- Science investigations use a variety of methods, tools, and techniques. (3-PS2-1)

Science Knowledge is Based on Empirical Evidence
- Science findings are based on recognizing patterns. (3-PS2-2)

Connections to Engineering, Technology, and Applications of Science
Interdependence of Science, Engineering, and Technology
- Scientific discoveries about the natural world can often lead to new and improved technologies, which are developed through the engineering design process. (3-PS2-4)

Crosscutting Concepts
Cause and Effect
- Cause and effect relationships are routinely identified. (3-PS2-1)
- Cause and effect relationships are routinely identified, tested, and used to explain change. (3-PS2-3)

Patterns
- Patterns of change can be used to make predictions. (3-PS2-2)

Grades 3-5. Engineering Design

Performance Expectations

Students who can demonstrate understanding can:

3-5-ETS1-1. Define a simple design problem reflecting a need or a want that includes specified criteria for success and constraints on materials, time, or cost.

PHYSICAL SCIENCE
Forces and Interactions

LIFE SCIENCE
Structure, Function, and Information Processing

EARTH SCIENCE
Weather and Climate

Pushes and Pulls

NEXT GENERATION SCIENCE STANDARDS | DISCIPLINARY CORE IDEA
PS2.A: Forces and Motion Each force acts on one particular object and has both strength and a direction. (3-PS2-1)

Objectives Students will be able to:
- Define a force as a push or a pull on an object.
- Know that every force has a strength and direction.

Science Vocabulary
force

ENGAGE

Tap Prior Knowledge

- Ask students to recall a time when they pushed a shopping cart. Ask: **What made the cart move?** (Possible answer: My hands pushing on the handle made the cart move.) **In which direction did the cart move?** (Possible answer: The cart moved forward. It moved in the same direction as my push.) **How can you make a shopping cart turn?** (You can turn a shopping cart by pushing it more on one side than the other.) Have students put their hands out as if they were pushing a cart. Ask: **How can you turn a cart to the right?** (by pushing more with your left hand) **How can you turn a cart to the left?** (by pushing more with your right hand)

- Ask: **Have you ever had a shopping cart move "by itself"? What do you think was happening?** (Possible answers: If you push a cart and let go, it can continue moving for a little while. Another way a cart can move without being pushed by you is if the ground is sloped. In that case, the cart will roll downhill. Wind can also provide a push to make a cart move.) **Was the cart really moving "by itself"?** (No; something moved the cart in each case.)

EXPLORE

Explore Pushes and Pulls

- Have students observe the image on pages 4–5. Ask probing questions to encourage exploration. For example, ask: **How many people are working to move the wheelchair across the sand?** (six) **What are they doing to make it move?** (The people in front of the

wheelchair are pulling it and the people behind the wheelchair are pushing it.)

Set a Purpose and Read

- Have students read in order to find out how forces act on objects.
- Have students read pages 4–5.

EXPLAIN

Define a Force as a Push or a Pull

- Have a volunteer reread the second sentence on page 4 aloud. Ask: **What does** *apply* **mean here?** (To *apply* a force means to use force on an object. Some people also say *exert a force*.) **What is a force?** (A force is a push or pull acting on an object.)

- Ask: **Is there any way to move an object without using a force?** Discuss this with students. There is no way to cause an object to move without using a force of some kind. However, students may not recognize different types of forces. Consider a few examples, and identify the force in each case. For example, ask: **Can you think of something you can move without using a push or a pull?** Students may say blowing on a piece of paper can move the paper without using a force. Explain that when you blow, you are pushing on the air with your lungs and mouth and the air is pushing on the paper to move it. Students may say kicking a ball can move the ball without a force. However, when you kick a ball you are pushing it with your foot. Students may say that sucking juice through a straw moves it without using a force. But sucking through a straw pulls the juice up through the straw. So even in these examples, a push or pull is applied.

- Summarize by quoting the text: **Every time an object moves, a force is acting on it.** Ask a volunteer to read the last sentence on page 4. Then give students a few moments to think of their own examples of applying forces to make objects move. Ask a few volunteers to share their examples.

PHYSICAL SCIENCE
Forces and Interactions

LIFE SCIENCE
Structure, Function, and Information Processing

EARTH SCIENCE
Weather and Climate

Know That Every Force Has a Strength and Direction

- Ask a volunteer to reread the first sentence on page 5 aloud. Say: **Look at the man in front on page 5. What type of force is he applying?** (a pull) **What is the direction of the force he is applying?** Have students gesture the direction in which the force is applied. **Does he look like he is applying a weak force or a strong force? Explain.** (Possible answer: The man looks like he is applying a strong force. He is leaning forward and pulling hard on the rope attached to the wheelchair.)

ELABORATE

Extend Your Thinking About Pushes and Pulls

Ask students to look again at the man in front on page 5. Have them write in their notebook the ways the man could change the strength and direction of force he is applying to the straps. (He could increase the strength of the force by leaning forward and pulling even harder, or he could decrease the strength of the force by not pulling as hard. He could change the direction of the force by turning his body toward the right and pulling that way, or turning his body toward the left and pulling that way.)

EVALUATE

Have students record their answers to the Wrap It Up questions in their science notebook.

Wrap It Up!

1. **DEFINE   What is a force?** (A force is a push or a pull.)

2. **RELATE   How does the direction of a push relate to the direction that the object moves?** (The object moves in the same direction as the push.)

3. **INFER   Suppose more team members pushed and pulled the cart. How might the force the people apply to the cart change?** (Each individual would not need to apply as much force if more people were pushing.)

SCIENCE MISCONCEPTIONS

What Is a Force?

Many students may not realize that anything that causes an object to move, change direction, or stop moving is exerting a force on that object. Students may think of a push only as a slow, forward pressure they apply with their hands. But any force that works to move a particular object away can be thought of as a push; any force that works to draw a particular object closer can be thought of as a pull. Some forces are contact forces, meaning that the objects must be touching in order to exert force on one another, such as a hand pushing on a door, or wind rustling the leaves of a tree. Other forces can act at a distance, such as electric force, magnetic force, and gravity.

READING CONNECTION

Use Text Features

Use text features and search tools (e.g., key words, sidebars, hyperlinks) to locate information relevant to a given topic efficiently.

Guide students to use text features to locate information in the text efficiently. For example, in the EXPLORE section when asking students probing questions about the photo, guide them to use the caption as a source of information. In the EXPLAIN section when asking students to define *force,* guide them to locate the bold word on the page and recognize that it is treated with bold type because it is a key word to this topic. The bold type is a text feature that makes it easier to find the word at a glance or look back at it later. The meaning of bold words can be gathered from context clues in the sentence or sentences around the word and in the glossary.

Balanced Forces

NEXT GENERATION SCIENCE STANDARDS | DISCIPLINARY CORE IDEA
PS2.A: Forces and Motion Each force acts on one particular object and has both strength and a direction. An object at rest typically has multiple forces acting on it, but they add to give zero net force on the object. Forces that do not sum to zero can cause changes in the object's speed or direction of motion. (3-PS2-1)
PS2.B: Types of Interactions Objects in contact exert forces on each other. (3-PS2-1)

Objectives **Students will be able to:**
- Recognize that objects in contact exert forces on each other.
- Define balanced force and net force.

Science Vocabulary
balanced forces; net force

ENGAGE

Tap Prior Knowledge

- Remind students that forces are pushes and pulls. Forces change an object's motion. Ask: **What forces are acting on objects in this room?** (Accept all reasonable answers at this time. Students will most likely point out objects they see moving and identify the force that caused the motion. They may not yet realize that objects at rest also have forces acting on them.)

EXPLORE

Preview the Lesson

- Have students observe the photos on pages 6–7. Ask: **What do you think this lesson is about?** (Students may say they think the lesson is about how forces can be used to break boards. Guide students to think about how this lesson may relate to forces and motion.)

Set a Purpose and Read

- Have students read in order to find out how multiple forces act together on an object.
- Have students read page 6.

EXPLAIN

Identify the Effects of Forces on Objects

- Have students look at the small photo of the boards at rest. Ask: **What forces are acting on the boards in this photo?** (The pull of gravity and the pressure of the concrete blocks.) **In**

which direction do these forces act? (Gravity pulls the boards downward. The concrete blocks push the boards upward.) **How do the directions of these forces relate to each other?** (The forces act in opposite directions.) **How do the strengths of these forces compare? How do you know?** (The strengths are the same. The boards aren't moving. If gravity were stronger, the boards would be falling to the ground.)

- Ask: **Are there any forces acting on your body right now?** (Yes; gravity is pulling me downward.) **What else?** (The chair is applying a force in the direction opposite to gravity to hold me up.) Explain that gravity is a force that pulls one object toward another object. Earth's gravity pulls all objects toward the planet's center.

- Explain that while it might not seem like chairs, tables, and floors can exert forces, they can. To help students grasp this concept, ask a volunteer to come to the front of the class and hold up a heavy object, such as a textbook. Have the student describe what it feels like to hold the book up. The student should notice that he or she can feel his or her muscles working to hold the book up. Ask the volunteer: **How does the feeling of holding something up compare with the feeling of pushing on something?** (It feels similar.) The student will notice that he or she must continue exerting force as long as he or she is holding the book up, and that this gets harder and harder as muscles fatigue. Ask the class: **What forces are acting on the book?** (Gravity and the force of the student's hand.) **In which directions are the forces acting?** (in opposite directions) **With what amounts of strength?** (with equal amounts of strength as long as the book is not moving)

Define Balanced Forces and Net Force

- Ask: **Are forces acting on the book even when the book is still?** (Yes.) **How can forces act on an object without moving the object?** (An object at rest typically has multiple forces acting on it, but they add to produce zero net force on the object.) **What does the term** *net force* **mean?** (Net force is the overall force that results when all the forces acting on an object are added together.)

- Have students look again at the photos on pages 6–7. Ask: **What is the net force on the boards in the small photo?** (zero) **In which direction is the net force on the boards in the larger photo?** (downward)

Crosscutting Concepts, Cause and Effect
Explain that cause-and-effect relationships are routinely identified by scientists. Ask: **Do you think the boards would break if you dropped a quarter on them?** (No. The quarter would not apply enough force to break the board.)

ELABORATE

Extend Your Thinking About Balanced Forces

 Have students conduct the following simple activity with a partner to demonstrate balanced forces. Have students place their hand against their partners' hand, palms facing each other.

Ask both students to apply a gentle pressure at the same time. Have students adjust their amount of force to match their partner's so that both students are using the same amount of force in opposite directions. Once the forces are balanced, the students' hands will not move. Have students describe their experiences in their science notebook.

EVALUATE

Have students record their answers to the Wrap It Up questions in their science notebook.

Wrap It Up!

1. **CAUSE AND EFFECT What caused the boards to move?** (Possible answer: The hand applied a force to the top board that caused the net force to no longer equal zero. This resulted in a downward force that caused the boards to move.)

2. **INFER The blackbelt's hand hits only the board on the top of the stack. What causes the other boards to break?** (When the top board moves down, it applies a force to the board beneath it, and so on.)

PHYSICAL SCIENCE
Forces and Interactions

LIFE SCIENCE
Structure, Function, and Information Processing

EARTH SCIENCE
Weather and Climate

TEACH WITH TECHNOLOGY

Diagramming Forces

Project the lesson on a whiteboard. Draw an arrow from the center of the boards downward. Say: **The strength and direction of forces can be represented with arrows. The length of an arrow shows how strong a force is. The direction of the arrow shows the direction of a force. This arrow represents a force pulling downward on the boards.** Ask: **What should I label this arrow?** (the force of gravity) Draw two arrows half the size of the first arrow from the cement blocks upward. Ask: **What should I label these arrows?** (force of the blocks) Ask: **Why do you suppose I drew the arrows pointing up half the size of the arrow pointing down?** (The length of the arrows represents the strength of the forces, and their strengths must add up to zero because the forces are balanced while the boards are at rest.) Have students draw an arrow to show the additional force added by the hand when the hand strikes the top board.

READING CONNECTION

Describe the Connection

Describe the logical connection between particular sentences and paragraphs in a text (e.g., comparison, cause/effect, first/second/third in a sequence).

Guide students to describe the logical connection between particular sentences and paragraphs in a text (e.g., cause/effect). For example, in the EVALUATE section when having students identify the cause of the boards' movement, guide them to look for specific sentences in the text that describe this connection. ("The hand striking the boards applies another force to them. The added force causes the boards to move.")

Unbalanced Forces

NEXT GENERATION SCIENCE STANDARDS | DISCIPLINARY CORE IDEA

PS2.A: Forces and Motion Each force acts on one particular object and has both strength and a direction. An object at rest typically has multiple forces acting on it, but they add to give zero net force on the object. Forces that do not sum to zero can cause changes in the object's speed or direction of motion. (3-PS2-1)

PS2.B: Types of Interactions Objects in contact exert forces on each other. (3-PS2-1)

Objectives Students will be able to:
- Define *unbalanced forces*.
- Describe the effects of net force.

Science Vocabulary
unbalanced forces

ENGAGE

Tap Prior Knowledge

- Have students look back at the previous lesson on pages 6–7 to stimulate their memory and make connections. Ask: **Do forces always cause motion?** (No.) **Give an example of a situation in which forces are applied, but no motion is produced.** Students may recall from the previous lesson that the boards had both the force of gravity and the force of the blocks acting on them, but they did not move. Students may also recall the demonstration in which a student needed to use force the whole time he or she held a book up, even while the book was still.) **What is the term for equal and opposite forces that add up to a net force of zero?** (*balanced forces*)

EXPLORE

Preview the Lesson

- Have students read the title of the lesson and observe the image on pages 8–9. Ask: **What do you think happens when forces are *not* balanced?** (Students will most likely realize that unbalanced forces cause a motion, or a change in motion.)

Set a Purpose and Read

- Have students read in order to find out how unbalanced forces change an object's motion.
- Have students read pages 8–9.

EXPLAIN

Define Unbalanced Forces

- Ask: **What does it mean to say that the forces acting on an object are unbalanced?** (All of the forces acting on an object do not add up to zero; there is a stronger force in one direction than the others.) **What happens when the forces acting on an object go from balanced to unbalanced?** (An object that was not moving starts moving.)

Describe the Effects of Net Force

- Refer students to the image on pages 8–9. Ask: **What happens to the rope when both teams pull in opposite directions with the same amount of force?** (The rope does not move.) **What is the net force?** (zero) **Are the forces on the rope balanced or unbalanced?** (balanced) **How can forces on the rope become unbalanced?** (If one team pulls with stronger force than the other team, then the forces will become unbalanced.) **What happened to the rope when there was more force on the right than on the left?** (The rope was moved to the right). **In which direction is the net force?** (to the right)

- Have students recall the hand breaking the boards in the previous lesson. Ask: **What happened to the net force on the boards when the blackbelt's hand struck the top board?** (When the blackbelt's hand struck the top board, the forces on the boards went from balanced to unbalanced. There was then a net force in the downward direction that caused the boards to move and break.)

ELABORATE

Extend Your Thinking About Unbalanced Forces

 Have students draw and label three diagrams in their notebook to describe the forces acting on a rope and the resulting motion. First, have students draw three horizontal lines to represent the rope. Have them draw a dot on each line to indicate the center of the rope.

- Diagram 1: Show balanced forces on the rope. (arrows of equal length pointing in opposite directions on either side of the dot)
- Diagram 2: Show a net force to the right. (a longer arrow pointing from the dot to the right)
- Diagram 3: Show a net force to the left. (a longer arrow pointing from the dot to the left)

Find Out More About Unbalanced Forces

Have groups of students use the Internet to research and select an image showing unbalanced forces, or research and select appropriate images for groups yourself. Examples might include diagrams of forces involved in tug-of-war, forces on a vehicle, and people pushing on a block. Ask groups to prepare a brief presentation to their class, describing the effects of the unbalanced forces on the object in the image. If arrows are shown in the diagram, have students include an explanation of the arrows in their discussion.

EVALUATE

Have students record their answers to the Wrap It Up questions in their science notebook.

Wrap It Up!

1. **DEFINE What is an unbalanced force?** (An unbalanced force is a net force that does not add up to zero; an unbalanced force is a force that changes an object's motion.)

2. **INFER Suppose the rope is moved to the left. In which direction is the net force?** (The net force is to the left.)

3. **APPLY Describe a situation in which forces are balanced and a situation in which forces are unbalanced.** (Possible answer: When a ball is not moving, the forces acting on it are balanced. When I kick the ball and it moves, the forces are unbalanced.)

An additional interactive assessment activity can be found in the Exploring Science Digital Book.

PHYSICAL SCIENCE
Forces and Interactions

LIFE SCIENCE
Structure, Function, and Information Processing

EARTH SCIENCE
Weather and Climate

SCIENCE MISCONCEPTIONS
Balanced and Unbalanced Forces

A common misconception among students is that forces always cause motion, and that if you apply any force to an object, the object will move in some way. However, only unbalanced forces change an object's motion. This can easily be demonstrated by pushing down on a tabletop and observing that the table does not move. Similarly, if you apply a force on an object that is balanced with gravity, you can hold the object still. To demonstrate that only unbalanced forces result in motion, hold a ball and alternate between slowly moving it up, down, in different directions, and holding it still. Have students call out *balanced* or *unbalanced* in each case. Every time the ball is moving students should say "unbalanced," and every time it is still they should say, "balanced."

READING CONNECTION
Use Photos to Demonstrate Understanding

Use information gained from illustrations (e.g., maps, photographs) and the words in a text to demonstrate understanding of the text (e.g., where, when, why, and how key events occur).

Guide students to use information gained from photographs to demonstrate understanding of the text. For example, in the EXPLAIN section when asking students to describe what is happening in the photograph, guide them to use details in the image to figure it out. When asked what happens to the rope when both teams pull in opposite directions with the same amount of force, students can look at the photo and imagine the people on both teams pulling equally hard and the rope staying still. Likewise, they can use the image to figure out what happens when there is more force on one side than the other.

Changing Direction

NEXT GENERATION SCIENCE STANDARDS | DISCIPLINARY CORE IDEA

PS2.A: Forces and Motion Each force acts on one particular object and has both strength and a direction. An object at rest typically has multiple forces acting on it, but they add to give zero net force on the object. Forces that do not sum to zero can cause changes in the object's speed or direction of motion. (3-PS2-1)

PS2.B: Types of Interactions Objects in contact exert forces on each other. (3-PS2-1)

Objective Students will be able to:
- Recognize that forces can change an object's speed or direction.

ENGAGE

Tap Prior Knowledge

- Have students recall the effects of unbalanced forces on objects. Ask: **What happens when you apply an unbalanced force to a soccer ball with your foot?** (The ball moves.) **What if the ball is already moving when you apply the force?** (Accept all reasonable responses at this time. Students may not yet realize that unbalanced forces can also stop, slow down, speed up, or change the direction of an object's motion.)

EXPLORE

Preview the Lesson

- Have students read the title of the lesson and observe the image on pages 10–11. Ask: **How do you think this lesson relates to forces?** (Students may say that forces can change an object's direction.)

Set a Purpose and Read

- Have students read in order to find out how forces change an object's motion.
- Have students read pages 10–11.

EXPLAIN

Recognize That Forces Can Change an Object's Speed or Direction

- Say: **Forces that do not add to zero can cause changes in the object's speed or direction of motion.** Ask: **How is the player on page 10 applying an unbalanced force to the ball?** (His foot is coming in contact with the ball and pushing it as he kicks.) **In which direction is the net force applied to the ball?** (away from the player's foot in the same direction his foot is moving)

- Say: **There are several different ways an object's speed can change. How is the ball's speed changing as it contacts the players foot?** (It is slowed down by the foot, stopped by the foot for a fraction of a second, and then sped up again as it is pushed away.) **What are some other ways that an object's speed can change?** (If an object is at rest, it can be put into motion. If an object is already in motion, it can be stopped completely, sped up, or slowed down.)

- Say: **There are also many ways an object's direction can change. How is the ball's direction changing as it contacts the players foot?** (The ball was moving in a direction toward the player, and now the ball will be moving in a direction away from the player.) Point out that the player can change the strength of the force he applies to the ball with his kick. Ask: **How does the strength of his kick change how the ball will move?** (A strong kick, or force, will cause the ball to move faster that a weaker kick, or force.)

- Have students think of an example of a time in which they used a force to change an object's direction. Ask a few volunteers to share their examples. (Possible answers: When I hit a tennis ball with a racket, I used a force to change the ball's direction. When I moved a pen up and down with my fingers to write, I used a force to change the pen's direction.)

- Have students complete the *SCIENCE in a SNAP* activity to experience changing the direction of an object's motion.

ELABORATE

Find Out More About the Ways Force Can Change Motion

 Have students select a sport and analyze one example of force used by the sport's players. Students can research and study photos and videos of the force in order to analyze it. Have them identify how the force is applied to a particular object, whether or not the net force on the object is zero, and the effects of the force on the object's motion. Have students share their analysis with the class.

EVALUATE

 Have students record their answers to the Wrap It Up questions in their science notebook.

Wrap It Up!

1. **RECALL** **Are the forces on the ball in the photo balanced or unbalanced? How do you know?** (The forces on the ball in the photo are unbalanced. I know this because the ball is in motion.)

2. **GENERALIZE** **In what ways can forces change an object's motion?** (Forces can change an object's speed or direction.)

SCIENCE in a SNAP

Changing Direction

Materials *For groups of 2:* small rubber or plastic ball; unsharpened pencil

Teaching Tips Before you begin, review the ways a force can change an object's motion. As a class, list all of the specific ways in which a force can change an object's motion. (speed an object up, slow it down, start it in motion, stop it, change its direction) Explain to students that there are many ways the ball's motion can change while keeping the ball in their working area. They do not need to use excessive force or send the ball across the room. Advise students that subtle movements are best for this activity. Students should record their observations in their science notebook, both in words and as diagrams.

What to Expect Students should observe that they were able to adjust the strength and direction of force applied to the ball to start the ball in motion, stop its motion, speed it up, slow it down, and change its direction.

Quick Questions Ask: **How did you apply a force to stop the ball?** (Possible answer: I held the pencil in a way so that the moving ball would collide with it and stop moving). Say: **Suppose you didn't apply a force to stop the ball. Would the ball keep moving?** (No, it would eventually stop.) **What are some other forces that could stop it**? (Possible answers: another object, such as a wall; the force of gravity)

PHYSICAL SCIENCE
Forces and Interactions

LIFE SCIENCE
Structure, Function, and Information Processing

EARTH SCIENCE
Weather and Climate

Plan and Conduct an Investigation

NEXT GENERATION SCIENCE STANDARDS | PERFORMANCE EXPECTATION

3-PS2-1. Plan and conduct an investigation to provide evidence of the effects of balanced and unbalanced forces on the motion of an object. [Clarification Statement: Examples could include an unbalanced force on one side of a ball can make it start moving; and, balanced forces pushing on a box from both sides will not produce any motion at all.] *[Assessment Boundary: Assessment is limited to one variable at a time: number, size, or direction of forces. Assessment does not include quantitative force size, only qualitative and relative. Assessment is limited to gravity being addressed as a force that pulls objects down.]*

Objective **Students will be able to:**
- Plan and conduct an investigation to provide evidence of the effects of balanced and unbalanced forces on the motion of an object.

cause an object to stay still. For example, they might show that by blowing on a cotton ball that is up against a block does not result in motion.

MANAGE THE INVESTIGATION

Materials *For groups of 4:* cotton ball; metric ruler; tape. Provide a drinking straw for each student. Also provide an assortment of materials from which student teams can select to build their course, such as cardboard boxes, pieces of cardboard, paper towel tubes, and wooden blocks of various shapes.

Time 20 minutes for planning; 30 minutes for observation and analysis; 20 minutes for sharing and explanation

Advance Preparation Collect materials that students can use to construct their courses.

Teaching Tips In order to meet the performance expectation, students must plan and conduct their own investigation. Coach students through the planning process without instructing them on specific steps to take or materials to use. Ask students to relate scientific ideas to their plans as they work.

What to Expect Students' investigations will provide evidence that unbalanced forces affect an object's motion. For example, they might show that blowing on a cotton ball through a straw or letting gravity pull it down a ramp causes the ball to move. They will also provide evidence that balanced forces

ENGAGE

Set the scene.

- Call attention to the photo on pages 12–13. Ask: **How are the men applying forces to the ball?** (They are pushing the ball with their feet.) **How do the forces affect the ball?** (The forces cause the ball to start moving, stop moving, speed up, slow down, and change direction.) Have students blow through the straw while holding their hand in front of it. Ask: **What do you feel?** (I feel air blowing on my hand.) **How could you use the air as a force to move the cotton ball?** (I could aim the straw at the cotton ball while I blow through it to push the air against the cotton ball.)

- Have a volunteer read the introductory paragraph and the first step on page 12. Ask: **What is your task?** (to design an obstacle course that demonstrates the effects of balanced and unbalanced forces on a cotton ball)

Ask a question.

My science notebook Have students record the question under step 1 in their science notebook.

PHYSICAL SCIENCE
Forces and Interactions

LIFE SCIENCE
Structure, Function, and Information Processing

EARTH SCIENCE
Weather and Climate

EXPLORE

Plan and conduct an investigation.

- Have a volunteer read the first sentence under step 2. Allow time for students to blow on the cotton ball in different ways and observe its motion.

- Have another volunteer read the second sentence and the list of possible ways they can move the cotton ball. Reiterate for students that they must design a course that shows how the cotton ball can move in at least three of those ways.

- Then read the last paragraph under step 2 aloud.

- As groups design their course, ask questions to stimulate critical thinking, such as:

  - **What will you use to build your course?** (Possible answer: We will use the cardboard and blocks to make a ramp and a wall, and we will use a paper towel tube as a tube for the ball to go through.)

  - **What are the three ways in which you will affect the ball with the air?** (Possible answer: We will make it move through a tube, down a ramp, and stay still while air is blown on it.)

  - **How will you use balanced and unbalanced forces?** (We will use unbalanced forces to make the ball move through a tube and down a ramp. We will use balanced forces to make the ball stay still while air is blown on it.)

- If students are having trouble identifying three ways they will affect the ball, point them back to the list under step 2 and tell them to choose three goals and write them in their notebook.

- Guide groups to develop a picture of their course as they work together, and encourage members to discuss their ideas with each

SCIENCE AND ENGINEERING PRACTICES

Planning and Carrying Out Investigations

- Have groups record the plan for their investigation and the steps they followed to carry it out. Ask groups to record how they are controlling variables in each trial. Discuss with students how the data generated by their investigation serve as the basis for evidence of the effects of balanced and unbalanced forces on the cotton ball.

Connections to Nature of Science
Science Investigations Use a Variety of Methods

- Discuss with students the fact that when scientists conduct investigations, they use a variety of methods, tools, and techniques. Ask: **What tools did you use to complete the investigation?** (Possible answer: I used blocks, paper towel tubes, and cotton balls as tools in this investigation.) Ask: **What techniques did you use to demonstrate the action of balanced and unbalanced forces on the cotton ball?** (Possible answer: I blew through a straw to move the cotton ball through a path to demonstrate unbalanced forces. I blew through the straw while the cotton ball was blocked by an object to show that balanced forces can cause the cotton ball to remain still.)

CROSSCUTTING CONCEPTS

Cause and Effect

- Say: **Cause-and-effect relationships are routinely identified by scientists during investigations.** Ask: **Did you identify any cause-and-effect relationships in this investigation?** (Possible answer: Yes. The unbalanced forces caused the cotton ball to move.)

- Encourage students to link concepts of cause and effect and unbalanced forces to other areas of science. For example, in life science, animals use muscles, joints, and bones to apply forces to various parts of their bodies, allowing movement and interaction with the environment.

Plan and Conduct an Investigation (continued)

EXPLORE (continued)

other. Have students render their final plan in their science notebook. Tell students it is okay to modify their design as they work with the materials and build their course. If they make modifications, have students record the changes in their notebook.

- Encourage students to test their course systematically by going through their list of goals and testing them one at a time. Have students record what they did and the effect it had on the ball each time.

Example:

The Effects of Forces on a Cotton Ball

Goal: Make the ball ...	What We Did	Observation
1. move through a tube.	We taped a tube on top of a book at the beginning of the course. Then we aimed the straw at the ball and applied a force by blowing through the straw.	The ball moved through the tube.
2. move down a ramp.	We taped a flat block at the end of the book to make a ramp. We held the straw so that the force would send the ball in the direction of the ramp and down the ramp.	The ball moved down the ramp. We needed less force to send it down the ramp than we did to send it through the tube. We had to be careful about the direction of force so the ball didn't fall off the book or the ramp.
3. stay still while air is blown on it.	We added a block wall and aimed the straw to make the ball stay still against the wall as we applied the force of air.	The ball moved along the side of the wall.

EXPLAIN

Analyze results and revise.

- Ask probing questions to help students interpret their results, such as: **Did the cotton ball move the way you wanted it to?** (Possible answer: The ball moved the way we wanted it to for goals 1 and 2, but not 3. We wanted the ball to

stay still, but it moved.) **How can your course be improved?** (Possible answer: We have to find a way to balance the forces so the ball doesn't move. We are going to try adding more blocks and blow with less force on the ball.) Allow time for students to revise their course and test it again. Remind them to record both their changes and their results. Students may need to make a second table.

- Revisit the question from the beginning of the investigation: *How can you use balanced and unbalanced forces to move a cotton ball through an obstacle course?* Have students look at their data tables and identify the times when they applied unbalanced forces on the cotton ball. Ask students to label these rows of their table, "unbalanced forces," or "UF." Then have students identify any times in which the forces on the cotton ball were balanced, and label those rows "balanced forces," or "BF." Have students explain their reasoning. (Example: When we made the ball move, the forces were unbalanced. I know this because unbalanced forces change motion. When the ball stayed still, the forces were balanced. I know this because balanced forces do not change motion.)

- Ask: **What does the word *evidence* mean?** (observations or facts that show a position is likely to be true) **How did your investigation provide evidence of the effects of balanced and unbalanced forces on the motion of an object?** (Possible answer: When forces were applied in different ways, the motion or lack of motion of the ball provided evidence of the effects of balanced and unbalanced forces on it.)

Share your results.

- Have each group share its course design, data, and conclusions with another group. Have students explain to each other how they used forces to control the motion of the ball, how they changed the strength and direction of forces, and how they used balanced and unbalanced forces. Ask students to use evidence from their data to support their discussions. Encourage students to listen to feedback and incorporate it.

Explain your findings.

- Have groups present their investigation and results to the class, including a demonstration of their course. Allow time for students to ask and answer questions about each other's work.

- Ask: **In what ways did you think like a scientist as you completed this activity?** (Possible answer: As part of the group, I planned and conducted an investigation to see how balanced and unbalanced forces affect the motion of a cotton ball, just like a scientist would.)

ELABORATE

- Extend the investigation by having students revise their course to meet all five goals under step 2. Have students describe how they will use forces to meet each goal. Then let them carry out their investigations and record their observations.

EVALUATE

 Check to make sure students have recorded their plans, modifications, and observations in their science notebook. Then ask students these questions. Have them record the answers in their science notebook.

1. **DEFINE What is evidence?** (Possible answer: Evidence is observations or facts that show a position is likely to be true.)

2. **IDENTIFY What evidence in the data you recorded shows that unbalanced forces change an object's motion?** (Possible answer: When the cotton ball was sitting still, the forces on it were balanced. When we blew through the straw toward the ball, the forces became unbalanced. The movement of the ball when we blew on it was evidence that unbalanced forces change an object's motion.)

3. **EXPLAIN What evidence from your data shows that every force has a strength and direction?** (By changing the strength and direction of the forces we used, we showed that forces have a strength and direction. When we blew harder, the ball moved farther and faster. When we turned the straw to blow on the ball from a different side, we changed the direction of the motion.)

RUBRICS

Teacher Rubric Use the scale descriptions to guide your assessment of each student's work. Assess each item separately, and then decide on one overall score, using the following scale:

4: Student performs with thorough understanding.
3: Student performs with adequate understanding.
2: Student performs with basic understanding.
1: Student performs with limited understanding.

Rubric	Scale			
The student planned and conducted an investigation to produce data that could serve to answer the question.	4	3	2	1
The student evaluated different ways of observing and/or measuring a phenomenon to determine which way can answer a question.	4	3	2	1
The student made observations and/or measurements to collect data that could be used to draw conclusions.	4	3	2	1
The student's presentation showed an understanding of how forces affect objects.	4	3	2	1
Overall Score	4	3	2	1

Student Rubric Have students complete a self-evaluation similar to that shown below.

Rubric	Yes	Not Yet
1. I can plan an investigation and carry out the steps.		
2. I can make and draw my observations.		
3. I can learn from my results.		
4. I can share my results and say how they show the ideas we have learned in this class.		

PHYSICAL SCIENCE
Forces and Interactions

LIFE SCIENCE
Structure, Function, and Information Processing

EARTH SCIENCE
Weather and Climate

Patterns of Motion

NEXT GENERATION SCIENCE STANDARDS | DISCIPLINARY CORE IDEA
PS2.A: Forces and Motion The patterns of an object's motion in various situations can be observed and measured; when that past motion exhibits a regular pattern, future motion can be predicted from it.

Objectives Students will be able to:
- Identify the pattern of an object's motion.
- Define regular motion.

Science Vocabulary
regular motion

ENGAGE

Tap Prior Knowledge

- Have students think of the motion of a swing. Ask: **What kind of pattern do you notice in the motion of a swing?** (The seat swings forward and back, over and over.)

EXPLORE

Preview the Lesson

- Have students read the title of the lesson and observe the image on pages 14–15. Ask: **How does the photo relate to the title?** (The photo shows a girl on a swing, and swinging motion is an example of a pattern of motion.)

Set a Purpose and Read

- Have students read in order to find out about patterns of motion.
- Have students read pages 14–15.

EXPLAIN

Identify the Pattern of an Object's Motion

- Say: **Look at the girl in the photo.** Ask: **Do you think she was in motion at the time the photo was taken?** (Yes.) **What makes you think so?** (The swing is shown in a position in which it cannot stay.) **What do you think will happen next?** (The girl will swing back.) **And after that?** (Then she will swing forward again, then back, and so on.) **What makes you think so?** (I know because the swing follows a pattern of back-and-forth motion. Because the swing's motion followed a pattern in the past, I can predict how it will move in the future.)

- Say: **A swing is an example of a pendulum. A pendulum is a weight that hangs on a cord or a rod from a point above it. The point at the top is still. The pendulum can swing freely from that point. Any object that is set up in this way will exhibit this pattern of motion.** Consider bringing in a yo-yo and swinging it back and forth to demonstrate. Ask: **If you think of the girl on the swing as part of a pendulum, what part is the weight?** (the girl) **Where is the still point at the top?** (It is beyond the image that is shown on the page, probably a knot where the fabric is tied to a tree branch.)

- Have students think back to the lessons on forces and motion. Say: **Recall that unbalanced forces are required to change an object's motion. What force do you think might have set the girl in motion?** (Possible answers: Another person might have given the girl a push to get her started. If the swing is low enough, she might have used her feet to push off the ground.) **Why doesn't she keep moving forward from the push?** (The swing is attached at the top and so it only lets her go so far.) **What force brings her back down?** (gravity)

Define Regular Motion

- Ask: **How can you describe the girl's pattern of motion on the swing?** (She is moving back and forth.) **What forces keep her going back and forth?** (Someone might be pushing her. She might also be moving her body to keep the swing in motion.) Explain that every time she reaches the highest point forward or back in the pattern, gravity pulls the girl back down again toward the center of the swing's path. Ask: **If no more forces are added, will she keep swinging forever?** (No, gravity would eventually stop her.)

- Ask: **Can all motion be predicted? Why or why not?** (No. Not all kinds of motion follow a repeating pattern.) **What is the term for motion that has a pattern that repeats over and over?** (*regular motion*)

- Ask a volunteer to read the caption on page 15. Ask: **Would you classify the motion of the swing as regular motion? Why?** (Yes. It follows a repeating pattern.)

ELABORATE

Extend Your Thinking About Patterns of Motion

Take students to the playground to observe their own motion on a swing. Have students push off only one time and then sit still on the swing as it gradually comes to a halt. Discuss their observations about what happened. Guide students to recognize that their motion became "less and less" at the same time they went back and forth. This is, though not perpetual, a predictable decreasing pattern.

EVALUATE

 Have students record their answers to the Wrap It Up questions in their science notebook.

Wrap It Up!

1. CONTRAST **How does the motion of a falling leaf differ from the motion of a swing?** (Possible answer: The motion of the falling leaf does not follow a predictable pattern. The motion of the swing follows a regular and predictable pattern.)

2. PREDICT **Look at the person in the photo. Describe how she will move next.** (Possible answer: She will swing back, in the direction of the place that is shown on the right page.)

PHYSICAL SCIENCE
Forces and Interactions

LIFE SCIENCE
Structure, Function, and Information Processing

EARTH SCIENCE
Weather and Climate

TEACH WITH TECHNOLOGY

Discuss Regular Motion

Project the lesson on a whiteboard. Say: **Underline the main idea of this lesson.** (*But some motion follows a pattern.*) **Circle terms and phrases that support the main idea.** (Answers may vary but might include *easier to predict, regular motion, pattern of repeating, back and forth, predictable pattern*.) **Draw an arrow to show the force of gravity on the girl.** (The arrow should start from the girl and point straight down.) **The force of gravity is pulling down on the girl, but she can't move straight down.** Ask: **Why?** (The swing is providing a force that opposes gravity. But she can still move forward and back.) **Draw a second arrow to show where she will move next.** (The arrow should show that she will swing back.)

READING CONNECTION

Determine Word Meaning

Determine the meaning of general academic and domain-specific words and phrases in a text relevant to a *grade 3 topic or subject area.*

Guide students to distinguish the academic meaning of the word *regular*, using the context provided by the text. For example, in the EXPLAIN section when asking students to consider the definition of *regular motion*, remind them that the term is bold, and therefore a vocabulary word for this lesson. Students are probably familiar with the word *regular* as it is commonly used to mean "ordinary" or "unremarkable." Guide students to the more specific meaning of *regular* as it pertains to a predictable pattern.

Motion

NEXT GENERATION SCIENCE STANDARDS | DISCIPLINARY CORE IDEA
PS2.A: Forces and Motion The patterns of an object's motion in various situations can be observed and measured; when that past motion exhibits a regular pattern, future motion can be predicted from it. (3-PS2-2)

Objectives Students will be able to:
- Observe and measure the pattern of an object's motion.
- Predict the future motion of an object moving in a regular pattern.

MANAGE THE INVESTIGATION

Materials *For groups of 4:* piece of foam tubing (pipe insulation), cut in half lengthwise (3 m); masking tape; meterstick; two chairs; metal mixing bowl (for the ELABORATE)

Time 40 minutes

Advance Preparation Cut the foam tubing to form ramps for the marbles. Test the marbles in the ramps before using them.

Teaching Tips Have groups help you clear enough space in the classroom to do the investigation. If space is limited, have groups take turns using fewer ramps.

What to Expect Students will observe that the marble exhibits a regular pattern of motion. They will use the past height reached by the marble to predict the marble's future height.

ENGAGE
Tap Prior Knowledge.
- Ask several students to recount their experiences bouncing a rubber ball. Ask: **Have you ever dropped a rubber ball and then caught it when it bounced back up?** (Yes.) **How did you know that the ball was going to move back up from the ground? How did you know how high up the ball would go?**

(Possible answer: I was able to predict what the ball would do based on my previous experiences observing a ball's patterns of motion.) Remind students that when an object is moving in a regular pattern, its past motion can be used to predict its future motion.

EXPLORE
- Guide students through the investigation. Read pages 16–17 together.

 Have students construct a table like the one shown at the top of page 17 for recording their observations in their science notebook.

- Before students begin, ask probing questions to help them connect what they are doing to the learning goals. Ask: **How will you measure the marble's motion?** (We will use a meter stick to measure how high up the marble starts and how high it rolls up the other side.) **How will you be able to observe a pattern?** (We will do this several times and at different heights and look for patterns in the data.)

- As students carry out step 2, remind them to pause and record their observations for each trial. Students may need to conduct a few practice trials before they start recording data.

- In steps 3 and 4, encourage students to record their predictions in their table.

EXPLAIN
- Help students calculate and record the average height the marble reached for each starting height. Ask students to compare the average height the marble reached with their predictions of how high it would reach.

Sample data table:

Height of Marble

Trial	Starting Point (cm)	Predicted Result (cm)	Actual Height Reached (cm)			
			Drop 1	Drop 2	Drop 3	Average
1						
2						
3						
4						

PHYSICAL SCIENCE
Forces and Interactions

LIFE SCIENCE
Structure, Function, and Information Processing

EARTH SCIENCE
Weather and Climate

- Ask: **How close were your predictions to the average height the marble reached?** (Possible answer: I predicted the marble would go higher than it did.) **Did your predictions get better as you went along?** (Possible answer: Yes.) **Did you notice any patterns in your data that helped you make your predictions? Explain.** (Possible answer: I noticed that the height the marble reached was a little lower than the height it was dropped from each time. After I noticed that pattern, my predictions were more accurate.) If students did *not* notice this pattern in their data, have them look again now.

- Have students compare their data tables with those of other groups and discuss any differences. Ask: **Do everyone's data show the same pattern?** Ask: **If your data did not show the same pattern, what might have caused the discrepancy?** Help students identify both experimental and human errors that may have caused outliers in their data. Guide students to recognize that patterns become easier to identify the more data you have to work with. With only a few data points, what looks like a pattern might really just be a coincidence.

ELABORATE

 Tell students to think again about their results. Ask: **Would you consider the motion of the marble to be an example of regular motion? Explain.** (Accept all answers with valid reasoning. The motion is regular in that it decreases quantifiably with each "dip" on the ramp.) **Would an object moving in a circle be considered regular motion?** (Yes, because it moves in a predictable, repeating pattern.) Have students

use the marble and the mixing bowl to produce a pattern of circular motion. Ask students to record their observations in their notebook.

EVALUATE

 Have students record their answers to the Wrap It Up questions in their science notebook.

Wrap It Up!

1. **PREDICT Did your results support your predictions? Explain.** (Possible answer: My results did not support my predictions. I predicted the marble would go higher than it did each time.)

2. **INTERPRET What pattern do you notice in your data?** (No matter what height I dropped the marble from, the marble did not reach the same height on the other side of the foam tube.)

READING CONNECTION

Use Text Features

Use text features and search tools (e.g., key words, sidebars, hyperlinks) to locate information relevant to a given topic efficiently.

Guide students to use text features to locate information efficiently. For example, in the EXPLORE section when asking students how they will take their measurements, refer them to the inset photos on page 17. Ask students how these small photos help them know what to do. (The photos in step 1 show how to arrange the foam tube and chairs. The photo in step 2 shows how to take the measurements.)

Make Observations

NEXT GENERATION SCIENCE STANDARDS | PERFORMANCE EXPECTATION

3-PS2-2. Make observations and/or measurements of an object's motion to provide evidence that a pattern can be used to predict future motion. [Clarification Statement: Examples of motion with a predictable pattern could include a child swinging in a swing, a ball rolling back and forth in a bowl, and two children on a see-saw.] [*Assessment Boundary: Assessment does not include technical terms such as period and frequency.*]

Objective **Students will be able to:**
- Make observations and measurements of an object's motion to provide evidence that a pattern can be used to predict future motion.

CLASSROOM MANAGEMENT

Materials *For groups of 4:* metal washer; string; masking tape; meterstick; stopwatch; 2–3 additional washers of various sizes and weights

Time 20 minutes for planning; 30 minutes for observation and analysis; 20 minutes for retesting; 20 minutes for sharing and explaining.

Advance Preparation Cut the string into 70 cm (about 28 in.) lengths. Clear chairs away from tables to make room for students' pendulums to move freely when they are hanging from the edges of the tables.

Teaching Tips In order to meet the performance expectation, students must plan and conduct their own investigation. Coach students through the planning process without instructing them on specific steps to take or materials to use. Ask students to relate scientific ideas to their plans as they work.

What to Expect Students will observe a pattern in the motion of their pendulum and use the pattern as evidence to predict its future motion. Examples of patterns include: the shorter the string, the faster the swing; the higher the weight is dropped from, the higher it goes; changing the mass at the end of the string does not change the speed of the pendulum's swing.

ENGAGE

Set the scene.

- Ask students to recall the term for a weight that swings from a point above it. (pendulum) Call attention to the photo on pages 18–19. Ask: **Is an artist on a trapeze an example of a pendulum?** (Yes.) **What type of motion does a pendulum demonstrate?** (regular motion; swinging back and forth) **Why might a trapeze artist need to predict the future motion of the trapeze?** (The ability of the artist to perform acts and move safely in the air depends on his or her being able to predict exactly how the trapeze will move.) **Why might other people need to predict the future motion of the trapeze?** (Possible answers: Choreographers predict how the trapeze will move so that they can plan the moves of the performers. Engineers who design the trapeze rig must be able to predict the motion of the trapeze to select ropes and fasteners that are strong enough to withstand the forces involved.)

- Have a volunteer read the introductory paragraph and the first step on page 18. Ask: **What is your task?** (to observe the motion of a swinging object and use the observations to predict its future motion) Preview the rest of the investigation together.

Ask a question.

Have students record the question under step 1 in their science notebook.

EXPLORE

Plan and conduct an investigation.

- Ask a volunteer to read the first paragraph under step 2. Instruct groups to use the string and one washer to set up their pendulum and give it a swing. Suggest that students start the pendulum in motion by pulling back on the washer while keeping the string straight and then simply letting it go. Let them know that they do not need to push on the washer. Ask: **What force pulls the washer down?** (gravity)

- Encourage students to think critically about their initial observations by asking probing questions such as:

  · **How long does the pendulum keep moving?**

  · **How high did you drop it from?**

  · **How high does it go on the other side? How fast does it swing?**

  · **How could you measure those variables?**

  · **How could you affect one of those variables?**

- Have another volunteer read the rest of step 2 aloud. Clarify for students what they will be doing first. Say: **First you will design an investigation, in which you change** **one variable at a time, to try and affect the motion of the pendulum. Choose one outcome to aim for—to make the pendulum move faster, higher, or longer. As you plan, think of one "swing" of a pendulum as both the forward movement and the movement back.** Have groups select an outcome and discuss and record the steps of their investigation. Encourage them to use words and diagrams to record their plan. Remind students to change only one variable at a time.

- If students choose to measure the length of the string, make sure they measure only the length that swings, that is the length of string from the edge of the table to the washer. To change this length, they don't need to cut the string. They can just pull up on the string and re-tape it to the table.

- Ask: **What variable will you change?** (Possible answer: We will change the length of

PHYSICAL SCIENCE
Forces and Interactions

LIFE SCIENCE
Structure, Function, and Information Processing

EARTH SCIENCE
Weather and Climate

SCIENCE AND ENGINEERING PRACTICES

Planning and Carrying Out Investigations

- In this activity, students make observations and measurements of the motion of a pendulum. Be sure that students understand that patterns they identify in the data serve as the basis for evidence that can be used to predict future motion. Have them use this evidence to make an explanation of how the pendulum moves, then use that explanation to formulate their predictions.

Connections to Nature of Science
Science Knowledge Is Based on Empirical Evidence

- Say: **Science findings are based on recognizing patterns. As you measured how a pendulum moves, you looked for patterns in the data.** Ask: **What pattern did you notice in this activity?** (Possible answer: I noticed that the pendulum would swing more times in ten seconds when the string is shorter than when the string is longer.)

CROSSCUTTING CONCEPTS

Patterns

- Say: **Patterns of change can be used to make predictions.** Ask: **What do you think will happen if you make the string 100 cm (1 m) long?** (Possible answer: It will probably swing less than 6 times in 10 seconds.)

- Encourage students to link concepts of patterns and the movement of objects to other areas of science. For example, in earth and space sciences, the regular motions of planets, moons, the sun and stars, have been observed and predicted by humans for thousands of years.

Make Observations (continued)

EXPLORE (continued)

the string.) **What variables will you measure?** (Possible answer: The length of the string and how fast it swings.) **How will you measure those variables?** (Possible answer: We will use the meterstick to measure the length of the string. We will use a stopwatch to count the number of swings in ten seconds to measure how fast it swings.) **How many tests will you conduct?** (Possible answer: four) Remind students that more tests provide more data, which makes it easier to spot patterns.

Example: Our group will change the length of the pendulum's string four times and measure how fast the pendulum swings each time.

1. We will tape the string to a table or other surface about one meter above the floor, leaving 80 cm between the edge of the surface and the washer.

2. We will pull back the string 90 degrees and let go.

3. We use the stopwatch to measure 10 seconds and count the number of times the pendulum swings during that time.

4. We will repeat steps 1–3 three more times changing the length of the string each time to 40 cm, 20 cm, and 10 cm.

- Guide students as they carry out their plan. Have students make a table in their notebook to record their observations as they carry out each test. One possible example is shown here:

Patterns of Pendulum Motion

Test	Length of String	Swings per 10 Seconds
1	80 cm	6
2	40 cm	8
3	20 cm	11
4	10 cm	15

EXPLAIN

Analyze and interpret data.

- Ask probing questions to help students interpret their results, such as: **What were your results?** (Students should cite their data and be able to generalize that as the length of the string got shorter, the pendulum swung faster.) **Can you use your data to predict the future motion of the pendulum?** (Possible answer: Yes, I predict that if I decrease the length of the string to 5 cm, the pendulum will swing at a rate faster than 15 swings per 10 seconds.) **Are there things you could do differently to improve your results?** (Possible answer: I could collect more data to see the pattern more clearly.)

- Allow time for students to study their data, find a pattern, make a prediction, and test it. Remind them to record variations to their plans and their observations. Students may need to add rows to their data table or make a second table.

Share your results.

- Have students share their results with a partner from another group. Instruct them to explain how they collected data, what pattern they observed, and how they made a prediction. Encourage students to incorporate feedback from their partners and let them test again as time allows.

Explain your findings.

- Have groups present their findings to the class, including a demonstration of their procedure. Ask students to share how they used their observations to predict the motion of the pendulum.

- Ask: **In what ways did you think like a scientist as you completed this activity?** (Possible answer: I discovered a pattern in the number of times a that the pendulum would swing depending on the length of the string, and I drew conclusions from my observations.)

ELABORATE

Extend the investigation by having students work in groups to build a marble roller coaster using what they have learned about forces and patterns in motion.

Step 1: Have groups discuss, develop, and draw their plans in their notebook, including a list of the materials they will need to build it. Students should include predictions about and measurements of the marble's motion.

Step 2: If time permits, have students build and demonstrate their roller coaster to the class, explaining how forces and motion affect the way it works.

EVALUATE

Check to make sure students have recorded their plans and data in their science notebook. Then ask students these questions. Have them record the answers in their science notebook.

1. **EXPLAIN How do you know that a pendulum's motion is regular motion?** (I know a pendulum's motion is regular motion because it follows a predictable pattern.)

2. **IDENTIFY What evidence from your data shows that a pattern can be used to predict future motion?** (Possible answer: My data showed a pattern in the pendulum's motion. The data showed that the shorter the string, the faster the pendulum moved. I was able to use that pattern to correctly predict the pendulum's future motion.)

RUBRICS

Teacher Rubric Use the scale descriptions to guide your assessment of each student's work. Assess each item separately, and then decide on one overall score, using the following scale:

4: Student performs with thorough understanding.
3: Student performs with adequate understanding.
2: Student performs with basic understanding.
1: Student performs with limited understanding.

Rubric	Scale			
The student planned and conducted an investigation to produce data that could serve to answer the question.	4	3	2	1
The student evaluated different ways of observing and/or measuring a phenomenon to determine which way can answer a question.	4	3	2	1
The student made observations and/or measurements to collect data that could be used to draw conclusions.	4	3	2	1
The student's presentation showed an understanding of patterns of motion.	4	3	2	1
Overall Score	4	3	2	1

Student Rubric Have students complete a self-evaluation similar to that shown below.

Rubric	Yes	Not Yet
1. I can plan an investigation and carry out the steps.		
2. I can make and draw my observations.		
3. I can learn from my results.		
4. I can share my results and say how they show the ideas we have learned in this class.		

PHYSICAL SCIENCE
Forces and Interactions

LIFE SCIENCE
Structure, Function, and Information Processing

EARTH SCIENCE
Weather and Climate

Magnets

NEXT GENERATION SCIENCE STANDARDS | DISCIPLINARY CORE IDEA
PS2.B: Types of Interactions Electric and magnetic forces between a pair of objects do not require that the objects be in contact. The sizes of the forces in each situation depend on the properties of the objects and their distances apart and, for forces between two magnets, on their orientation relative to each other. (3-PS2-3), (3-PS2-4)

Objectives Students will be able to:
- Identify magnetic force as a force that can act at a distance.
- Recognize that the forces between two magnets depend on their orientation relative to each other.

Science Vocabulary
magnet, attract, magnetic force, pole, repel

ENGAGE

Tap Prior Knowledge

- Have a few students share their experiences with magnets. Ask: **How have you used a magnet?** (Possible answers: to attach things to a refrigerator; to operate a game or toy) **What do magnets do?** (Possible answer: They attract some metals.) **Do you think magnets can exert forces? Explain.** (Yes, because they can pull on things, and a pull is a force.)

EXPLORE

Explore Magnetic Force

- Have students observe the images on pages 20–21. Ask: **What is happening in the photo on page 20?** (Several objects are being pulled to a magnet.) **Where is the magnet in the photo?** (It is at the top of the photo.) **How can you tell the objects are being pulled by the magnet?** (You can tell because the objects are not falling down.) **What are the magnets doing in the photos on page 21?** (pulling on a paper clip and holding small pieces together to form a sculpture)

Set a Purpose and Read

- Have students read in order to find out about the force of magnetism.
- Have students read pages 20–21.

EXPLAIN

Identify Magnetic Force

- Ask: **What does _attract_ mean?** (to pull together) **What kinds of objects can magnets attract?** (Magnets can attract other magnets and certain kinds of metals.) **What evidence in the photo on page 20 shows that magnets attract certain kinds of metals?** (All of the objects that are attracted to the magnet in the photo look like they have parts made of similar kinds of metal.) **What does _repel_ mean?** (to push apart) **What kinds of objects can magnets repel?** (Magnets can repel other magnets.)

- Have students look again at the photos. Ask: **Does a magnet have to be touching another object in order to exert a force on it?** (No.) **What evidence in the photos shows that magnets do not have to be in contact with objects in order to exert forces on them?** (The paper clip in the photo on page 21 is being pulled by the magnet even though it is not touching the magnet.) **How could you provide further evidence that the magnet is exerting a force on the paper clip?** (You could change the direction of the force exerted by the magnet by moving it to the right or left, and observe whether the paper clip moves with it.) Give students a moment to imagine this, or if you have the materials on hand to do so, perform the simple demonstration.

- **What do you predict would happen if you moved the magnet closer to the paper clip in the photo on page 21?** (It would still be attracted to the magnet.) **What would happen if you moved the magnet farther away?** (If you moved it far enough, the paper clip would fall down to the surface to which it is attached.)

Consider the Orientation of Magnetic Force

- Have students study the diagram on page 20. Ask: **What do the letters _S_ and _N_ mean on the magnets?** (south pole and north pole) **How are arrows used to show forces in this illustration?** (The arrows pointing toward each other show attraction, and the arrows pointing away from each other show repulsion.) Say: _Orientation_ means the way the magnets are facing. Ask: **How does the orientation of the magnets affect their forces?** (If unlike poles are facing each other, the magnets attract. If like poles are facing each other, the magnets repel.)

ELABORATE

Extend Your Thinking About Magnets

 Have students think of a time when they encountered evidence of magnets acting at a distance. Have students write their stories in their notebook and then share them with a partner. Ask a few students to share their stories with the class. (Possible answers may include feeling the pull of a magnet closure before a lid or refrigerator door was closed, or using two like poles of magnetic trains to push each other without touching.)

EVALUATE

 Have students record their answers to the Wrap It Up questions in their science notebook.

Wrap It Up!

1. **DEFINE What does _attract_ mean? What does _repel_ mean?** (_Attract_ means "to pull together," and _repel_ means "to push apart.")

2. **CONTRAST How is the force applied in the kick of a soccer ball different from the force a magnet exerts on a paper clip?** (Possible answer: The force applied to kick a soccer ball requires contact with the ball; the force a magnet exerts on a paper clip does not require contact.)

3. **EXPLAIN Tell what the phrase "opposites attract" means about magnets.** (Opposite poles of magnets pull toward each other.)

An additional interactive assessment activity can be found in the Exploring Science Digital Book.

SCIENCE BACKGROUND

Magnetism

In the same way gravity exerts non-contact forces on all objects, magnetism exerts non-contact forces on magnetic materials. Unlike gravity, which only attracts objects, magnetic force can attract or repel objects. The strength of a magnet's magnetic field decreases as the distance from the magnet increases. Only a few types of metals react strongly to magnetic fields, most commonly cobalt, iron, and nickel, though the strongest magnets include "rare earth" metals such as neodymium and samarium. These metals are attracted to magnets, and will also become _temporary magnets_ themselves when a magnetic filed is present. A _permanent magnet_ can be created when one of these metals (or an alloy containing multiple metals) is heated to a certain temperature, and then allowed to cool while in the presence of a strong external magnetic field.

READING CONNECTIONS

Determine Word Meaning

Determine the meaning of general academic and domain-specific words and phrases in a text relevant to a _grade 3 topic or subject area._

Guide students to determine the meaning of general academic and domain-specific words and phrases in the text. For example, in the EXPLAIN section when asking students to define _attract_ and _repel,_ guide students to use context clues to determine the meaning of the words. Encourage students to use their own words to further explain the meaning of each word.

PHYSICAL SCIENCE
Forces and Interactions

LIFE SCIENCE
Structure, Function, and Information Processing

EARTH SCIENCE
Weather and Climate

Magnetic Force

NEXT GENERATION SCIENCE STANDARDS | DISCIPLINARY CORE IDEA
PS2.B: Types of Interactions Electric and magnetic forces between a pair of objects do not require that the objects be in contact. The sizes of the forces in each situation depend on the properties of the objects and their distances apart and, for forces between two magnets, on their orientation relative to each other. (3-PS2-3), (3-PS2-4)

Objectives Students will be able to:
- Identify evidence that magnetic forces do not require that objects be in contact.
- Observe the effects of a magnet's distance apart from an object, and orientation on the force it exerts.

CLASSROOM MANAGEMENT

Materials *For groups of 4:* metric ruler; 2 strong bar magnets, 5 paper clips, small bar magnet

Time 30 minutes

Teaching Tips Preserve the strength of your classroom magnets by storing them properly. Magnets should be stored at room temperature in a dry place. Store each type of magnet separately, and always keep like poles apart. Be careful not to drop magnets as mechanical shock can cause them to lose their magnetism.

What to Expect Students will observe that a magnet must be near an object, but does not have to touch it, in order to exert a pull or a push on it. They will also observe that the strength of the force can vary depending on the magnet's size, distance apart from an object, and orientation relative to it. The exact distances needed for magnets to exert forces depend on the properties of the individual magnets you are using.

ENGAGE

Tap Prior Knowledge

- Ask: **What types of objects can magnets attract?** (Magnets attract other magnets and certain types of metals.) **What types of objects can magnets repel?** (other magnets) **What determines whether a magnet will attract or repel another magnet?** (the way in which the two magnets are oriented relative to each other)

EXPLORE

- Guide students through the investigation. Read pages 22–23 together.

 Have students construct a table for recording their observations in their science notebook.

Example:

Observations of Magnetic Force

Objects	Orientation	Predictions	Observations
2 bar magnets	north poles facing each other		

- Guide students as they carry out step 1. Show students how to record data in their table by demonstrating what to write in the beginning of the first row, as shown in the example.
- Tell students to record their observations in numbers and words. For example, they should write down the distance between the two magnets when they could first detect a force between them and also describe what happened.
- In steps 3 and 4, students make predictions. Remind them to record their predictions in their notebook.

EXPLAIN

- Ask students probing questions to help them interpret their data: **When did the magnets repel each other?** (when their like poles were facing each other) **How close were the magnets when they started to exert a force on each other?** (Answers will vary.) **When did you observe magnetic attraction?** (when the opposite poles of the magnets were facing each other and when a magnet came near a paper clip)

- Ask: **How did your observations of the small magnet compare with your observations of the large magnet?** (Possible answer: The larger magnet attracted paper clips from farther away and could hold more paper clips end-to-end than the small one.)

- **What can affect the size (strength) of a magnet's force on an object?** (The strength can be affected by how far it is from the object. The strength of the force increases as the magnet gets closer to the object that is attracted to it. Also, the direction in which the poles of two magnets are facing affects the magnet's force.) Remind students that another word for "which way something is facing" is *orientation*.

ELABORATE

 Provide other objects for students to test for magnetism. Include both magnetic and nonmagnetic materials, such as coins, bolts, aluminum foil, pencils, erasers, and washers. Have students plan and carry out an investigation to determine which materials are magnetic. They can use one or all of the magnets from the *Investigate*. Guide students to record predictions and observations in their notebook.

- If students are interested in knowing more about how an object can exert a force without contact, tell them that the way magnets exert a force at a distance is through something called a magnetic field that surrounds the magnet. Other forces that can act at a distance, such as gravity and electric force, also have fields of force.

EVALUATE

Have students record their answers to the Wrap It Up questions in their science notebook.

Wrap It Up!

1. **DESCRIBE Identify evidence from your investigation that magnets can exert forces without touching.** (Possible answer: Opposite poles of the magnets started pulling toward each other before they were touching. Like poles of the magnets pushed apart without touching. The paper clips began to move toward the magnet before the magnet touched them.)

2. **COMPARE AND CONTRAST How are the large and small magnets alike? How are they different** (They both have north and south poles and both exert magnetic forces. The large magnets may exert a stronger force than the small magnet.)

3. **CAUSE AND EFFECT What would happen if you brought the north pole of a bar magnet toward the north pole of another magnet that was attached to a toy car?** (The magnets would repel each other and the car would move.)

READING CONNECTION

Use Text Features

Use text features and search tools (e.g., key words, sidebars, hyperlinks) to locate information relevant to a given topic efficiently.

Guide students to use text features to locate information efficiently. For example, in the EXPLAIN and EVALUATE sections when asking students to discuss their results, tell them to feel free to page back to information in the previous lessons. Say: **Graphics and their captions, such as the one showing forces between magnets on pages 20–21, can be easy and quick sources of information for refreshing your memory.**

PHYSICAL SCIENCE
Forces and Interactions

LIFE SCIENCE
Structure, Function, and Information Processing

EARTH SCIENCE
Weather and Climate

Electromagnets

NEXT GENERATION SCIENCE STANDARDS | DISCIPLINARY CORE IDEA

PS2.B: Types of Interactions Electric and magnetic forces between a pair of objects do not require that the objects be in contact. The sizes of the forces in each situation depend on the properties of the objects and their distances apart and, for forces between two magnets, on their orientation relative to each other. (3-PS2-3), (3-PS2-4)

Objectives Students will be able to:
- Identify evidence that electromagnets can exert a force without being in contact with an object.
- Change the size of force produced by an electromagnet.

MANAGE THE INVESTIGATION

Materials For groups of 4: iron bolt (3 in.); D-cell battery; battery holder; 20 paper clips; piece of insulated copper wire with ends stripped (about 3 ft.) **For teacher:** wire stripper and cutter

Time 30 minutes

Advance Preparation Cut wire into pieces about 3 ft. long. Strip about an inch of insulation off both ends of each wire.

Teaching Tips Caution students that when the circuit is complete, the metal connections between battery holder and wires can get very hot. If any part of the electromagnet becomes hot, disconnect the battery.

What to Expect Students will observe that electricity can produce a magnetic force and that the size of the force can be changed by changing the number of times the wire is wrapped around the bolt. The more coils, the stronger the force.

ENGAGE

Tap Prior Knowledge

- Ask: **What are some things that affect the strength of a magnet's force on an object?** (The sizes of the forces depend on the properties of the magnet, the distance the magnet is from the object, and the orientation of one magnet with another magnet.) Tell students that an electric circuit set up in a certain way makes a special type of magnet called an electromagnet. One of the properties of an electromagnet is the number of times its wire is wrapped into a coil around a piece of metal.

EXPLORE

- Guide students through the investigation. Read pages 24–25 together.

 Have students construct a table for recording their observations in their science notebook.

Example:

Observations of Electromagnetic Force

Wraps of Wire	Number of Paper Clips	
	Predicted	Observed
15		
25		
35		

- Demonstrate step 1 for students. Show students how to hold the bolt and the end of the wire with one hand while they wrap the wire around with the other hand. The wraps of wire can be touching, but should not overlap.

- In step 2, you may need to clarify for students how to attach the wire to the battery holder, especially if your holders differ from the one shown on page 25. Make sure students put the battery in correctly.

PHYSICAL SCIENCE
Forces and Interactions

LIFE SCIENCE
Structure, Function, and Information Processing

EARTH SCIENCE
Weather and Climate

- Remind students to record their predictions and observations in their science notebook. Tell students they don't need to make any predictions until step 4. Encourage them to use their observations from step 3 to help them make their predictions in step 4.

EXPLAIN

- Have students share predictions, observations, and ideas within groups and with the class. Ask: **Did your results support your predictions? Explain.** (Answers will vary. Have students provide evidence that either supports or refutes their predictions.)

- Help students explain their observations by asking probing questions such as: **What happened to the force of the electromagnet as you added wraps around the bolt?** (The force got stronger.) **Does the electromagnet work without the battery?** If students are unsure, let them try it. (No, the electromagnet doesn't work without the battery.) **Why do you think that might be so?** (Encourage students to explain their reasoning. Possible answer: The electromagnet only works when there is electricity running through the wire. The electricity running around the bolt turns the bolt into a magnet.)

ELABORATE

 Extend the investigation by supplying groups with a switch, a ring stand, string, and a piece of metal that responds to a magnet, such as a toy car. Challenge students to use the materials to design and build a model junkyard electromagnet. Depending on your students' experience with circuits, you may want to add the switches to their circuits yourself and let them design the rest. Have students draw and label their model in their notebook. (Possible solution: Students can tie one end of the string to the top of the bolt, and string the other end through the ring stand. They can use the electromagnet to pick up the car, pull on the string to lift it, and turn the switch to let it go.)

EVALUATE

 Have students record their answers to the Wrap It Up questions in their science notebook.

Wrap It Up!

1. **EXPLAIN** **How did you measure the strength of the electromagnet's force? When was it weakest? Strongest?** (Possible answer: I measured the strength of the force by counting the number of paper clips the electromagnet would hold. It was weakest when I wrapped the wire 15 times. It was strongest when I wrapped the wire 35 times.)

2. **GENERALIZE** **Can an electromagnet exert a force without touching an object? Explain.** (Yes. If electricity is flowing through the electromagnet, it can exert a magnetic force from a distance.)

3. **CAUSE AND EFFECT** **What might happen if you had a longer bolt and wrapped the wire around 50 times?** (The electromagnet would be even stronger.)

READING CONNECTION

Use Text Features

Use text features and search tools (e.g., key words, sidebars, hyperlinks) to locate information relevant to a given topic efficiently.

Guide students to use text features to locate information efficiently. For example, in the EVALUATE section when asking students about what they did, have them refer back to the steps of the procedure. Point out that the procedure is written in short, numbered paragraphs, which makes it easier to follow and locate information.

Electric Forces

NEXT GENERATION SCIENCE STANDARDS | DISCIPLINARY CORE IDEA
PS2.B: Types of Interactions Electric and magnetic forces between a pair of objects do not require that the objects be in contact. The sizes of the forces in each situation depend on the properties of the objects and their distances apart and, for forces between two magnets, on their orientation relative to each other. (3-PS2-3), (3-PS2-4)

Objectives **Students will be able to:**
- Identify electric force as a force that can act at a distance.
- Recognize that the electric force between two objects depends on the properties of the objects.
- Observe the effect of distance on the force exerted by a charged object.

Science Vocabulary
static electricity

ENGAGE
Tap Prior Knowledge
- Ask students to recount an experience with static electricity. Ask: **Have you ever seen someone's hair stand up like the cat's fur in the photo? What was happening when the person's hair stood up?** Have a few students share their experiences.

EXPLORE
Preview Electric Forces
- Have students observe the image on pages 26–27. Ask: **What is happening to the cat's fur?** (It is standing up.) Say: **Remember that every time an object moves, a force is acting on it. The cat's fur is moving up.** Ask: **What kind of force is acting on the cat's fur?** (a pull) **What do you think might be causing the pull?** Give students a moment to think. Then tell students the balloon is exerting a pulling force.

Set a Purpose and Read
- Have students read in order find out about electric force.
- Have students read pages 26–27.

EXPLAIN
Identify Electric Force
- Have students look again at the large photo on pages 26–27. Ask: **What type of force is the balloon exerting on the cat's fur?** (electric force) **What evidence can you see in the photo that shows that objects can exert electric forces without touching?** (Possible answer: Most of the fur being pulled up by the balloon is not touching the balloon.)

Recognize That Electric Forces Depend On Objects' Properties
- Ask: **What are electric charges?** (Tiny particles that exert a force and are either positive or negative.) Say: **When an object has more positive charges than negative charges, then the net charge is positive. When an object has more negative charges than positive charges, then the net charge is negative.** Ask: **How can an object become charged?** (by contacting certain materials) Ask: **What is an electric charge that builds up on an object called?** (static electricity) **From the photo and your experiences, what types of objects and materials do you think can easily become charged?** (balloons, hair, door knobs and other metal objects, flannel, wool, paper)
- Tell students that the ability to take or give charges is simply a property of some materials. The material an object is made of either has the property or it does not. Likewise, magnetism is a property of some objects.
- Ask: **How can you charge a balloon?** (Possible answer: I can rub it on my hair.) **What did you do with the electric force?** (Possible answer: I used it to pull the balloon toward the wall and hold it there.)
- Guide students through the *SCIENCE in a SNAP* activity.

ELABORATE

Extend Your Thinking About Electric Force

 Provide groups of students with a stopwatch and a latex balloon filled with air. Have students rub the balloon against their hair for varying amounts of time and test how long the balloon hangs on a wall. Ask students to record their observations and explain their results in terms of forces. Have groups share their results.

EVALUATE

 Have students record their answers to the Wrap It Up questions in their science notebook.

Wrap It Up!

1. **COMPARE** **How are the forces exerted by electric charges similar to the forces exerted by magnets?** (Magnets and electric charges can both exert forces from a distance. With magnets, opposite poles attract and like poles repel. With electric charges, opposite charges attract and like charges repel.)

2. **IDENTIFY** **Where have you seen the effects of static electricity at home or at school?** (Possible answer: I had a sock stuck to my shirt when it came out of the dryer at home.)

READING CONNECTION

Ask and Answer Questions to Demonstrate Understanding

Ask and answer questions to demonstrate understanding of a text, referring explicitly to the text as the basis for the answers.

Guide students in asking and answering questions to demonstrate understanding of a text. For example, in the EXPLAIN section as you ask students how an object can become charged, have students point to the text, illustrations, or captions where they found their answers. Ask students if they have any other questions about electric forces and static electricity.

SCIENCE in a SNAP

Electric Forces

Materials *For groups of 2:* tissue paper; scissors, balloon full of air, wool cloth

Teaching Tips Plan enough time to blow up and tie the balloons prior to the activity. Before you begin, review electric forces by asking: **What determines the strength of an electric force between two objects?** (the properties of the objects and their distance apart) Tell students that you have selected for this activity objects with properties that allow them to become charged and exert electric forces. Tell students that they will get to build the charge and manipulate the distance between the two objects themselves. Have students record their observations in their science notebook using both words and diagrams.

What to Expect Students will observe no electric force between the pieces of tissue paper and balloon in step 2. After they charge the balloon with the wool cloth in step 3, they will observe an electric force between the balloon and the tissue that gets stronger as they move the balloon toward the paper.

PHYSICAL SCIENCE
Forces and Interactions

LIFE SCIENCE
Structure, Function, and Information Processing

EARTH SCIENCE
Weather and Climate

Electric Forces

NEXT GENERATION SCIENCE STANDARDS | DISCIPLINARY CORE IDEAS

PS2.B: Types of Interactions Electric and magnetic forces between a pair of objects do not require that the objects be in contact. The sizes of the forces in each situation depend on the properties of the objects and their distances apart and, for forces between two magnets, on their orientation relative to each other. (3-PS2-3), (3-PS2-4)

Objectives **Students will be able to:**
- Identify evidence that electric forces between a pair of objects do not require that the objects be in contact.
- Observe attractive and repulsive effects of electric forces.

CLASSROOM MANAGEMENT

Materials *For groups of 4:* 2 latex balloons inflated with air; 2 pieces of string (1 m); masking tape; wool cloth

Time 40 minutes

Advance Preparation Blow up the balloons before the activity. Cut string into pieces about a meter long.

Teaching Tips The balloons will charge best if students rub them with the cloth in one direction, 10–20 times.

What to Expect Students will observe that when one balloon is rubbed with the cloth, it attracts the other balloon. This happens because the balloon gains charges from the cloth when they are in contact. The positively charged balloon exerts an electric force on the other balloon, pulling the balloons toward each other. When both balloons are rubbed with the cloth, they repel each other. This happens because both balloons become positively charged and like charges repel each other.

ENGAGE

Tap Prior Knowledge

- Have students observe the large photo on pages 28–29. Ask: **What is happening in this photo?** (Pieces of packing foam are sticking to the woman's arms.) **What force is holding the foam pieces on her arms?** (static electricity) **What is static electricity?** (an electric charge that builds up on an object)

EXPLORE

- Guide students through the investigation. Read pages 28–29 together.

  My science notebook Have students construct a table for recording their observations in their science notebook.

  Example:

  Observations of Electric Force

What I Did	Predictions	Observations

- Guide students as they make their observations and predictions. Ask probing questions to encourage critical thinking and connections, such as: **What forces are acting on the balloons in step 1?** (gravity and the string holding it up) **Are the forces balanced or unbalanced in step 1?** (balanced) **What unbalanced force is acting on the balloons in step 2?** (my hands) **What was the effect of that force?** (The balloons moved together and then fell back to their original position when I removed the force.) **What happened to the balloons when you rubbed one of them with the wool cloth?** (The balloons moved together and stayed there.) **What happened to the balloons when you rubbed both balloons with the wool cloth?** (The balloons moved away from each other and stayed there.)

- Ask students to record their observations both in words and as drawings. Encourage students to use the terms *attract* and *repel* in their descriptions.

EXPLAIN

- Have students share their predictions and observations within groups and with the class. Ask: **Did your results support your predictions? Were there any results that surprised you? Explain.** (Answers will vary. Have students point out evidence from their observations to either support or refute their predictions.)

- Ask questions to help students explain their observations: **How did rubbing the balloons with the wool cloth change the balloons?** (It built up a charge on them.) **What might have caused the balloons to attract each other after you rubbed one of the balloons with the cloth?** (The charged balloon exerted an electric force on the other balloon, attracting it.) **What might have caused the balloons to repel each other after you rubbed both balloons with the cloth?** (Both balloons had the same type of charge, so they repelled each other.)

- **What evidence from your observations shows that objects do not have to be touching to exert electric forces on each other?** (Possible answer: In step 3, the balloons started moving toward each other before they were touching. In step 4, the balloons affected each other without touching at all.)

ELABORATE

 If a faucet is available in your classroom, ask the class to stand around it and have a few volunteers demonstrate the effect of a charged balloon on running water. The stream of water will move toward the balloon. Probe the class for explanations of what they observe. If students have trouble explaining that the balloon and water must have opposite charges to attract, help them relate the situation to step 3 of the *Investigate*. Have students draw their observations and record in their science notebook an explanation for what they observed.

EVALUATE

 Have students record their answers to the Wrap It Up questions in their science notebook.

Wrap It Up!

1. EXPLAIN **Why did you observe the hanging balloons before you rubbed them?** (so I would have something to compare my results with after I rubbed one of them)

2. DESCRIBE **In steps 3 and 4, what happened when the balloons were hanging freely? What did you do to cause this difference?** (In step 3 they moved together, and in step 4 they moved apart. In step 3 only one balloon was charged and exerted a force on the other balloon. In step 4 both balloons had the same type of charge.)

3. INFER **What can you infer about the charges on the balloons in step 3? In step 4?** (In step 3 the charges were opposite; in step 4 the charges were the same.)

PHYSICAL SCIENCE
Forces and Interactions

LIFE SCIENCE
Structure, Function, and Information Processing

EARTH SCIENCE
Weather and Climate

Determine Cause-and-Effect Relationships

NEXT GENERATION SCIENCE STANDARDS | PERFORMANCE EXPECTATION

3-PS2-3. Ask questions to determine cause and effect relationships of electric or magnetic interactions between two objects not in contact with each other. [Clarification Statement: Examples of an electric force could include the force on hair from an electrically charged balloon and the electrical forces between a charged rod and pieces of paper; examples of a magnetic force could include the force between two permanent magnets, the force between an electromagnet and steel paperclips, and the force exerted by one magnet versus the force exerted by two magnets. Examples of cause and effect relationships could include how the distance between objects affects strength of the force and how the orientation of magnets affects the direction of the magnetic force.] [Assessment Boundary: Assessment is limited to forces produced by objects that can be manipulated by students, and electrical interactions are limited to static electricity.]

Objective   Students will be able to:

- Ask questions to determine cause-and-effect relationships of electric or magnetic interactions between two objects not in contact with each other.

CLASSROOM MANAGEMENT

Materials   For groups of 4: Assemble a variety of materials from which students can choose to test their question, including metric rulers; graph paper; magnets of varying sizes, strengths, and shapes; plastic bags full of paper clips or steel washers; stopwatches; inflated balloons; wool cloths; string; scissors; masking tape; plastic bags full of shredded paper or packing peanuts.

Time   15 minutes for planning; 30 minutes for testing and observation; 15 minutes for analysis and retesting; 20 minutes for sharing and explanation

Advance Preparation   Prepare plastic bags of small supplies, such as paper clips, washers, shredded paper, and packing peanuts.

Teaching Tips   In order to meet the performance expectation, students must plan and conduct their own investigation. Coach students through the planning process without instructing them on specific steps to take or materials to use. Ask students to relate scientific ideas to their plans as they work.

What to Expect   Students will observe that magnetic and electric forces can act at a distance and that every force has a strength and a direction. They will ask and answer questions to identify a cause-and-effect relationship about a force. For example, they could measure the strength of a magnet's force by tying a paper clip to a string and pulling it away from a magnet to measure how far the paper clip remains suspended because of the force of the magnet. They could then test multiple magnets to determine that a magnet with a stronger force causes the paper clip to be suspended a greater distance from the magnet.

ENGAGE

Set the scene.

- Call students' attention to the photo on pages 30–31. Have a volunteer read the caption aloud. Ask: **What is happening in the photo?** (A bunch of paper clips are hanging from someone's hand.) Explain that even though it may look like there is something sticking into or through the person's hand, there is not. The magnet and paper clips are not pushing against the person's hand hard enough to be painful.) **What is holding the paper clips up?** (the force of the magnet acting through the person's hand)

- Prepare students for the type of thinking they will be doing in this activity. Ask: **How could you measure the strength of this magnet so that you could compare its strength to another magnet's strength?** (Possible

PHYSICAL SCIENCE
Forces and Interactions

LIFE SCIENCE
Structure, Function, and Information Processing

EARTH SCIENCE
Weather and Climate

answer: You could count how many paper clips it can hold up.) Say: **You can plan and conduct an investigation to answer your question and determine a cause-and-effect relationship. For example, complete this cause-and-effect statement: A magnet with a stronger force will hold (more or fewer) paper clips.** (more) Ask: **How could you test that?** (Possible answer: You could try different magnets and count the number of paper clips each can hold through a material such as a piece of cardboard or a plastic cup.)

- Have a volunteer read the introductory paragraph and the first step on page 30. Ask: **What is your task?** (to test a question about magnetic or electric forces) Preview the rest of the investigation together.

Ask a question.

 Have students discuss with their group members which question under step 1 they would like to test and record it in their science notebook.

EXPLORE

Plan and conduct an investigation.

- Guide students as they plan their investigation. Have them make a list of materials in their notebook. Encourage students to set up their investigation so that they can measure quantities in numbers, whenever possible. Refer back to the example in the ENGAGE section. Ask: **How did we say we could measure the force of the magnet through the hand?** (by the number of paper clips a magnet could

attract) Tell students numbered data are useful because they can be compared easily.

- Ask: **How will you set up your test?** (Possible answer: We will tie a paper clip to a string and place the paper clip on a magnet. We will pull the paper clip away from the magnet and measure how far the paperclip can remain suspended before it drops to the desk.) Ask: **Which items are you planning to test?** (Possible answer: the large and small bar magnet, and the disc magnet) **How will you make sure your test is fair?** (Possible answer: We will change only one variable—the type of magnet tested—and keep all other variables the same.) **How will you record your data?** (Possible answer: We will make a table.)

- Have students write their plan as a series of numbered steps.

Example:

1. We will tie a paper clip to a piece of string. We will tape a magnet to a desk so the magnet stays in place. We will place a ruler next to the end of the magnet.

2. To test the strength of the magnet, we will put the paper clip on the magnet and pull the string until it is tight. Then we will slowly pull the string and paper clip away from the magnet. The paper clip will be held in the air by the magnet. We will slowly pull the paper clip away until it falls to the desk. We will use the ruler to measure how far the magnet was able to pull on the paper clip until the paper clip fell.

3. We will repeat step 2 two more times with different magnets and record our data.

SCIENCE AND ENGINEERING PRACTICES

Asking Questions and Defining Problems

- In this activity, students asked questions to determine cause-and-effect relationships of electric or magnetic interactions between two objects not in contact with each other. Have groups of students generate a new question from their results and discuss how that question could be investigated.

CROSSCUTTING CONCEPTS

Cause and Effect

- Say: **Cause-and-effect relationships are routinely identified, tested, and used to explain change.** Ask: **What change did you notice when you completed your activity?** (Answers will vary depending on the chosen activity. Accept reasonable responses related to the effects they noticed and what caused them.)

Determine Cause-and-Effect Relationships (continued)

EXPLORE (continued)

- Guide students as they carry out their plan. Have students make a table similar to the one shown on page 31a in their notebook to record their observations.

  Example:

  ### Strength of Magnets

Test	Magnet	Distance Magnet Held Paper Clip Up
1	large bar magnet	1.3 cm (13 mm)
2	small magnet	0.9 cm (9 mm)
3	disc magnet	0.7 cm (7 mm)

EXPLAIN

Analyze and interpret data.

- Ask questions to help students interpret their data. **What did you results show?** (Possible answer: The large bar magnet was the strongest of the magnets we tested.) **Were you able to measure the strength of a magnet or an electric charge, or the direction of a magnet's force?** (Possible answer: We measured the strength of a magnet.)

- **Did your investigation show the relationship between a cause and its effect?** (Possible answer: Yes. Our investigation showed that a stronger magnet held the paper clip in the air for a greater distance.) **If not, how could you change your investigation so that it shows such a relationship and answers your question?** Students may need to adjust their test so they are changing only one variable at a time.

- Say: **If you change only one variable and keep all the others the same, it is called a fair test. A fair test is the *only* kind of test that can show a cause-and-effect relationship. If your test produces an effect, you know the effect was caused by the variable you changed because it was the only one you changed.**

- Ask: **What variable did you change?** (Possible answer: We changed the type of magnet to attract the paper clip.) **What variable did you measure?** (Possible answer: We measured the distance each magnet was able to hold up the paper clip.) **What variables did you keep the same each time?** (Possible answer: We used the same string and paper clip each time. We taped the magnet to the desk so it would remain in place. We had the same person pull each time, and she pulled at the same rate each time. We had the same person read the measurement on the ruler each time.)

Share your results.

- Have students share their results with a partner from another group, explaining how they collected data and what cause-and-effect relationship they observed. Encourage students to give each other feedback and suggestions for improvement.

- Have students revisit the question they selected at the beginning of the lesson, for example: *How can I measure the strength of a magnet?* Ask: **How can you use your results to answer your question?** (Example: In our investigation, we designed a way to test the strength of a magnet, and we used it to obtain strength data for several magnets.)

- If time allows, have groups trade tests with each other to corroborate their data. Explain that, when a variable is tested with different tests and responds the same way each time, the results are more likely to be valid. For example, ask: **Which groups tested the strength of a magnet's force?** Have those groups exchange tests and retest their magnets using the same method. Have each group give a short demonstration so the other group knows what to do. They can also read the steps as they are written out in each other's notebooks. Have students record their new observations. After students have tested their objects using each other's tests, have them compare the new data to their original data. If their science is sound, the patterns in both sets of data should match.

Explain your findings.

- Have groups present their findings to the class. Have them demonstrate their test and explain how they showed a cause-and-effect relationship.

- Ask: **In what ways did you think like a scientist as you completed this activity?** (Possible answer: I performed a fair test to investigate the forces related to magnets, took measurements, and analyzed my observations for cause and effect, just like a scientist would.)

ELABORATE

 Extend the investigation by bringing out a new magnet or electrically charged object for students to test using a procedure similar to the one they used in the activity. The charged object could be a plastic rod rubbed with fur or a glass rod rubbed with silk (rubbing the object in only one direction works best). Have students make a prediction, test the new object, and explain their observations.

EVALUATE

 Check to make sure students have recorded their procedures and data in their science notebook. Then ask students these questions. Have them record the answers in their science notebook.

1. **DESCRIBE How did your data show a cause-and-effect relationship?** (Possible answer: Each time we changed one variable, the variable we were measuring changed. We controlled the other variables the best we could. This shows a cause-and-effect relationship. The variable we changed was the type of magnet. The variable we measured was the distance the magnet was able to hold the paper clip in the air before it fell to the desk. We saw that different magnets were able to hold the paper clip in the air for different distances. We concluded that the stronger the magnet, the further we could pull the paper clip before it fell to the desk.

2. **EXPLAIN What evidence did your data provide that an object can exert magnetic or electric forces on another object without contacting it?** (Possible answer: As we pulled the paper clip away from each magnet, the paper clip remained held in the air. The magnet was exerting a force on the paper clip even though they were not in contact.)

RUBRICS

Teacher Rubric Use the scale descriptions to guide your assessment of each student's work. Assess each item separately, and then decide on one overall score, using the following scale:

4: Student performs with thorough understanding.
3: Student performs with adequate understanding.
2: Student performs with basic understanding.
1: Student performs with limited understanding.

Rubric	Scale			
The student planned and conducted an investigation to produce data that could serve to answer the question.	4	3	2	1
The student evaluated different ways of observing and/or measuring a phenomenon to determine which way can answer a question.	4	3	2	1
The student made observations and/or measurements to collect data that could be used to draw conclusions.	4	3	2	1
The student's presentation showed an understanding of forces.	4	3	2	1
Overall Score	4	3	2	1

Student Rubric Have students complete a self-evaluation similar to that shown below.

Rubric	Yes	Not Yet
1. I can plan an investigation and carry out the steps.		
2. I can make and draw my observations.		
3. I can learn from my results.		
4. I can share my results and say how they show the ideas we have learned in this class.		

PHYSICAL SCIENCE
Forces and Interactions

LIFE SCIENCE
Structure, Function, and Information Processing

EARTH SCIENCE
Weather and Climate

Define and Solve a Problem

NEXT GENERATION SCIENCE STANDARDS | PERFORMANCE EXPECTATION

3-PS2-4. Define a simple design problem that can be solved by applying scientific ideas about magnets. [Clarification Statement: Examples of problems could include constructing a latch to keep a door shut and creating a device to keep two moving objects from touching each other.]

3-5-ETS1-1. Define a simple design problem reflecting a need or a want that includes specified criteria for success and constraints on materials, time, or cost.

Objectives **Students will be able to:**
- Define a design problem that can be solved by applying scientific ideas about magnets.
- Specify criteria for success and constraints on materials, time, or cost.

CLASSROOM MANAGEMENT

Materials *For groups of 4:* Assemble a variety of magnets from which students can choose, such as disc magnets, bar magnets, horseshoe magnets, cut sections of magnet sheet, and magnets with adhesive backs. Also assemble a variety of basic model-building materials, such as string, glue, tape, scissors, cardboard pieces, cardboard boxes, recycled containers, binder clips, and toy cars.

Time 20 minutes for planning; 30 minutes for making, testing, and analyzing; 20 minutes for retesting; 20 minutes for sharing and explanation

Teaching Tips In order to meet the performance expectation, students must define a problem, and plan and conduct their own investigation to solve the problem. Coach students through the planning process without instructing them on specific steps to take or materials to use. Ask students to relate scientific ideas to their plans as they work.

What to Expect Students will define a problem that can be solved with magnets and design a solution. They will observe that the problem-solving cycle often involves many stages of analysis, refinement, and retesting.

ENGAGE

Set the scene.

- Have students look at the photos on pages 32–33 and ask volunteers to read the accompanying captions aloud. Ask: **How do the ball and goal use magnets?** (The ball detects a magnetic field when it enters into the goal.) **What problem does this design solution solve?** (Presumably it solves the problem of a referee not always being able to see for sure whether a ball crossed into the goal or not.) **How does it solve the problem?** (The moment when the ball crosses into the goal, it sends a signal to the referee's watch, so the referee knows with certainty that a goal has been scored.)

- Have a volunteer read the introductory paragraph and the first step on page 32. Ask: **What is your task?** (To design a new use for magnets.) Preview the rest of the investigation together.

Ask a question.

 Have students record the question under step 1 in their science notebooks.

EXPLORE

Plan and carry out an investigation.

- Say: **Engineers design solutions to problems. You will be using magnets to design a solution. But first you will need to identify and define the problem you wish to solve. Think of the uses that magnets lend themselves to, such as clasping or attaching things. Think of problems you have encountered that needed this type of solution.** Brainstorm possible problems that could be solved with magnets. Have a volunteer read the ideas under step 2 on page 32 to get you started.

PHYSICAL SCIENCE
Forces and Interactions

LIFE SCIENCE
Structure, Function, and Information Processing

EARTH SCIENCE
Weather and Climate

- Write the word *Problem* on the board. Have students copy it into their notebook. Once groups come up with a problem to solve, have them write it under this heading. (For example: The problem we will solve is that our coat zippers often fall down when we want the zipper to stay up.)

- Say: **A *prototype* is a preliminary model of a solution.** Have students examine the materials available and begin to work with their group members to sketch out a prototype in their notebook. From the materials available, students may need to build a model of the problem as well as the solution. For example, if students are designing a way to keep a mailbox shut, they will need to build a model of the mailbox as well as a prototype of their solution. Assist students with this, if necessary. They may not realize they only need to model the problem area. For example, in the case of the mailbox, they would need a flap or lid that closes up from the bottom. They do not necessarily need something that looks like an actual mailbox. Tell students they can also look for objects in the classroom that suitably model the problem.

- To stimulate critical thinking, ask probing questions, such as: **How could you use these materials to make a prototype of your design solution?** (We could attach a magnet to the zipper, and attach something metal to the coat collar for the magnet to stick to.)

- Ask follow-up questions based on students' responses. These follow-up questions are essential for modeling self-questioning and getting students used to the logic of the engineering cycle. For example: **What could you use to attach the magnet to the zipper?** (Possible answer: Maybe we could use some type of cord or string.) **What type of magnet might work best for your needs? Study the materials again if you need to. Take your time.** (Possible answer: Maybe one with a hole in the middle.) **Why do you think so?** (Possible answer: We could use the hole to tie a string through the magnet and attach it to the zipper pull.) **What type of metal will you use on the coat collar and how will you attach it?** (Possible answer: We could use a binder clip.) **What are your reasons for that decision?** (Possible answer: We tested it and the clip is attracted to the magnet. Also, it can clip easily to a coat collar.) **What scientific ideas about magnets will you make use of in your design?** (Possible answer: We will use the force that magnets exert on some metal objects to hold the zipper up.)

- Write the word *Solution* on the board. Have students copy it into their science notebook. Have students draw a picture of their prototype in their science notebook.

- Say: **How will you test your prototype?** (Possible answer: We will use Lauren's coat because her zipper falls down. We will have her

SCIENCE AND ENGINEERING PRACTICES

Asking Questions and Defining Problems

- Say: **Engineers solve problems by developing new or improved tools.** Ask: **What simple problem can you think of that can be solved through the development of a new or improved object or tool?** (Answers will vary, but accept reasonable responses for possible solutions to problems. An example may be a magnetic stand for their tablet device so it stands at an angle without needing to hold it.)

CROSSCUTTING CONCEPTS

Connections to Engineering, Technology, and Applications of Science
Interdependence of Science, Engineering, and Technology

- Say: **Scientific discoveries about the natural world can often lead to new and improved technologies, which are developed through the engineering design process.** Ask: **What are some tools or devices you have seen that could have been inspired by nature?** (Possible answers include: Airplanes inspired by birds, hook and loop tape inspired by burr, parachutes inspired by dandelion seeds, barbed wire inspired by thorn bushes.)

Define and Solve a Problem (continued)

EXPLORE (continued)

wear the coat and jump up and down ten times. She will try to jump the same way each time.)

- **How will you determine whether or not your prototype works?** (Possible answer: We will have Lauren jump up and down ten times without our solution. Then we will have her jump up and down ten times with our solution attached to her coat. We will use a ruler to measure how far down the zipper drops each time. We will compare the two measurements.)

- Write the word *Criteria* on the board. Have students copy it into their science notebook. Say: **What are the criteria for success?** Under that heading, have students specify the criteria for a successful solution. (Possible answer: We will know we have a successful solution if the zipper has dropped more without our solution than with our solution, after being subjected to ten jumps.)

- Write the word *Constraints* on the board. Have students copy it into their science notebook. Say: **What are the constraints of your design?** Under that heading, have students specify the constraints they are working under. (Time is limited to the class period and materials are limited to those that are available.)

- Have students write their plans for building and testing their prototype in their science notebook.

Analyze and interpret data.

- Guide students as they make and test their prototype. Have students create a table in their science notebook to record their observations.

Example:

Zipper Solution Test 1

Description	How Far Zipper Dropped (cm)	Observations
original design solution	10	The magnet fell off and the zipper fell down quickly.
no solution	7	The zipper dropped down a little bit with each jump.

- Guide students as they analyze their data. Ask: **Does your solution work the way you want it to?** (Possible answer: No.) **How do you know?** (Possible answer: The zipper dropped farther with the design than without it.) **How can you explain your results?** (We think the magnet might be too heavy.) **How can you improve your design?** (We will try using a smaller, lighter magnet and taping it to the string.)

- Have students make changes to their prototype and test it again. Encourage multiple iterations.

Example:

Zipper Solution Test 2

Description	How Far Zipper Dropped (cm)	Observations
smaller magnet	9	The string came off the magnet and the zipper dropped down a little with each jump.
no solution	7	The zipper dropped down a little bit with each jump.

Zipper Solution Test 3

Description	How Far Zipper Dropped (cm)	Observations
sticky magnets	0	It worked well. The zipper did not drop.
no solution	7	The zipper dropped down a little bit with each jump.

EXPLAIN

Construct an explanation from evidence.

- Have students share their results and discuss their final design, how their solution uses magnetic forces to solve a problem, and how they arrived at their solution. (Possible answer: Our solution uses magnetic force to attract a zipper to the top of a coat and keep it from falling down. Through our testing, we determined that the type of magnet we chose was important to a successful design. Some magnets were too heavy and others kept coming off during testing. We ended up using two sticky square magnets and sticking them, back-to-back directly to the zipper pull. We gave up on the string. Our final solution works like this: the magnets stick to the metal part of the binder clip on the collar of the coat, and that keeps the zipper from falling.)

Communicate information.

- Have groups present their findings to the class, including a demonstration of their final design solution. Allow time for questions and answers.

- Ask: **In what ways did you think like an engineer as you completed this activity?** (Answers will vary depending on the problem being solved. Students' answers should include designing a solution by creating and testing a prototype.)

ELABORATE

- Allow students to conduct "phase 2" or "beta testing" of their final design. Accommodate for students to set up a situation in the real world, or as close to it as possible, to try out their solution. For example, if they are improving a mailbox, have them run tests using an actual mailbox. If they are improving a zipper, have the student wear a coat using the solution as he or she normally would. Have students plan the investigation, record their observations, and interpret their results in their science notebook. Have students share their results with the class.

EVALUATE

 Check to make sure students have recorded their plans and data in their science notebook. Then ask students these questions. Have them record the answers in their science notebook.

1. **DEFINE** **What problem did you set out to solve? How did you think of that problem?** (Possible answer: We set out to solve the problem of coat zippers falling down. We thought of the problem because one of our group members has a coat that does this.)

2. **IDENTIFY** **What observation from your data was most useful in improving your design? What did it teach you?** (Possible answer: The observation from our first test when the magnet fell off was the most useful because it taught us that we needed to find just the right magnet for the job. Once we were able to do that, we had solved the problem.)

RUBRICS

Teacher Rubric Use the scale descriptions to guide your assessment of each student's work. Assess each item separately, and then decide on one overall score, using the following scale:

4: Student performs with thorough understanding.
3: Student performs with adequate understanding.
2: Student performs with basic understanding.
1: Student performs with limited understanding.

Rubric	Scale			
The student planned and conducted an investigation to produce data that could serve to answer the question.	4	3	2	1
The student evaluated different ways of observing and/or measuring a phenomenon to determine which way can answer a question.	4	3	2	1
The student made observations and/or measurements to collect data that could be used to draw conclusions.	4	3	2	1
The student's presentation showed an understanding of the force of magnetism.	4	3	2	1
Overall Score	4	3	2	1

Student Rubric Have students complete a self-evaluation similar to that shown below.

Rubric	Yes	Not Yet
1. I can plan an investigation and carry out the steps.		
2. I can make and draw my observations.		
3. I can learn from my results.		
4. I can share my results and say how they show the ideas we have learned in this class.		

PHYSICAL SCIENCE
Forces and Interactions

LIFE SCIENCE
Structure, Function, and Information Processing

EARTH SCIENCE
Weather and Climate

Roller Coaster Designer

NEXT GENERATION SCIENCE STANDARDS | CONNECTIONS TO NATURE OF SCIENCE
Scientific Investigations Use a Variety of Methods Science investigations use a variety of methods, tools, and techniques.

Objective **Students will be able to:**
- Connect concepts about forces, motion, and patterns to the career of a roller coaster designer.

ENGAGE

Tap Prior Knowledge

- Ask students to share some of their personal experiences with roller coasters. Ask: **What are some of the effects of the motions you experienced?** (Possible answers: I felt myself moving so fast that I could feel it in my stomach. I felt a strange sensation when the coaster fell quickly. I felt jerked around in my seat when the coaster turned quickly.) **What science concepts do you think roller coaster designers need to know?** (They need to know about the forces and the patterns of motion of roller coaster cars in order to make the structures safe and their movements safe and fun.)

EXPLORE

Preview the Lesson

- Have students observe the photo on pages 34–35. Ask probing questions to encourage exploration. For example, ask: **How are the people oriented?** (They are upside-down.) **Do you think they are moving?** (Yes.) **Fast or slow?** (They are probably moving very fast.) **In what ways is their motion changing?** (They are changing direction and they may also be changing speed.)

Set a Purpose and Read

- Have students read in order to describe the career of a roller coaster designer.
- Have students read pages 34–35.

EXPLAIN

Describe the Work of a Roller Coaster Designer

- Ask: **What does Cynthia Emerick do?** (She oversees the design and installation of roller coasters.) **What type of classes did Ms. Emerick take in college to help her in her career?** (She took math and science classes. She also took classes about materials, how to put them together, and what happens when they break down.) **In addition to figuring out how to make rides fun, what is another problem she and her team work to solve?** (how to make rides safe) **What is a constraint that Ms. Emerick and her team are working under?** (Cost. They are figuring out how to make rides in a way that is not too expensive.)

Connect Concepts About Forces, Motion, and Patterns to the Career of a Roller Coaster Designer

- Direct students' attention again to the photo on page 35. Say: **The people in the photo are in motion, and their motion is changing in speed and direction.** Ask: **Are the forces on the people balanced or unbalanced?** (They are unbalanced.) **How do you know?** (I know because only unbalanced forces result in a change of motion.) **What force pulled the people to the top of the first hill?** (a pull supplied by motors) **What force will pull them back down?** (gravity) **What patterns of motion would a roller coaster designer need to identify in order to predict future motion?** (Possible answers: what happens to the riders when they move up and down and turn quickly; how much time and space the roller coaster needs to slow down to a stop at the end)

PHYSICAL SCIENCE
Forces and Interactions

LIFE SCIENCE
Structure, Function, and Information Processing

EARTH SCIENCE
Weather and Climate

Find Out More

- Ask: **Is this a career you would find interesting? Why or why not?** (Allow students to share their answers. Accept all positive and negative responses.) For students who find this to be an interesting career, ask: **Why would you like to be a roller coaster designer?** (Possible answer: I love riding roller coasters and would like to be part of a team that designs bigger, better, and faster roller coasters but uses science to make sure that the rides are still safe.)

ELABORATE

Learn More About Roller Coasters

 Have students do research to find out about three different roller coasters. Suggest that they try to answer each of the following questions about each coaster: **When was it built? Where is it located? How many hills does it have? How high is its highest hill? What is its maximum speed? Is it made mostly of metal or wooden materials? How many loops does it have? Would you ever want to ride on this coaster?** Then have students make a detailed drawing of their ideal roller coaster and write a few sentences to explain how forces, motion, and patterns relate to their drawings.

EVALUATE

 Ask students these questions. Have them record their answers in their science notebook.

1. **RECALL What does Cynthia Emerick do as a roller coaster designer?** (She oversees the design and installation of roller coasters to make sure they are thrilling and safe but not too expensive.)

2. **EXPLAIN What did Ms. Emerick study in college to help her make sure that roller coasters are always safe for the riders?** (She studied math and science. She also studied materials, how to put them together, and what happens when they break down.)

3. **CAUSE AND EFFECT What causes roller coaster cars to move up a hill?** (Powerful motors pull the cars up the hill.)

DIFFERENTIATED INSTRUCTION

Extra Support Have pairs of students use the terms *force, motion, pull,* and *predict* to describe Cynthia Emerick's career and the science involved in it.

Challenge Have partners prepare a mock interview with a roller coaster designer. Have one partner play the role of the reporter and the other partner play the designer. Have partners perform their interviews for the class.

READING CONNECTION

Ask and Answer Questions to Demonstrate Understanding

Ask and answer questions to demonstrate understanding of a text, referring explicitly to the text as the basis for the answers.

Guide students to ask and answer questions to demonstrate understanding of a text, referring explicitly to the text as the basis for the answers. As they read, encourage students to ask questions about explicit pieces of the text that they don't understand. In the EXPLAIN section when asking students to identify the forces involved in the roller coaster's motion, tell them that they can refer to the caption as a basis for their answers.

Life Science

Grade 3. Interdependent Relationships in Ecosystems

Performance Expectations

Students who demonstrate understanding can:

3-LS2-1. Construct an argument that some animals form groups that help members survive.

3-LS4-1. Analyze and interpret data from fossils to provide evidence of the organisms and the environments in which they lived long ago. [Clarification Statement: Examples of data could include type, size, and distributions of fossil organisms. Examples of fossils and environments could include marine fossils found on dry land, tropical plant fossils found in Arctic areas, and fossils of extinct organisms.] [*Assessment Boundary: Assessment does not include identification of specific fossils or present plants and animals. Assessment is limited to major fossil types and relative ages.*]

3-LS4-3. Construct an argument with evidence that in a particular habitat some organisms can survive well, some survive less well, and some cannot survive at all. [Clarification Statement: Examples of evidence could include needs and characteristics of the organisms and habitats involved. The organisms and their habitat make up a system in which the parts depend on each other.]

3-LS4-4. Make a claim about the merit of a solution to a problem caused when the environment changes and the types of plants and animals that live there may change. [Clarification Statement: Examples of environmental changes could include changes in land characteristics, water distribution, temperature, food, and other organisms.] [*Assessment Boundary: Assessment is limited to a single environmental change. Assessment does not include the greenhouse effect or climate change.*]

Disciplinary Core Ideas

LS2.C: Ecosystem Dynamics, Functioning, and Resilience
- When the environment changes in ways that affect a place's physical characteristics, temperature, or availability of resources, some organisms survive and reproduce, others move to new locations, yet others move into the transformed environment, and some die.(secondary to 3-LS4-4)

LS2.D: Social Interactions and Group Behavior
- Being part of a group helps animals obtain food, defend themselves, and cope with changes. Groups may serve different functions and vary dramatically in size (Note: Moved from K–2). (3-LS2-1)

LS4.A: Evidence of Common Ancestry and Diversity
- Some kinds of plants and animals that once lived on Earth are no longer found anywhere. (Note: moved from K-2) (3-LS4-1)
- Fossils provide evidence about the types of organisms that lived long ago and also about the nature of their environments. (3-LS4-1)

LS4.C: Adaptation
- For any particular environment, some kinds of organisms survive well, some survive less well, and some cannot survive at all. (3-LS4-3)

LS4.D: Biodiversity and Humans
- Populations live in a variety of habitats, and change in those habitats affects the organisms living there. (3-LS4-4)

Science and Engineering Practices

Engaging in Argument from Evidence
Engaging in argument from evidence in 3–5 builds on K–2 experiences and progresses to critiquing the scientific explanations or solutions proposed by peers by citing relevant evidence about the natural and designed world(s).
- Construct an argument with evidence, data, and/or a model. (3-LS2-1)
- Construct an argument with evidence. (3-LS4-3)
- Make a claim about the merit of a solution to a problem by citing relevant evidence about how it meets the criteria and constraints of the problem. (3-LS4-4)

PHYSICAL SCIENCE
Forces and Interactions

LIFE SCIENCE
Interdependent Relationships in Ecosystems
Inheritance and Variation of Traits : Life Cycles and Traits

EARTH SCIENCE
Weather and Climate

Analyzing and Interpreting Data
Analyzing data in 3–5 builds on K–2 experiences and progresses to introducing quantitative approaches to collecting data and conducting multiple trials of qualitative observations. When possible and feasible, digital tools should be used.

- Analyze and interpret data to make sense of phenomena using logical reasoning. (3-LS4-1)

Crosscutting Concepts

Cause and Effect
- Cause and effect relationships are routinely identified and used to explain change. (3-LS2-1), (3-LS4-3)

Scale, Proportion, and Quantity
- Observable phenomena exist from very short to very long time periods. (3-LS4-1)

Systems and System Models
- A system can be described in terms of its components and their interactions. (3-LS4-4)

Connections to Nature of Science
Scientific Knowledge Assumes an Order and Consistency in Natural Systems
- Science assumes consistent patterns in natural systems. (3-LS4-1)

Connections to Engineering, Technology, and Applications of Science
Interdependence of Engineering, Technology, and Science on Society and the Natural World
- Knowledge of relevant scientific concepts and research findings is important in engineering. (3-LS4-4)

Grade 3. Inheritance and Variation of Traits: Life Cycles and Traits

Performance Expectations

Students who demonstrate understanding can:

3-LS1-1. Develop models to describe that organisms have unique and diverse life cycles but all have in common birth, growth, reproduction, and death. [Clarification Statement: Changes organisms go through during their life form a pattern.] [*Assessment Boundary: Assessment of plant life cycles is limited to those of flowering plants. Assessment does not include details of human reproduction.*]

3-LS3-1. Analyze and interpret data to provide evidence that plants and animals have traits inherited from parents and that variation of these traits exists in a group of similar organisms. [Clarification Statement: Patterns are the similarities and differences in traits shared between offspring and their parents, or among siblings. Emphasis is on organisms other than humans.] [*Assessment Boundary: Assessment does not include genetic mechanisms of inheritance and prediction of traits. Assessment is limited to non-human examples.*]

3-LS3-2. Use evidence to support the explanation that traits can be influenced by the environment. [Clarification Statement: Examples of the environment affecting a trait could include normally tall plants grown with insufficient water are stunted; and, a pet dog that is given too much food and little exercise may become overweight.]

3-LS4-2. Use evidence to construct an explanation for how the variations in characteristics among individuals of the same species may provide advantages in surviving, finding mates, and reproducing. [Clarification Statement: Examples of cause and effect relationships could be plants that have larger thorns than other plants may be less likely to be eaten by predators; and, animals that have better camouflage coloration than other animals may be more likely to survive and therefore more likely to leave offspring.]

Disciplinary Core Ideas

LS1.B: Growth and Development of Organisms
- Reproduction is essential to the continued existence of every kind of organism. Plants and animals have unique and diverse life cycles. (3-LS1-1)

LS3.A: Inheritance of Traits

- Many characteristics of organisms are inherited from their parents. (3-LS3-1)
- Other characteristics result from individuals' interactions with the environment, which can range from diet to learning. Many characteristics involve both inheritance and environment. (3-LS3-2)

LS3.B: Variation of Traits

- Different organisms vary in how they look and function because they have different inherited information. (3-LS3- 1)
- The environment also affects the traits that an organism develops. (3-LS3-2)

LS4.B: Natural Selection

- Sometimes the differences in characteristics between individuals of the same species provide advantages in surviving, finding mates, and reproducing. (3-LS4-2)

Science and Engineering Practices

Developing and Using Models

Modeling in 3–5 builds on K–2 experiences and progresses to building and revising simple models and using models to represent events and design solutions.

- Develop models to describe phenomena. (3-LS1-1)

Analyzing and Interpreting Data

Analyzing data in 3–5 builds on K–2 experiences and progresses to introducing quantitative approaches to collecting data and conducting multiple trials of qualitative observations. When possible and feasible, digital tools should be used.

- Analyze and interpret data to make sense of phenomena using logical reasoning. (3-LS3-1)

Constructing Explanations and Designing Solutions

Constructing explanations and designing solutions in 3–5 builds on K–2 experiences and progresses to the use of evidence in constructing explanations that specify variables that describe and predict phenomena and in designing multiple solutions to design problems.

- Use evidence (e.g., observations, patterns) to support an explanation. (3-LS3-2)

Constructing Explanations and Designing Solutions

Constructing explanations and designing solutions in 3–5 builds on K–2 experiences and progresses to the use of evidence in constructing explanations that specify variables that describe and predict phenomena and in designing multiple solutions to design problems.

- Use evidence (e.g., observations, patterns) to construct an explanation. (3-LS4-2)

Connections to Nature of Science
Scientific Knowledge is Based on Empirical Evidence

- Science findings are based on recognizing patterns. (3-LS1-1)

Crosscutting Concepts

Patterns

- Patterns of change can be used to make predictions. (3-LS1-1)
- Similarities and differences in patterns can be used to sort and classify natural phenomena. (3-LS3-1)

Cause and Effect

- Cause and effect relationships are routinely identified and used to explain change. (3-LS3-2), (3-LS4-2)

PHYSICAL SCIENCE
Forces and Interactions

LIFE SCIENCE
Interdependent Relationships in Ecosystems
Inheritance and Variation of Traits : Life Cycles and Traits

EARTH SCIENCE
Weather and Climate

Ecosystems

NEXT GENERATION SCIENCE STANDARDS | DISCIPLINARY CORE IDEAS
LS4.D: Biodiversity and Humans Populations live in a variety of habitats, and change in those habitats affects the organisms living there. (3-LS4-4)

Objective Students will be able to:
- Describe how populations live and interact in a variety of ecosystems.

Science Vocabulary
ecosystem

ENGAGE

Tap Prior Knowledge

- Ask students to share what they know about where things live. Ask: **Where have you seen living things?** (Accept any reasonable responses. Possible answers: a yard, a pond, an aquarium, a house, etc.) Ask: **Were there things that are not living in those same places?** (Yes.) **What are they?** (Possible answers: rocks, soil, water, sunlight, furniture, etc.)

EXPLORE

Explore Populations and Ecosystems

- Have students observe the picture on pages 38–39. Ask probing questions to encourage exploration. For example, ask: **What living things do you see in the picture? What nonliving things do you see? Do you see anything that was once living, but is not anymore?**

- Have students share their observations. Students may notice living things such as the European salamander, trees, and leaves. They may notice nonliving things such as water and light, and things that were once living, like sticks and the downed tree.

Set a Purpose and Read

- Have students read in order to describe how populations survive in a variety of environments where their needs are met. Students will learn more about habitats and ecosystems on page 46.

- Have students read pages 38–39.

EXPLAIN

Describe Populations and Ecosystems

- After students read pages 38–39, say: **The picture shows living things surrounded by nonliving things. Another word for "living things" is organisms. Plants, animals, and other living things are all organisms.** Ask: **What do you call all the living and nonliving things in a certain area and the ways they interact?** (an ecosystem)

- Remind students that ecosystems can vary in size. Have students identify a small and a large ecosystem in the picture.

- Ask: **What type of ecosystem is pictured?** (a forest)

- Say: **Explain what a population is.** (A population is a group of the same type of living thing.)

- Ask: **What populations are in this forest ecosystem?** (trees, salamanders; Some students may mention the shelf-like organisms growing on the log. Explain that these organisms are fungi.)

- Remind students that an important aspect of ecosystems is how the various populations interact with each other and nonliving things. Ask: **How are the populations in this forest ecosystem interacting with each other and with nonliving things?** (Possible answers: The fungi are growing on the tree. The trees are using the water and light to live and grow.)

ELABORATE

Extend Your Thinking About Ecosystem Interactions

- Have students extend their thinking about the interactions between organisms within an ecosystem. Say: **Remember that ecosystems contain both living and nonliving things.** Ask: **What are some ways living things might interact?** (They might compete for food. They might help each other survive. One might eat the other.) **How might living things interact with nonliving things?** (Living things use nonliving things to grow and survive, such as plants using energy from sunlight to make food or animals drinking water. They also use nonliving things for shelter.) **What are some ways two nonliving things might interact?** (The sun dries out water. Water makes soil damp.)

Research Ecosystems

Step 1: Have small groups of students use the Internet or library resources to research different types of ecosystems: tropical rainforest, grassland, desert, tundra, and coral reef. Have them research the living and nonliving things in each ecosystem and how they interact.

Step 2: If time permits, have each group create a collage and present it to the class.

EVALUATE

Have students record their answers to the Wrap It Up questions in their science notebook.

Wrap It Up!

1. **DEFINE** **What is an ecosystem?** (An ecosystem is all the living and nonliving things in an area and the ways they interact.)

2. **INTERPRET PHOTOS** **Look at the photo of the forest. What are some of the living things in this forest ecosystem?** (trees, European salamander, etc.)

3. **INFER** **Name some of the nonliving things you cannot see that may live in this forest ecosystem.** (mud, sand, or stones at the bottom of the river, air, sunlight, water in the air.)

PHYSICAL SCIENCE
Forces and Interactions

LIFE SCIENCE
Interdependent Relationships in Ecosystems
Inheritance and Variation of Traits : Life Cycles and Traits

EARTH SCIENCE
Weather and Climate

READING CONNECTION

Ask and Answer Questions to Demonstrate Understanding

Ask and answer questions to demonstrate understanding of a text, referring explicitly to the text as the basis for the answers.

Guide students in asking and answering questions, referring to the text as the basis for the answer. For example, in the EVALUATE section when students are recording the answers to Wrap It Up, remind them to refer to the text when considering their answers. Also encourage them to share any questions they may still have and invite students to answer questions or do further research if the answers cannot be found in the text.

SCIENCE BACKGROUND

Food Chains and Webs

A major way that organisms within an ecosystem interact is through their feeding dynamics, or "who eats what or whom." These feeding interactions can be graphically represented in food chains and food webs. A food chain shows how living things get food and how nutrients and energy are passed from creature to creature. For example, a food chain might show a mouse eating acorns, a snake eating the mouse, and an owl eating the snake. A food web is a more complex representation that shows how the food chains within an ecosystem overlap and affect each other.

Forests Change

NEXT GENERATION SCIENCE STANDARDS | DISCIPLINARY CORE IDEAS
LS2.C: Ecosystem Dynamics, Functioning, and Resilience When the environment changes in ways that affect a place's physical characteristics, temperature, or availability of resources, some organisms survive and reproduce, others move to new locations, yet others move into the transformed environment, and some die. (secondary to 3-LS4-4)
LS4.D: Biodiversity and Humans Populations live in a variety of habitats, and change in those habitats affects the organisms living there. (3-LS4-4)

Objectives **Students will be able to:**
- Describe how natural events can change an environment.
- Explain how changes in an environment's physical characteristics, temperature, or availability of resources affect the organisms living there.

ENGAGE

Tap Prior Knowledge

- Ask students to share what they know about natural events that change the physical characteristics of a place. Ask: **What are some natural events that have major effects on the physical characteristics of a place?** (Possible answers: fires, tornadoes, hurricanes, tsunamis, floods, etc.) Ask: **How do these events change a place?** (Accept any reasonable responses. Possible answers: Tornadoes and hurricanes can rip trees from the ground. Tsunamis and floods wash away soil and drown plant and animal life. Fires burn and destroy trees and other plants and can clear large areas of land.)

EXPLORE

Preview the Lesson

- Have students observe the pictures on pages 40–41. Point to the small picture on page 40 and ask: **Was this picture taken before or after the fire in the larger picture? Why do you think so?**
- Have students share their answers. Students may say that they know the small picture was taken after the fire because the bigger trees are black and bare and many burnt tree trunks are on the ground. They might also point out the new, young plant life.

Set a Purpose and Read

- Have students read in order to describe how changes in the forest affect the organisms living there.
- Have students read pages 40–41.

EXPLAIN

Describe How Forests Change

- After students read pages 40–41, ask: **What can you tell about how the forest in the picture looked like before the fire?** (It had tall trees that were full of leaves and needles.)
- Say: **Physical characteristics are things that you can see. Describe the physical characteristics that the fire changed in this forest.** (There a fewer trees. The larger trees are bare and black. New trees, grasses, and wildflowers are beginning to grow.)
- Ask: **Are there effects from the fire that you cannot see?** (Yes.) **Can you find any discussed in the text?** (The soil is enriched, and some seeds sprout faster than normal.)

Explain the Effects of Change in an Environment

- Ask: **How can physical changes affect the living things in an environment?** (Living organisms' food supply is threatened, and their shelter is destroyed.)
- Ask: **What are three things that could happen to a population of animals left in this forest after the fire?** (Some might stay and have babies. Others move away to find food and shelter. Others might die.)
- Ask: **Why would many animals be forced out of this forest after the fire?** (The animals have to go somewhere else to find food.)
- Ask: **A fire like the one shown on pages 40–41 is not bad for all living organisms. How does it benefit some living things?** (A fire helps some things grow because the burned wood adds nutrients to the soil and the heat can make seeds of certain pine trees sprout.)

ELABORATE

Research Benefits of Wildfires

 Despite the danger that wildfires pose to human development and animal life, fire also serves many positive functions in nature. Have pairs of students use the Internet or other resources to research the benefits of wildfires. Have each pair share one fact that they learn.

Compare Effects of Natural Disasters

• Besides forest fires, other natural disasters can extensively change environments. As a class, do Internet research for video and photos of ways that tornadoes change environments. Focus your search on changes to natural environments as opposed to those built by humans. Have students describe how the changes might unexpectedly benefit some organisms.

EVALUATE

 Have students record their answers to the Wrap It Up questions in their science notebook.

Wrap It Up!

1. **DESCRIBE** **How does a fire change a forest?** (It burns the trees and other plants and turns the ground black and bare.)

2. **CAUSE AND EFFECT** **How does a fire affect the deer in a forest?** (It affects the deer's food supply, the available shelter, and potentially its ability to reproduce.)

3. **INFER** **After a forest fire, wildflowers soon begin to grow. How might the wildflowers eventually affect the number of rabbits in the area? Why?** (The number of rabbits might eventually increase as their food supply increases.)

READING CONNECTION

Use Photos and Text to Demonstrate Understanding

Use information gained from illustrations (e.g., maps, photographs) and the words in a text to demonstrate understanding of the text (e.g., where, when, why, and how key events occur).

Guide students to use photos and the text on pages 40–41 to demonstrate understanding. For example, in the EXPLAIN section, have students reference the photographs when they describe the changes a fire makes in a forest. Also, ask students to explain how the inset photo and its caption shows and tells what happens soon after a fire.

ELL SUPPORT

Affect vs. Effect

Beginning Explain the difference between *effect* and *affect*. Have students find an example of each word in a sentence online.

Intermediate Have students fill in the blank with either *affect* or *effect: One (effect) of forest fires is the ground becomes black and bare. Fires also (affect) the plant and animal life.* Ask students to explain their choices.

Advanced Help students write four sentences about forest fires, two using *affect* and two using *effect*.

PHYSICAL SCIENCE
Forces and Interactions

LIFE SCIENCE
Interdependent Relationships in Ecosystems
Inheritance and Variation of Traits : Life Cycles and Traits

EARTH SCIENCE
Weather and Climate

Searching for Water

NEXT GENERATION SCIENCE STANDARDS | DISCIPLINARY CORE IDEAS
LS2.C: Ecosystem Dynamics, Functioning, and Resilience When the environment changes in ways that affect a place's physical characteristics, temperature, or availability of resources, some organisms survive and reproduce, others move to new locations, yet others move into the transformed environment, and some die. (secondary to 3-LS4-4)
LS4.D: Biodiversity and Humans Populations live in a variety of habitats, and change in those habitats affects the organisms living there. (3-LS4-4)

Objective   Students will be able to:
- Describe how the availability of water changes habitats.
- Explain how availability of water in an environment affects the organisms living there.

Science Vocabulary
migrate

ENGAGE

Tap Prior Knowledge

- Ask students to share their knowledge of how the availability of water affects an environment. Ask: **In general, how are the places that get more rain different from the places where it does not rain much?** (Accept any reasonable responses. Possible answers: In general, there is less plant and animal life in places where it rains less. Plants may appear more brown and less green. The ground is drier, and there are fewer bodies of water.)

EXPLORE

Preview the Lesson

- Have students observe the pictures on pages 42–43. Say: **Look at the pictures of the herd of gnu and the herd of elephants.** Ask: **Which picture was taken during the dry season and which was taken during the rainy season? How can you tell?**

- Have students share their observations. Students may say they can tell that the elephants are pictured during a rainy season because there is water on the ground and the trees in the back are green. They might also notice that the plants in the picture of the gnu are brown, there is no water on the ground, and a fire is burning in the background. Lead students to the conclusion that fires start easily in dry land.

Set a Purpose and Read

- Have students read in order to describe how the availability of water affects organisms living in an environment, or habitat, where their needs can be met. Students will learn more about habitats on page 46.

- Have students read pages 42–43.

EXPLAIN

Describe How Water Availability Changes the Environment

- After students read pages 42–43, ask: **How does the availability of water change throughout the year in the grasslands of East Africa?** (Part of the year is rainy, and part is dry.)

- Say: **Describe the East African grasslands during the rainy season.** (In the rainy season, water fills the rivers and ponds, and the soil is moist. Grasses and other plants grow well during this time.)

- Say: **Describe the East African grasslands during the dry season.** (Rivers and ponds dry up. The soil is dry, so grasses and plants turn brown.)

Explain How Water Availability Affects Organisms

- Say: **What does it mean to migrate?** (To migrate means to move to a different place to meet basic needs such as food, water, or shelter.)

- Ask: **Why do animals in the East African grasslands migrate during the dry season?** (They migrate because they need water to live and can't find it where they are living.)

- Ask: **Where do they migrate?** (They migrate to someplace with more water and greener grass to eat.)

- Say: **Explain how the presence or absence of water can control an organism's behavior.** (Since animals need water to live, some animals that live in dry places spend a lot of energy searching for it. Other organisms, such as camels and cacti, have special features to conserve water.)

ELABORATE

Learn More About Droughts

 Droughts can cause extreme changes in habitats and ecosystems. As a class, do an Internet search for educational videos about the effects of drought. Then have students contribute to a discussion about how droughts affect habitats and the organisms that live there.

Extend Your Thinking About the Effects of Too Much or Too Little Water

- Have students extend their thinking about how the effects of too much and not enough water are similar and different. Ask: **How do droughts and floods change habitats and affect the organisms that live there in different and similar ways?** (Floods and droughts have opposite causes of destruction, but both can cause widespread devastation and have the effect of killing organisms or forcing them to leave.)

EVALUATE

 Have students record their answers to the Wrap It Up questions in their science notebook.

Wrap It Up!

1. IDENTIFY **What are the two main seasons in the grasslands of East Africa?** (There is a dry season and a rainy season.)

2. CAUSE AND EFFECT **How does the dry season affect the grasses? Why?** (The grasses turn brown in the dry season because they don't have as much water as in the wet season.)

3. INFER **What might happen to the population of wildebeests if they did not migrate? Explain.** (Most likely many of them would die or become dangerously weak from lack of water and food.)

PHYSICAL SCIENCE
Forces and Interactions

LIFE SCIENCE
Interdependent Relationships in Ecosystems
Inheritance and Variation of Traits: Life Cycles and Traits

EARTH SCIENCE
Weather and Climate

READING CONNECTION

Use Photos and Text to Demonstrate Understanding

Use information gained from illustrations (e.g., maps, photographs) and the words in a text to demonstrate understanding of the text (e.g., where, when, why, and how key events occur).

Guide students to use photos and text to demonstrate understanding. In the EXPLAIN section when you are asking questions, remind them to use the photos and captions as another source of information. You might also ask them to explain how the photos support the information in the main text.

SCIENCE BACKGROUND

Monsoons

Monsoons are the result of predictable shifts in the direction of global winds at certain times of the year. During dry seasons, wind blows from the land toward the ocean, which makes the air dry. During the wet seasons, winds blow toward the land from the ocean, making the air moist and causing excessive rainfall. West Africa, Asia, and Australia are the areas best known for their monsoons. Although rain often comes as a relief from months of drought, heavy rains can bring about other types of destruction and devastation.

Changes in Temperature

NEXT GENERATION SCIENCE STANDARDS | DISCIPLINARY CORE IDEAS
LS2.C: Ecosystem Dynamics, Functioning, and Resilience When the environment changes in ways that affect a place's physical characteristics, temperature, or availability of resources, some organisms survive and reproduce, others move to new locations, yet others move into the transformed environment, and some die. (secondary to 3-LS4-4)
LS4.D: Biodiversity and Humans Populations live in a variety of habitats, and change in those habitats affects the organisms living there. (3-LS4-4)

Objective Students will be able to:
- Describe how shifts in temperature change habitats.
- Explain how changes in temperature in an environment affect organism living there.

Science Vocabulary
deciduous, hibernate

ENGAGE

Tap Prior Knowledge

- Ask students to share their personal experience with changes in temperature. Ask: **What changes do you notice outside in the winter?** (Accept any reasonable responses. Possible answers: The air is cold. Some trees lose their leaves. Different animals and insects are around.)

EXPLORE

Preview the Lesson

- Have students observe the pictures on pages 44–45. Ask: **Which of the animals shown do you think is experiencing cold temperatures? Why?**
- Have students share their observations and thoughts. Students might say that the dormouse seems to be experiencing cold temperatures because it is curled up and hibernating, which some animals do in the winter. By contrast, they might notice that the bees look busy, which is a behavior associated with warmer temperatures. They also might notice that the dormouse picture is darker, which could signal fewer hours of daylight in winter.

Set a Purpose and Read

- Have students read in order to describe how environmental shifts in temperature affects habitats (the environment where an organism's needs are met.)
- Have students read pages 44–45.

EXPLAIN

Describe How Shifts in Temperature Change Environments

- After students read pages 44–45, ask: **How do colder temperatures change the environment?** (The air grows cold, and the ground can freeze. There are also fewer hours of daylight.)
- Ask: **Do you think all climates experience the same changes in the winter?** (No. Some places may experience rainy or windy winters instead of cold or snowy winters.)

Explain How Shifts in Temperature Affect Organisms

- Say: **Name two ways plants change in colder temperatures.** (Some plants die. Some trees loose their leaves.)
- Ask: **What happens to plants when warmer temperatures arrive?** (Seeds left from plants that died will sprout and grow into new plants. Trees that lost their leaves will grow new ones.)
- Ask: **What is a deciduous tree?** (It is a tree that sheds its leaves in the fall.)
- Explain that some animals, such as the dormouse shown on pages 44–45, hibernate during the winter. Hibernation is an adaptation for winter survival during which an animal becomes inactive and all body processes slow down. Ask: **Why do some animals hibernate in the winter?** (Lead students to understand that some animals hibernate to conserve energy because food is scarce during the winter.)
- Ask: **How do the dormouse and a deciduous tree behave similarly in the winter?** (Both go into a dormant, or resting, state to conserve energy.)
- Remind students that to migrate means to move to a different place to meet basic needs. Ask: **Why do some birds migrate to warmer climates in the winter?** (Some birds migrate to areas with warmer climates in the winter because food is more available.)

ELABORATE

Research Deciduous Trees

 Have pairs of students use the Internet to research deciduous trees in areas that experience extreme weather changes during the four seasons. Have each pair print four pictures of the same kind of deciduous tree, one picture for each season. Have students paste the pictures onto one page with the definition of *deciduous* tree at the top of the page.

Extend Your Thinking About Migration and Hibernation

- Have students extend their thinking about migration and hibernation. Say: **Both migration and hibernation are ways that animals adapt to survive winter food shortages. Hedgehogs, for example, deal with the decreased food supply by hibernating. They slow down their heartbeats and breathing and enter an inactive state for the whole winter. Other animals, like the gray whale, migrate in the winter, moving to warmer areas with more food. Then there are other animals, like the snowshoe rabbit, that don't migrate or hibernate.** Ask: **Why do you think some animals hibernate while others migrate?** (Whether an animal migrates or hibernates depends on how they are equipped to deal with the food shortage. Animals that migrate can travel long distances and are able to navigate well, while animals that hibernate eat extra in the fall and slow their heartbeat, breathing, and other body functions to conserve energy.) **How do you think animals that neither migrate nor hibernate get through the winter season?** (These animals may have other ways to adapt, such as growing new fur or eating food they stored in the fall.)

EVALUATE

Have students record their answers to the Wrap It Up questions in their science notebook.

Wrap It Up!

1. DESCRIBE **What are two ways that plants respond to changes in the environment, such as fewer hours of daylight and the cold weather of winter?** (They die and leave behind their seeds, or they shed their leaves and become dormant.)

2. EXPLAIN **How does hibernation help a dormouse survive?** (The dormouse doesn't use much energy while it is hibernating, so it doesn't need to eat.)

3. GENERALIZE **How does the cold weather of winter affect the amount of food available to most animals?** (Food supplies generally decrease with the colder weather of winter.)

READING CONNECTION

Ask and Answer Questions to Demonstrate Understanding

Ask and answer questions to demonstrate understanding of a text, referring explicitly to the text as the basis for the answers.

Guide students to ask and answer questions to demonstrate understanding of the text. Encourage them to refer explicitly to the text as the basis for answers. For example, when asking questions in the EXPLAIN section, ask students to point out where in the text they are drawing their answers from. Also encourage them to share questions they many have about how shifts in temperature affect organisms.

SCIENCE MISCONCEPTION

Bears and Hibernation

There has been debate in the scientific community about whether bears, though often used as a prime example of an animal that hibernates, should be considered true hibernators. Some scientists believe that since a bear's body temperature doesn't drop as much as smaller animals that hibernate, the bear is not truly hibernating. However, bear biologists are now thinking that since bears can go six or seven months without eating, drinking, urinating, or defecating, they must be considered hibernators. The new misconception is not that bears are hibernators, but that the process of hibernation is the same for all species.

PHYSICAL SCIENCE
Forces and Interactions

LIFE SCIENCE
Interdependent Relationships in Ecosystems
Inheritance and Variation of Traits : Life Cycles and Traits

EARTH SCIENCE
Weather and Climate

Living Things Make Changes

NEXT GENERATION SCIENCE STANDARDS | DISCIPLINARY CORE IDEAS
LS2.C: Ecosystem Dynamics, Functioning, and Resilience When the environment changes in ways that affect a place's physical characteristics, temperature, or availability of resources, some organisms survive and reproduce, others move to new locations, yet others move into the transformed environment, and some die. (secondary to 3-LS4-4)
LS4.D: Biodiversity and Humans Populations live in a variety of habitats, and change in those habitats affects the organisms living there. (3-LS4-4)

Objective **Students will be able to:**
- Describe how living things make changes to the environments that affect the organisms living there.

Science Vocabulary
habitat, predators

ENGAGE

Tap Prior Knowledge

- Ask students to share what they know about how animals change their environments. Ask: **How is a bird building a nest an example of an animal changing its environment?** (Accept all reasonable responses. Possible answer: A bird gathers sticks and leaves and other things from its environment to build its nest, which is a change to the environment.)

EXPLORE

Preview the Lesson

- Have students observe the pictures on pages 46–47. Ask: **What is the beaver on page 46 doing with the tree limb in its mouth? What do you think the area pictured on page 47 looked like before beavers built this dam?**

- Have students share their observations. Students may say that the beaver is taking the stick to add to the dam pictured on page 47. They may say that before the beaver built the dam, the water ran freely in a stream instead of forming a pond.

Set a Purpose and Read

- Have students read in order to describe how living things make changes to the environment.

- Have students read pages 46–47.

EXPLAIN

Describe How Living Things Make Changes

- After students read pages 46–47, ask: **How was the dam on page 47 built?** (Beavers built it using sticks and mud.)

- Ask: **How does a beaver dam change the environment?** (The beavers chew down small trees in the area and dig holes for mud. Also, the dam holds back water and can turn a stream into a pond.)

- Ask: **What is a habitat?** (A habitat is the place where a plant or animal lives and gets everything it needs to survive.)

- Say: **Name two ways a dam improves the beaver's habitat.** (The dams give beavers a place to live with a constant level of water. It also protects beavers from predators.)

- Ask: **Why do beavers need protection from predators?** (Beavers need protection from predators because predators eat them.)

Explain How Changes Affect Other Living Things

- Ask: **Name three other living things that a beaver dam benefits.** (Possible answers include marsh plants, turtles, dragonflies, sunfish, frogs, birds, and small mammals.)

- Ask: **How does the dam benefit these other living things?** (Possible answers: It creates a wetland habitat, or place for them to live and get what they need to survive.)

ELABORATE

Research Beavers' Effect on Ecosystems

Step 1: Have small groups of students perform research on the behavior of beavers. Have each group create a list of ways a beaver dam benefits the beavers and the ecosystem.

Step 2: Have each group use the Internet or other resources to research potential ways that beaver dams could hurt the ecosystem.

Extend Your Thinking About How Plants Make Changes

- Animals change the environment in ways such as building dams, digging holes, and grazing grasslands. Plants change their environments in other ways. Say: **Redwoods are some of the largest and tallest trees in the world. These trees also have extensive root systems that are shallow but spread out sideways and often intertwine with one another.** Ask: **How do you think the introduction of redwood trees could change an environment and ecosystem?** (Over time, the introduction of redwood trees would drastically change an ecosystem. The tall trees would decrease the amount of sunlight reaching the ground, making it difficult for some smaller plants to survive. The large roots would also push out some species. The trees might also attract different wildlife and insects than previously in the area.)

EVALUATE

Have students record their answers to the Wrap It Up questions in their science notebook.

Wrap It Up!

1. **DESCRIBE How does a beaver dam change a stream?** (It holds back water and changes a stream into a pond.)
2. **CAUSE AND EFFECT How do beaver dams affect the other animals in the ecosystem?** (The dam provides a good habitat for some animals, including turtles, dragonflies, and sunfish.)
3. **APPLY Beavers use their teeth to cut down trees to make their dams. How might cutting down trees affect the animals in the nearby forest?** (Animals in the forest might loose shelter or protection when the beavers cut down trees.)

PHYSICAL SCIENCE
Forces and Interactions

LIFE SCIENCE
Interdependent Relationships in Ecosystems
Inheritance and Variation of Traits : Life Cycles and Traits

EARTH SCIENCE
Weather and Climate

READING CONNECTION

Describe Logical Connections

Describe the logical connection between particular sentences and paragraphs in a text (e.g., comparison, cause/effect, first/second/third in a sequence).

Guide students to describe the logical connections between particular sentences and paragraphs in a text. For example, when reading the text, point out particular sentences that express a cause, such as *The dam holds back the water and turns the stream into a pond*. Guide students to the discovery that the first and last sentences in the second paragraph express effects of the dam turning the stream into a pond.

DIFFERENTIATED INSTRUCTION

Extra Support Have students make a chart that shows how the pond is a good habitat for marsh plants, turtles, dragonflies, and sunfish. If needed, help students conduct simple research on these organisms.

Challenge Have students use the Internet or library resources to do research about how beaver dams can contribute to flooding. Have them draw a flow chart that begins with a beaver dam and ends with the potential effects of increased flooding.

People Change Land

NEXT GENERATION SCIENCE STANDARDS | DISCIPLINARY CORE IDEAS
LS2.C: Ecosystem Dynamics, Functioning, and Resilience When the environment changes in ways that affect a place's physical characteristics, temperature, or availability of resources, some organisms survive and reproduce, others move to new locations, yet others move into the transformed environment, and some die. (secondary to 3-LS4-4)
LS4.D: Biodiversity and Humans Populations live in a variety of habitats, and change in those habitats affects the organisms living there. (3-LS4-4)

Objective **Students will be able to:**
- Describe how humans make changes to the land that affect the organisms living there.

ENGAGE

Tap Prior Knowledge

- Ask students to share what they know about how humans change the environment. Ask: **What do you think the land in your community looked like before people started living there?** (Accept any reasonable responses. Possible answers: There were more plants and trees. There were also more animals and probably different kinds of animals and insects. There would have been no buildings or roads.)

EXPLORE

Explore How People Change Land

- Have students observe the picture on pages 48–49. Ask probing questions to encourage exploration. For example, ask: **What is happening in the pictures on pages 48–49? How are humans changing the land?**

- Have students share their observations. Students may say humans are cutting down the forest in the picture on page 48 and that they are planting a forest in the picture on page 49. Students may recognize that humans are changing the land in both pictures.

Set a Purpose and Read

- Have students read in order to describe how people change the land.

- Have students read pages 48–49.

EXPLAIN

Describe How People Change Land

- After students read pages 48–49, say: **Name four things humans do that change the environment.** (People build roads, build houses, plant crops, and build dams.)

- Say: **These actions take space.** Ask: **What was the space used for before humans changed it?** (It was probably a habitat for other living things.)

- Ask: **What happens to the living things that were there before humans?** (Some forest animals move to other places. Others die.)

- Remind students that, just like beavers that built dams, humans can have both a negative and a positive impact on the environment and an ecosystem.

- Ask: **What is one way humans can help preserve an area's ecosystem?** (They can plant young trees that are native to the area to replace the trees they remove.)

- Ask: **Why is planting native trees important?** (Planting native trees helps preserve the original ecosystem and helps provide food and shelter for birds, insects, and other animals.)

ELABORATE

Research Climate Change

Step 1: Have small groups of students use the Internet or other resources to research climate change. Have students look for three ways that people change the land and contribute to climate change.

Step 2: If time permits, have each group create a simple graphic representation of their findings and share their pictures with the class.

Find Out More About Earth Day

- Help students use the Internet or other resources to find out more about Earth Day and how their communities observe it. Encourage students to participate in Earth Day events and also to think of ways they can have a positive impact on the planet beyond Earth Day. Ask: **What is one way you could change the land that would have a positive effect?** (Accept all reasonable responses. Possible answers: I could plant trees or a garden, use reusable containers, recycle, etc.) Prompt students to think critically about the connections between their behaviors and resulting effects on the environment.

EVALUATE

Have students record their answers to the Wrap It Up questions in their science notebook.

Wrap It Up!

1. **LIST** **What are some human activities that change the environment?** (People build roads and houses. They also plant crops and build dams.)

2. **CAUSE AND EFFECT** **How does cutting down trees in a forest affect the animals that live there?** (When the trees are cut down, it changes the forest so that some animals are forced to leave. Others may die from lack of food, shelter, or protection. Some animals may survive and reproduce.)

3. **MAKE JUDGMENTS** **What do you think is a good way to protect the animals that live in forests? Explain.** (A good way to protect the animals in the forest is to study their behavior and try to use practices that have the least disruptive effect on them.)

READING CONNECTION

Use Photos and Text to Demonstrate Understanding

Use information gained from illustrations (e.g., maps, photographs) and the words in a text to demonstrate understanding of the text (e.g., where, when, why, and how key events occur).

Guide students to use information gained from photos and the words in the text to demonstrate understanding of the text. For example, after students have read through the text, ask: **How do the words in the text help you understand what is occurring in the pictures?** (The text helps me understand that in the bigger picture, cutting of trees is changing the forest environment, and in the smaller picture, the land is being changed by people who are planting young trees that may someday be a new forest.)

ELL SUPPORT

Adjectives with the Suffixes –ed/–ing

Beginning Have students choose *tired* or *tiring* to fill in the blanks. *The people felt (tired) after planting trees. Planting trees is (tiring).*

Intermediate Have students answer questions in complete sentences, using the words *tired* and *tiring* as adjectives. Ask: **How did the people feel after planting trees?** (The people felt tired after planting trees.) Ask: **How would you describe planting trees?** (Planting trees is tiring.)

Advanced Have students write sentences using the following words: *tired/tiring, confused/confusing,* and *excited/exciting.* If needed, help them with sentence starters such as: *The people felt . . ., Planting trees is . . ., The deer looked . . ., The forest path was . . ., My friends were . . ., The Earth Day celebration was . . .*

People Change Ecosystems

NEXT GENERATION SCIENCE STANDARDS | DISCIPLINARY CORE IDEAS
LS2.C: Ecosystem Dynamics, Functioning, and Resilience When the environment changes in ways that affect a place's physical characteristics, temperature, or availability of resources, some organisms survive and reproduce, others move to new locations, yet others move into the transformed environment, and some die. (secondary to 3-LS4-4)
LS4.D: Biodiversity and Humans Populations live in a variety of habitats, and change in those habitats affects the organisms living there. (3-LS4-4)

Objective **Students will be able to:**
- Describe how changes people make affect living things and change ecosystems.

ENGAGE

Tap Prior Knowledge

- Ask students to share what they learned in the previous lesson. Say: **Remember that human activities can change the environment.** Ask: **What did you learn in the last lesson about the effects of humans changing the land?** (Accept any reasonable responses. Possible answers: Humans can have both positive and negative effects on the land when they change it. If they cut down a forest, for example, animals can lose their homes. On the other hand, if they plant trees, they give animals homes and help the environment.)

EXPLORE

Explore How People Change Ecosystems

- Have students observe the pictures on pages 50–51. Ask probing questions to encourage exploration. For example, ask: **In what ways can you tell that humans have worked to preserve parts of the ecosystems of the areas these pictures were taken in?**
- Have students share their observations. Students may notice that the community shown on page 50 has visible green space and people have planted trees within the community. Students may also notice the rooftop garden pictured on page 51, which attempts to restore a natural element to the city.

Set a Purpose and Read

- Have students read in order to describe how changes people make affect living things and change ecosystems.
- Have students read pages 50–51.

EXPLAIN

Describe How People Change Ecosystems

- After students read pages 50–51, ask: **What are two ways that buildings and roads affect an environment?** (Buildings and roads change the environment physically. They can also affect the living things in the ecosystem.)
- Ask: **How are cities different from the environment that was there before humans built the city?** (Cities are covered with buildings and pavement that did not used to be there.)
- Ask: **How do buildings and pavement affect plant life in the area?** (Little can grow when the ground is covered with buildings and pavement.)
- Ask: **What is a rooftop garden?** (It is a garden built on the roof of a building.)
- Ask: **What are four ways that rooftop gardens benefit a city ecosystem?** (They help clean the air. They help keep the buildings on which they grow cool. They capture rainwater. They can provide people with food.)
- Say: **Describe how people changed the ecosystems in each picture on page 51.** (In the top picture, the city most likely forced out lots of animals and vegetation. In the bottom picture, people in the city are attracting new insects and birds by providing them with habitats in rooftop gardens.)

PHYSICAL SCIENCE
Forces and Interactions

LIFE SCIENCE
Interdependent Relationships in Ecosystems
Inheritance and Variation of Traits : Life Cycles and Traits

EARTH SCIENCE
Weather and Climate

ELABORATE

Research the Importance of Trees

Step 1: Trees are important to the health of the global ecosystem. Have pairs of students research why trees are important. Have each pair make a Venn diagram showing ways that trees benefit wildlife, people, and both.

Step 2: Combine the research of the pairs of students into one Venn diagram on the board. Discuss why it is in the best interest of all living organisms to protect our forests.

Extend Your Thinking About Habitat Conservation

- Have students extend their thinking about habitat conservation. Say: **Imagine that a building is being built on land where hummingbirds are a common sight.** Ask: **What could be done to help keep the hummingbirds in the area, even when the building is there?** (Plants that are common food for hummingbirds could be planted around the building. Hummingbird feeders could be hung in the trees. Water could be made available to them. A garden with plants that attract hummingbirds could be planted.)

EVALUATE

Have students record their answers to the Wrap It Up questions in their science notebook.

Wrap It Up!

1. **DESCRIBE How do rooftop gardens change the rooftop environment?** (They give off oxygen and help keep the air clean.)

2. **COMPARE In the summer, how would the temperature of a rooftop garden differ from that of a bare roof?** (Buildings with rooftop gardens would be cooler than buildings without them.)

3. **INFER How might building rooftop gardens affect the number of birds in a city? Why?** (Rooftop gardens might increase the number of birds in the city by providing them with shelter and food. They might also affect the types of birds that are seen in the city.)

READING CONNECTION

Describe the Relationship

Describe the relationship between a series of historical events, scientific ideas or concepts, or steps in technical procedures in a text, using language that pertains to time, sequence, and cause/effect.

Guide students to describe the cause-and-effect relationship referenced in the text. For example, when asking questions in the EXPLAIN section, ask students to identify human activities that are causes of ecosystem changes, and then relate those causes to the effects they produce.

ELL SUPPORT

Prepositions (on, in, for, from, at, to)

Beginning Have students choose an answer from the given choices:

1. *A garden is (<u>on</u>) the roof. (on/in); 2. I live far (<u>from</u>) the city. (for/from); 3. Let's drive (<u>to</u>) the country. (at/to)*

Intermediate Give students a word bank of the above prepositions. Then have them fill in the answers to the Beginning sentences.

Advanced Give students a list of the above prepositions. Then have them use each one in a conversation with a partner.

Compare Solutions and Make a Claim

NEXT GENERATION SCIENCE STANDARDS | PERFORMANCE EXPECTATION

3-LS4-4. Make a claim about the merit of a solution to a problem caused when the environment changes and the types of plants and animals that live there may change. [Clarification Statement: Examples of environmental changes could include changes in land characteristics, water distribution, temperature, food, and other organisms.] [Assessment Boundary: Assessment is limited to a single environmental change. Assessment does not include the greenhouse effect or climate change.]

Objective Students will be able to:
- Make a claim about the merit of solutions to the drop in salmon population in the Columbia River.

CLASSROOM MANAGEMENT

Time 50 minutes

Teaching Tips Before guiding students through the process of making a claim, make sure they understand river systems and the migration pattern of salmon. Draw a diagram to illustration these concepts as you read the paragraph under "Set the scene."

What to Expect Students will define as a problem the decreasing salmon population in the Columbia River caused by the dams built in the river system. They will make a table that summarizes and compares attempted solutions to the problem, and they will make a claim about which solutions are best. Finally, they will share their conclusion with the class and defend their claim.

ENGAGE

Set the scene.

- Tell students that they are going to read about a problem and then make a claim about which solutions are the best. Have a volunteer read the paragraph under "Set the scene" on page 52.
- After reading the paragraph, say: **A major river and the smaller rivers and streams that flow into it are collectively called a river**

system. Describe the Columbia River system. (The Columbia River system is made up of the Columbia River and the hundreds of streams and rivers that flow into it.)

- Say: **Hundreds of streams and rivers flow into the Columbia River.** Ask: **What body of water does the Columbia River flow into?** (The Columbia River flows into the Pacific Ocean.)

- Say: **Describe the migration route of salmon in the Columbia River.** (Salmon swim up the Columbia River from the ocean to lay their eggs in freshwater streams. When the eggs hatch, the young salmon also swim to the ocean until they become adults and return to lay their eggs in the streams.) Explain that there are many different types, or species, of salmon. In some salmon, the adults return to the ocean after the eggs are laid. The adult salmon of the species that spawn in the Columbia River die a few days after laying the eggs.

Define the problem.

- Have a volunteer read the paragraph under "Define the problem" on page 52.

- After reading the paragraph, make sure that students associate the number of salmon in the population with the number of salmon that are able to successfully migrate in order to reproduce. Ask: **How many salmon migrated up the Columbia in the past?** (In the past, more than ten million salmon migrated up the Columbia every year.)

- Ask: **How many salmon make the trip now?** (Today, fewer than two million salmon swim up the river each year.)

- Say: **Define the problem.** Ask: **Why are fewer salmon migrating up the Columbia River now**

PHYSICAL SCIENCE
Forces and Interactions

LIFE SCIENCE
Interdependent Relationships in Ecosystems
Inheritance and Variation of Traits : Life Cycles and Traits

EARTH SCIENCE
Weather and Climate

than in the past? (The dams that people have built in the Columbia River system keep the fish from swimming up and down the rivers.) **How does fewer migrating salmon relate to the total number of salmon?** (If the salmon cannot migrate, they cannot successfully reproduce, so their total numbers decline.)

- Ask: **How does the decreased salmon population affect the river ecosystem?** (The decrease in numbers of salmon disrupts the ecosystem because it decreases the amount of food available to animals that typically feed on salmon. Decreasing salmon numbers also increases populations of aquatic life that the salmon feed upon.)

- Have volunteers read the captions on pages 52–53.

EXPLORE

Compare solutions.

- Have a volunteer read the paragraph under "Compare solutions" on page 54.

- Next, have volunteers read the captions on page 55.

- Guide students to draw a table like the one below in their science notebook.

Ways to Increase Salmon in the Columbia River

Solution	How It Works	Benefit
spillways		
fish hatcheries		
fish screens		
fish ladders		

SCIENCE AND ENGINEERING PRACTICES

Engaging in Argument from Evidence

- Remind students that real solutions must be relevant and meet the criteria and constraints of the problem at hand. Ask students to turn to a partner and constructively compare the solutions they chose. Why might one be better than another?

CROSSCUTTING CONCEPTS

Systems and System Models

- Say: **This activity focused on the effects of dams on salmon individuals and populations.** Ask: **What other parts of a river ecosystem might be impacted by dams?** (Possible answers: neighboring farm land; the rate of water flow; animals that feed on the salmon)

- Encourage students to link concepts of systems and system models, as well as solutions to environmental changes, to other disciplines of science. For example, in earth science, engineers and scientists develop systems for reducing impacts of natural hazards, such as spillways and levees for flooding, or early-warning systems and shelters for tornadoes.

Compare Solutions and Make a Claim (continued)

EXPLORE (continued)

Make a claim.

- Have a volunteer read the paragraph under "Make a claim" on page 54.

- Guide students to make a claim about which two solutions would be the best to include in a new dam design. Ask: **Which designs do you think are the most helpful by themselves? Explain.** (Answers will vary but should be supported. For example, students may argue that spillways help young fish get to the ocean; fish hatcheries help increase the salmon population and keep the ecosystem more balanced; fish screens protect the fish from physical harm; and fish ladders are the least disturbing to the fish's natural migration.) **Do some designs make a better pair than others? Explain.** (Students may say that some designs make up for other designs' shortcomings. For example, spillways and fish hatcheries address the young fish, but do not address the fish migrating upstream, so these solutions might work best if combined with technology like a fish ladder.)

- Assign time for students to write a paragraph that makes and explains their claim.

EXPLAIN

Support your claim.

- After students have written their paragraph, have a volunteer read the "Support your claim" section of the text on page 54.

- Organize students in groups of four or five, and have them take turns sharing and defending their claims. Remind students to use details from their paragraphs to support their choices.

- Ask: **In what ways did you think like a scientist as you completed this activity?** (Possible answer: I evaluated the different designs for helping salmon migrate over dams. I evaluated the trade-offs of the different solutions and picked the two I thought would best solve the problem.)

ELABORATE

My science notebook Help students conduct Internet research to explore the debate over dams in the Columbia River Basin. Have small groups prepare informal arguments to share with the class about whether the dams are more helpful or harmful and whether efforts to restore declining fish populations are effective enough. Encourage students to explore potential drawbacks that might not be readily apparent for each solution. For example, the air bubbles created in water flowing over spillways can increase the nitrogen content, which can harm the young fish. Fish can also produce water pollution from overpopulating a condensed area. Finally, some scientists argue that after climbing fish ladders, adult salmon might be too exhausted to reproduce. Remind students to support their arguments with facts from reliable sources.

EVALUATE

My science notebook

Check to make sure students have completed comparison tables in their science notebook. Assess the paragraphs they have written to make a claim about the merit of solutions to the drop in salmon population in the Columbia River. Then, ask students these questions. Have them record the answers in their science notebook.

1. **EXPLAIN Why has there been a drop in the Columbia River salmon population?** (because dams are keeping fish from migrating up the river to reproduce and down the river after they hatch)

2. **SUMMARIZE How do fish ladders address the decreasing salmon population?** (Fish ladders help the adult salmon get over dams so that they can migrate upstream to reproduce.)

3. **COMPARE What is a similarity between the way spillways and fish hatcheries address the decreasing salmon population?** (Spillways and fish hatcheries both are focused on increasing the number of young salmon that make it back to the ocean.)

RUBRICS

Teacher Rubric Use the scale descriptions to guide your assessment of the student's work. Assess each item separately, and then decide on one overall score, using the following scale:

4: Student performs with thorough understanding.

3: Student performs with adequate understanding.

2: Student performs with basic understanding.

1: Student performs with limited understanding.

Rubric	Scale			
The student defined the problem that dams built in the Columbia River system are blocking salmon from their typical migration patterns.	4	3	2	1
The student analyzed and compared solutions to help increase the Columbia River salmon population.	4	3	2	1
The student made a claim about which two solutions would be the best to include in a new dam design.	4	3	2	1
The student shared his or her recommendation with classmates, supporting and defending his or her claim.	4	3	2	1
Overall Score	4	3	2	1

Student Rubric Have students complete a self-evaluation similar to that shown below.

Rubric	Yes	Not Yet
1. I can define the problem of how dams are affecting the Columbia River salmon population.		
2. I can analyze and compare solutions to help increase the Columbia River salmon population.		
3. I can make a claim about which two solutions would be the best to include in a new dam design.		
4. I can share my recommendation with my classmates, and support and defend my claim.		

PHYSICAL SCIENCE
Forces and Interactions

LIFE SCIENCE
Interdependent Relationships in Ecosystems
Inheritance and Variation of Traits: Life Cycles and Traits

EARTH SCIENCE
Weather and Climate

Living in Groups

NEXT GENERATION SCIENCE STANDARDS | DISCIPLINARY CORE IDEAS
LS2.D: Social Interactions and Group Behavior Being part of a group helps animals obtain food, defend themselves, and cope with changes. Groups may serve different functions and vary dramatically in size.

Objective Students will be able to:
- Explain how being part of a group helps animals obtain food, defend themselves, and cope with changes.

ENGAGE

Tap Prior Knowledge

- Ask students to share what they know about animals that live in groups. Encourage them to share firsthand experience, or knowledge from photographs and other media. Ask: **What animals have you seen in a group? What were they doing?** (Possible answers: birds flying in a v-shaped formation, fish swimming, lions resting, deer grazing)

EXPLORE

Explore Living in Groups

- Have students observe the picture on pages 56–57. Ask probing questions to encourage exploration. For example, ask: **What animals do you see in the pictures? What does it look like they are doing?**

- Have students share their observations. Students may notice that the meerkats seem to be on the lookout for danger, the zebras are grazing, and the penguins are taking care of their young.

Set a Purpose and Read

- Have students read in order to explain how being part of a group helps animals obtain food, defend themselves, and cope with changes.

- Have students read pages 56–57.

EXPLAIN

Explain the Benefits of Living in Groups

- After students read pages 56–57, say: **What are three examples of names for different groups of animals?** (Possible answers: flock of birds, herd of elephants, school of fish, swarm of bees, pod of whales)

- Ask: **Is a wolf pack usually smaller or larger than a flock of birds?** (A wolf pack is usually smaller than a flock of birds.)

- Ask: **How do you think a swarm of bees is different in size from a herd of elephants?** (A herd of elephants numbers far fewer than a swarm of bees.)

- Ask: **What are three reasons animals live in groups?** (Living in groups can help them get food. It can help them defend themselves and care for their young. It can help them cope with changes in weather or in their environment.)

- Remind students of the gnu and the elephants from pages 42–43 that travel in herds to look for food and water. Then, point out that a colony of beavers built the dam on pages 46–47.

ELABORATE

Research Rules for Living in a Group

Scientists who study animal behavior have discovered that animal groups seem to have rules. Members of the group that aren't cooperative, for instance, could end up alone in the wild. Have student pairs research social behavior of animals such as the fox, chimpanzee, cat, and elephant. Have students share their findings about how these animals' actions support group living.

Extend Your Thinking About Disadvantages to Living in Groups

- Have students extend their thinking about possible disadvantages to living in a group. Say: **We have learned about the benefits animals get from living in a group.** Ask: **What do you think some possible disadvantages are to group living?** (Accept all reasonable responses. Possible answers: In a large group, there is more competition for food, water, mates, and other resources, like places to nest or sleep. Predators can also spot large groups of animals more easily than individuals or small groups, and disease spreads more quickly among members of a group.)

EVALUATE

Have students record their answers to the Wrap It Up questions in their science notebook.

Wrap It Up!

1. **NAME** **What are some of the names used for groups of animals?** (Possible answers: flock of birds, herd of elephants, school of fish, swarm of bees, pod of whales)

2. **CONTRAST** **Animal groups come in different sizes. Describe how the size of a wolf pack is different from the size of a large flock of birds.** (A wolf pack is fewer than 50 members, and usually is closer to 20 members. A large flock of birds could have more than one million members.)

3. **SUMMARIZE** **How does living in groups help animals survive?** (Living in groups can help animals get food. It can help them defend themselves. It can help them care for their young. It can help them cope with changes in weather or in their environment.)

An additional interactive assessment activity can be found in the Exploring Science Digital Book.

PHYSICAL SCIENCE
Forces and Interactions

LIFE SCIENCE
Interdependent Relationships in Ecosystems
Inheritance and Variation of Traits : Life Cycles and Traits

EARTH SCIENCE
Weather and Climate

READING CONNECTION

Determine Word Meaning

Determine the meaning of general academic and domain-specific words and phrases in a text relevant to *a grade 3 topic or subject area.*

Guide students to determine the meanings of domain-specific words in the text. For example, point out that different animal groups are called by different names. Have volunteers identify the different group names listed in the first paragraph on page 56. (flock, herd, school, swarm, pod) Share some additional group names, such as band of gorillas, tower of goats, gang of elk, and a crash of rhinoceroses. Explain that these names are arbitrary, that is, they have no real relationship to any physical characteristic of the group.

TEACHING WITH TECHNOLOGY

List the Benefits of Group Living

Project the lesson on a whiteboard. Ask one student to circle the title of the lesson. (Living in Groups) Then, ask another student to put a box around the paragraph that tells about the benefits of living in a group. (the second paragraph) Ask three more volunteers to write the numbers 1 through 3 next to phrases that tell the benefits of living in a group. (1. get food; 2. defend themselves and care for their young; 3. cope with changes in the weather or their environment) Ask: **What is the main idea of this paragraph?** (the benefits of group living) Say: **Yes, the main idea of this paragraph is that living in a group has benefits. The benefits are listed as details in the paragraph's text.** Then ask a volunteer to read the numbered phrases.

Getting Food

NEXT GENERATION SCIENCE STANDARDS | DISCIPLINARY CORE IDEAS
LS2.D: Social Interactions and Group Behavior Being part of a group helps animals obtain food, defend themselves, and cope with changes. Groups may serve different functions and vary dramatically in size.

Objective Students will be able to:
- Explain how being part of a group helps animals obtain food.

Science Vocabulary
pack, prey

ENGAGE
Tap Prior Knowledge

- Ask students to share what they remember from the lesson Living Things Make Changes on pages 46–47 about what animals who want to eat another animal are called. Say: **Remember that one reason the beavers shown in the lesson *Living Things Make Changes* built the dam was to protect them from other animals that wanted to eat them.** Ask: **What is an animal called that hunts and eats another animal?** (An animal that hunts and eats another animal is called a predator.)

EXPLORE
Preview Getting Food

- Have students observe the picture on pages 58–59. Ask: **What is happening in these pictures? Which animals are the predators?**

- Have students share their observations. Students may say that it looks like the wolves are hunting the bison and the cheetahs are hunting the gazelle. This makes the wolves and cheetahs predators.

Set a Purpose and Read

- Have students read in order to explain how being part of a group helps animals obtain food.

- Have students read pages 58–59.

EXPLAIN
Explain How Animals Get Food

- After students read pages 58–59, say: Ask: **What do you call the group of wolves surrounding the bison?** (The group of wolves surrounding the bison is called a pack.)

- Remind students that groups of different types of animals have different names.

- Ask: **How do the wolves in a pack work together to chase down the bison?** (The wolves take turns chasing the bison until the bison is too tired to run. Then, the wolves surround the bison. They share a fresh meal.)

- Ask: **In the picture on page 59, which animal is the prey? Explain.** (The bison is the prey because it is the one being hunted.)

- Ask: **Do wolves need to hunt mice and rabbits in packs?** (No. Individual wolves can catch mice and rabbits.)

- Say: **Explain why the pack is needed to hunt bison.** (Bison can weigh ten times as much as a single wolf. They are too big for a single wolf to capture, but no match for the pack.)

- Ask: **What other animals do wolves hunt in packs?** (Wolves hunt other large animals, such as moose and elk, in packs.)

- Say: **Name four other animals that hunt in groups.** (lions, hyenas, orcas, and army ants)

- Ask: **Why don't all animals hunt in groups all the time?** (Possible answers: Animals don't need to hunt in groups when hunting smaller animals. Also, when the prey is smaller, hunting in a group would increase competition for food.)

ELABORATE

Research Pack Hunters

Have pairs of students use the Internet or library resources to research another type of animal mentioned in the lesson that also hunts in packs. Allow pairs to choose between lions, hyenas, orcas, and army ants. Ask students to tell the class what kind of prey the animal they researched hunts as a group, why they need the group to hunt this prey, and how the group works together to hunt it.

Extend Your Thinking About Hunting Animals and Their Prey

Have students extend their thinking about the relationships of predators and prey. Say: **Animals that hunt and eat other animals are known as predators. The animals they hunt are their prey.** Ask: **Can an animal be both a predator and prey? Explain.** (Yes. An animal might be a predator of one animal and the prey of another.) **What is an example of an animal that is both predator and prey?** (Accept all reasonable answers. Possible answer: A snake is a predator of mice, and may be the prey of a hawk.)

EVALUATE

Have students record their answers to the Wrap It Up questions in their science notebook.

Wrap It Up!

1. **DEFINE What is a pack?** (A pack is a group of closely related animals that live and hunt together.)

2. **CONTRAST What kind of prey can a single wolf catch? How is this different from the prey that a pack of wolves can catch?** (A single wolf can catch mice and rabbits and other small animals. Packs of wolves can catch bigger animals.)

3. **GENERALIZE How does hunting in groups help animals survive?** (Hunting in groups allows animals to catch larger prey and share it with the whole group.)

PHYSICAL SCIENCE
Forces and Interactions

LIFE SCIENCE
Interdependent Relationships in Ecosystems
Inheritance and Variation of Traits : Life Cycles and Traits

EARTH SCIENCE
Weather and Climate

READING CONNECTION

Determine Word Meaning

Determine the meaning of general academic and domain-specific words and phrases in a text relevant to a *grade 3 topic or subject area.*

Guide students to use the text and context clues to determine word meaning. For example, this lesson has two vocabulary words—*pack* and *prey*—and another highly relevant word, *predator*. Help students build understanding of these terms by asking them to use these words when describing what is happening in the photos on pages 58–59.

DIFFERENTIATED INSTRUCTION

Extra Support Have students circle the predators in each of the following pairs of animals: cheetah/gazelle, mouse/snake, crow/worm, catfish/humans, coyote/house cat.

Challenge Have students circle the predators in each of the pairs above. Then, have them do research to find predators for the animals they circled and prey of the animals that they did not circle. Have them create new pairs with the information they find. If any animals don't have predators (humans), have them write the animal's name alone with a box around it.

Protection and Defense

NEXT GENERATION SCIENCE STANDARDS | DISCIPLINARY CORE IDEAS
LS2.D: Social Interactions and Group Behavior Being part of a group helps animals obtain food, defend themselves, and cope with changes. Groups may serve different functions and vary dramatically in size.

Objective Students will be able to:
- Explain how being part of a group helps animals protect and defend themselves.

Science Vocabulary
school

ENGAGE

Tap Prior Knowledge

- Ask students to share what they know about how animals protect and defend themselves. Ask: **What are some ways you know of that animals defend themselves?** (Accept any reasonable responses. Possible answers: Some animals defend themselves by growling or barking or using their sharp teeth or claws. Some have hard shells or spines that poke predators. Others play dead, sting predators, or release poisonous spray or venom.)

EXPLORE

Explore Protection and Defense

- Have students observe the picture on pages 60–61. Ask probing questions to encourage exploration. For example, ask: **Which animal is the predator and which is the prey in this picture? Which mackerel are at risk of being eaten and which are the safest?**

- Have students share their observations. Students may say the dolphins are the predators and the mackerel are the prey. They may say that the mackerel on the outside of the group are at risk of being eaten, but the ones inside the group are safe.

Set a Purpose and Read

- Have students read in order to explain how being part of a group helps animals protect and defend themselves.

- Have students read pages 60–61.

EXPLAIN

Explain How Animals Protect and Defend

- After students read pages 60–61, say: **Remember that animal groups have different names.** Ask: **What do you call a group of fish swimming close together?** (A group of fish swimming close together is called a school of fish.)

- Ask: **What does "safety in numbers" mean?** ("Safety in numbers" means that animals are safer in a group than alone.)

- Ask: **How does swimming in a school provide safety in numbers?** (In a school, there are more eyes to spot predators, and the large number of fish makes it harder for a predator to target a single fish.)

- Ask: **What land animals live in herds to protect themselves from predators such as lions?** (Wildebeests and zebras live in large herds to protect themselves from predators.)

- Remind students that, like the bison that the wolves were hunting in the previous lesson, a herd of zebras would be more likely to fight off a lion than an individual zebra would be.

- Ask: **What is a group of birds flying together called?** (A group of birds flying together is called a flock.)

- Ask: **How is a flock of blackbirds being hunted by a hawk similar to the mackerel in the picture on pages 60–61?** (A flock of blackbirds would make it difficult for a hawk to reach the blackbirds at the center of the flock. The flock would also have more eyes with which to spot the hawk and make it harder for the hawk to target one bird.)

PHYSICAL SCIENCE
Forces and Interactions

LIFE SCIENCE
Interdependent Relationships in Ecosystems
Inheritance and Variation of Traits: Life Cycles and Traits

EARTH SCIENCE
Weather and Climate

ELABORATE

Research Ways Animals Protect and Defend

Animals have other ways to protect and defend themselves besides living in groups. Have small groups of students search the National Geographic Kids Website for information on how red-eyed tree frogs, pufferfish, skunks, and cichlid fish defend themselves. Have each group of students create a chart to record their findings. As a class, discuss how these organisms' defense mechanisms are similar and how they are different.

Extend Your Thinking About Defense and Protection

- Have students extend their thinking about how animals defend themselves. Say: **Some animals rely on safety in numbers as their main way to defend themselves, while others have individual ways to keep themselves safe.** Ask: **Do you think safety in numbers or another type of defense is best for animals? Explain.** (Accept all reasonable responses. Possible answer: It depends on the animal. Safety in numbers is good defense for animals with no other way to defend themselves. Venomous animals don't need the protection of a group, though, because they have an effective individual way to keep themselves safe.)

EVALUATE

Have students record their answers to the Wrap It Up questions in their science notebook.

Wrap It Up!

1. **DEFINE What is a school of fish?** (A school of fish is a group of fish that swim very close together.)

2. **EXPLAIN How does swimming in a school help protect fish?** (Swimming in a school means there are many eyes to spot predators. The huge number of fish also makes it more difficult for a predator to target a single fish.)

3. **INFER How might swimming in a large school not help fish survive?** (Predators might be more likely to see a school of fish. Also, the fish on the outside of the school are left vulnerable.)

READING CONNECTION

Use Photos and Text to Demonstrate Understanding

Use information gained from illustrations (e.g., maps, photographs) and the words in a text to demonstrate understanding of the text (e.g., where, when, why, and how key events occur).

Guide students to use information gained from the photograph on pages 60–61 and the words in the text to demonstrate understanding of how living in groups can help animals defend and protect themselves. For example, when asking questions in the EXPLORE section, ask students to explain how the photograph helps them understand which mackerel are in danger and which are safe. In the EXPLAIN section encourage students to use direct phrases from the text and to use the photograph as an example in their answers.

SCIENCE MISCONCEPTION

Porcupine

It is a misconception that porcupines are able to shoot or throw their quills at attackers to defend themselves. Porcupines do use the sharp quills as a defense, of course, but they do not propel them in any way. Instead, when a porcupine is threatened, it turns its back to an aggressor and raises its quills. If this warning is not heeded, the porcupine will run backward toward the predator in an effort to poke it with the quills. The quills come out of the porcupine easily, but not the attacker. Porcupine quills have barbs on the end that make them difficult to remove from skin. Luckily for the porcupine, any spines it looses in a battle will grow back.

61

Coping with Change

NEXT GENERATION SCIENCE STANDARDS | DISCIPLINARY CORE IDEAS
LS2.D: Social Interactions and Group Behavior Being part of a group helps animals obtain food, defend themselves, and cope with changes. Groups may serve different functions and vary dramatically in size.

Objective Students will be able to:
- Explain how being part of a group helps some animals cope with changes.

Science Vocabulary
swarm

ENGAGE
Tap Prior Knowledge

- Ask students to share what they know from previous lessons about how living things cope with change. Ask: **What are the two behaviors you learned about in a previous lesson that some living things do when the weather changes?** (Some living things migrate to warmer climates when the weather becomes cooler. Other animals cope with the change by hibernating.)

EXPLORE
Preview Coping With Change

- Have students read the title and then look at the picture on pages 62–63. Ask: **From the title, what do you think you will learn about in this lesson? What can you guess about the bees in the picture, based on the title? What kind of change do you think the bees are coping with?**

- Have students share their observations. Students may say that they will learn about how animals react to and deal with changes in the weather and in their environment. They might say that the bees in the picture must be dealing with some kind of change. They might notice that the bees seem to be huddled together, so they might be protecting something, keeping warm, or resting.

Set a Purpose and Read

- Have students read in order to explain how being part of a group helps animals cope with changes.

- Have students read pages 62–63.

EXPLAIN
Explain How Animals Cope With Change

- After students read pages 62–63, say: **Remember that *to migrate* means "to move to a different place to meet basic needs."** Ask: **What is one basic need that migration helps some birds meet?** (Possible answer: Migration helps birds meet their needs for food.)

- Remind students that a group of birds flying together is called a flock. Say: **Flocks of birds migrate to warmer places for the winter.** Ask: **When do you think they migrate back to cooler climates?** (They probably migrate back to cooler climates in the spring or summer when temperatures get warmer and food is more abundant.)

- Ask: **In addition to moving to cope with weather changes, what is another change that might cause animals to need to move?** (Overcrowding of space can cause animals to move.)

- Ask: **What animal moves in a group to cope with overcrowded space?** (Possible answer: Bees move in a group when a nest gets too crowded.)

- Say: **Explain what a swarm is.** (A swarm is a large group of small animals moving together.)

- Ask: **Why is it important that a swarm include a queen bee?** (It is important that a swarm includes a queen bee so that she can lay eggs and the bees can start a new colony.)

- Ask: **What are the bees in the photograph doing?** (They are resting while scout bees find a good place for the swarm to live. They are also probably protecting the queen bee.)

ELABORATE

Research Orca Migration

Step 1: Have pairs of students use the Internet or other resources to research orca migration along the North American Pacific coast. Have pairs work together to draw a map of the whales' migration route. Have students label the most southern and northern points of the map with months of the years.

Step 2: As a class, discuss what a group of whales is called. (pod) Also discuss why the orca migrate (for food and to give birth), and other ways they cope with the change of weather (added layers of fat).

Find Out More About Coping With Changes in the Environment

- Have students find out more about how living in a group can help one another cope with change. Say: **Remember that some animals hibernate to cope with change. Some animals hibernate alone. Others, like some lizards and snakes, hibernate in groups.** Ask: **What are some advantages to hibernating in a group?** (Animals that hibernate in groups can help keep one another warm.)

EVALUATE

Have students record their answers to the Wrap It Up questions in their science notebook.

Wrap It Up!

1. **DEFINE What is a swarm of bees?** (A swarm of bees is a large group of bees moving together.)
2. **CAUSE AND EFFECT What condition causes bees to swarm?** (Overcrowding of a nest causes bees to swarm.)
3. **INFER What change in their habitat makes it necessary for birds to migrate in the fall?** (Birds migrate in the fall to find food and shelter because the weather turns cooler.)

PHYSICAL SCIENCE
Forces and Interactions

LIFE SCIENCE
Interdependent Relationships in Ecosystems
Inheritance and Variation of Traits : Life Cycles and Traits

EARTH SCIENCE
Weather and Climate

READING CONNECTION

Describe the Relationship

Describe the relationship between a series of historical events, scientific ideas or concepts, or steps in technical procedures in a text, using language that pertains to time, sequence, and cause/effect.

Guide students to describe the relationship between changes in conditions in an area and how those changes result in behavioral changes in animals in terms of cause and effect. Have students make a two-column chart in their science notebook with column headings "Cause: Change in Conditions" and "Effect: How Animals Cope." As you work through the EXPLAIN section, have students complete the chart with examples from the text. For example, Cause: Weather cools in fall. Effect: Some birds migrate to warmer areas where food is more plentiful. Repeat by having a volunteer identify the cause-and-effect relationship pertaining to bees described in the text.

TEACHING WITH TECHNOLOGY

Main Idea and Details

Project the lesson on a whiteboard. Ask one student to circle the title. (Coping with Change) Ask another student to circle the paragraph that is about animals moving to cope with changes in the weather. (the first paragraph) Have a third volunteer underline a detail in the paragraph that supports the main idea of the paragraph. (Possible answer: Flocks of birds migrate to warmer places where they spend the winter can get what they need to survive.) Then ask a student to put a box around the paragraph that is about animals that move to cope with other changes in their environment. (the second paragraph) Have a volunteer underline a detail that supports the main idea of the paragraph. (Possible answer: When a nest of bees gets too crowded, thousands of bees fly away in a swarm.)

Construct an Argument

NEXT GENERATION SCIENCE STANDARDS | PERFORMANCE EXPECTATION
3-LS2-1. Construct an argument that some animals form groups that help members survive.

Objective Students will be able to:
- Construct an argument that some animals form groups that help members survive.

CLASSROOM MANAGEMENT

Time 40 minutes

Teaching Tips Organize the class into groups of 2–4 students. Encourage students to work together to carefully follow the steps in the text and construct an argument about how some animals form groups that help members survive. Guide students through the steps one at a time, leaving time for groups to complete each step before moving on as a class to the next one.

What to Expect Students will ask the question *Why do sandhill cranes form groups at various times?* Next, they will gather information and prepare a list of ways that migrating and living in groups are helpful. Then, they will construct an argument that describes how forming groups at various times benefits sandhill cranes. Arguments will vary, but should address all three situations mentioned in the text.

ENGAGE

Set the scene.

- Remind students that they have learned some reasons why various animals form groups. Ask: **How can forming groups help living things survive?** (Groups can help living things get food, protect members of the group, and cope with change.) **What is an example of a living thing benefiting from forming a group?** (Accept all reasonable responses. Possible answer: Wolves that hunt in packs are better able to kill large prey that a single wolf would not be able to kill on its own.)

EXPLORE

Preview the lesson.

- Have students look at the pictures of the cranes on pages 64–65. Ask: **How many cranes do you see in each picture?** (There are four cranes in the big picture, six in the small picture on the right, and too many to count in the small picture on the left.) **How do the three groups pictured differ from each other?** (The groups vary in size. Also, each group seems to be doing something different.)

EXPLAIN

Ask a question.

- After reading the introductory paragraph on page 64, ask: **What is one first step for constructing an argument?** (One step is to ask a question.)

- Have a volunteer read the question in step 1. Then, say: **You will work in small groups of two to four to construct an argument that answers this question.**

Gather information.

- Ask: **What is another step for constructing an argument?** (Another step is to gather information.)

- Have a volunteer read the text in step 2. Then, ask: **What will you prepare a list of as you read the captions that go with the pictures?** (Students will prepare a list of the ways that migrating and living in groups probably helps sandhill cranes survive.)

- Say: **Tables can help you organize information you gather so that you can easily use it as evidence later.** Ask: **How can you use a table to organize the information you gather on these pages about why cranes form groups?** (Accept reasonable solutions. See page 65a for an example table.) Guide students to draw their tables in their science notebook.

Why Cranes Form Groups

Description of Group	How It Helps the Cranes Survive

- Have students take turns reading the captions on pages 64–65 in their groups.

- After students have read the captions, guide them to discuss the question at the end of each caption within their groups. First, ask: **What is migration?** (Migration is animals moving to a different place to meet their basic needs.)

- Then, say: **With your group, discuss the question at the end of each caption, and fill in your tables with your answers.**

Construct an argument.

- After students have filled in their tables, ask: **What is the final step?** (The final step is to construct an argument.)

- Have a volunteer read the text in step 3. Then, ask: **What information will you use to construct an argument describing how the formation of groups helps sandhill cranes survive?** (Students will use the information they collected in their tables to construct their arguments.)

- Remind students to include information about the different-sized groups that sandhill cranes form at different times of the year, both during and in between migrations.

- Have students present their arguments to the class. Allow students to give one another constructive feedback. Encourage students to rebut challenges to their arguments using data from their research. As necessary, have students redraft their arguments to address flaws in logic and reasoning or misinterpretation of data.

- When students finish presenting, tell them that when constructing an argument they do not always need to follow this specific order of steps. At any stage, students and scientists may choose to redefine the question or generate arguments to replace an idea that isn't working out.

- Ask: **In what ways did you think like a scientist as you completed this activity?** (Possible answer: I used my knowledge about animal behaviors and the reasons animals form groups to hypothesize why sandhill cranes might also form groups.)

SCIENCE AND ENGINEERING PRACTICES

Engaging in Argument from Evidence

- Explain that scientists construct arguments using evidence, data, and models. Ask students what they used to support their argument. What else could they have used as support? (Possible answers: students used data as support; they could have used a model of the bird population.)

CROSSCUTTING CONCEPTS

Cause and Effect

- Ask students to restate their argument to explain the effects migrating in large groups might have on the survival of sandhill cranes. (Possible answer: Because sandhill cranes migrate in large groups, they can protect and raise their young together, and find food more quickly as a group.)

PHYSICAL SCIENCE
Forces and Interactions

LIFE SCIENCE
Interdependent Relationships in Ecosystems
Inheritance and Variation of Traits: Life Cycles and Traits

EARTH SCIENCE
Weather and Climate

Construct an Argument (continued)

ELABORATE

Extend Your Thinking About How Sandhill Cranes Form Groups

My science notebook The groups that sandhill cranes form for migration and nesting are often large and can include hundreds of thousands of birds. An individual family of sandhill cranes is a much smaller group consisting of two parent birds and their young. Ask: **Why do you think sandhill cranes form large groups to migrate, but raise their young in smaller groups? How does the size of each group satisfy a particular need?** (When sandhill cranes are raising their young, it makes sense that they would live in small groups and that each pair of parents puts its focus on feeding and protecting their young. Also, the birds are settled in one place during the months they are raising their young, so safety in numbers is less of a concern than when they are on the move, in constantly changing environments. When the birds are migrating, a larger group is better because the focus moves to protection of the whole flock. When migrating, the cranes are not staying in one place, so large groups of the birds do not deplete the environment of food. When raising young, the cranes must stay in the same place for a considerable amount of time. If they were in large groups at this time, the cranes would likely run out of food.)

EVALUATE

My science notebook Check to make sure students have recorded the information they have gathered and the argument they have constructed in their science notebook. Then, ask students these questions. Have them record the answers in their science notebook.

1. **LIST Name three behaviors that sandhill cranes do in groups.** (They fly, flock, and nest in groups.)

2. **EXPLAIN How is migration a way that living things cope with change?** (Migration is a way living things cope with changes in the weather. When the weather is too cold, they move to other areas to find food and shelter.)

3. **MAKE JUDGMENTS Which picture is the best representation of safety in numbers?** (Possible answer: The bottom left picture is the best representation of safety in numbers because there are the most birds in the picture. The bigger the group, the more eyes for spotting danger and the more birds to scare or fight off predators.)

RUBRICS

Teacher Rubric Use the scale descriptions to guide your assessment of the student's work. Assess each item separately, and then decide on one overall score, using the following scale:

4: Student performs with thorough understanding.

3: Student performs with adequate understanding.

2: Student performs with basic understanding.

1: Student performs with limited understanding.

Rubric	Scale			
The student worked with a group to gather information about why cranes form groups.	4	3	2	1
The student worked with a group to successfully organize the information they gathered in a table.	4	3	2	1
The student constructed an argument that describes how forming groups at various times benefits sandhill cranes.	4	3	2	1
The student presented his or her argument and rebutted challenges using data from research.	4	3	2	1
If warranted, the student revised his or her argument to address lapses in logic or factual errors.	4	3	2	1
Overall Score	4	3	2	1

Student Rubric Have students complete a self-evaluation similar to that shown below.

Rubric	Yes	Not Yet
1. I can work with a group to gather information about why cranes form groups.		
2. I can work with a group to successfully organize the information they gathered in a table.		
3. I can construct an argument that describes how forming groups at various times benefits sandhill cranes.		
4. I can present my argument and rebut challenges using data from my research.		
5. I can revise my argument to address misunderstandings or errors.		

PHYSICAL SCIENCE
Forces and Interactions

LIFE SCIENCE
Interdependent Relationships in Ecosystems
Inheritance and Variation of Traits : Life Cycles and Traits

EARTH SCIENCE
Weather and Climate

Fossils

NEXT GENERATION SCIENCE STANDARDS | DISCIPLINARY CORE IDEAS
LS4.A: Evidence of Common Ancestry and Diversity
- Some kinds of plants and animals that once lived on Earth are no longer found anywhere. (3-LS4-1)

- Fossils provide evidence about the types of organisms that lived long ago and also about the nature of their environments. (3-LS4-1)

Objectives **Students will be able to:**
- Explain that some kinds of plants and animals that once lived on Earth are no longer found anywhere.

- Explain that fossils provide evidence about the types of organisms that lived long ago and the nature of their environments.

Science Vocabulary
fossils

ENGAGE
Tap Prior Knowledge

- Ask students to share what they know about fossils. Ask: **If you stepped in wet concrete, what would be left behind?** (A footprint would be left behind if you stepped in wet concrete.) Ask: **What would happen when the concrete dried?** (When the concrete dried, the footprint would remain.) Explain that some fossils are similar to footsteps in concrete in that they show evidence of the presence of ancient organisms.

EXPLORE
Explore Fossils

- Have students observe the picture on pages 66–67. Ask probing questions to encourage exploration. For example, ask: **Do any of the animals in the picture remind you of animals that are familiar to you? How do you think the small picture on page 66 relates to the rest of the picture?**

- Have students share their observations. Students may notice that some of the animals in the picture look like octopi or squids. Others look like snails and snakes. They might say that the small picture on page 66 is an example of the remains of an animal shown in the larger image.

Set a Purpose and Read

- Have students read in order to explain that some kinds of plants and animals that once lived on Earth are no longer found anywhere and that fossils provide evidence about them and the nature of their environments.

- Have students read pages 66–67.

EXPLAIN
Explain Extinct Organisms

- After students read pages 66–67, ask: **How long ago did the creatures in the picture live?** (The animals in the picture lived between 450 and 500 million years ago.)

- Ask: **What does it mean when an animal is extinct?** (When an animal is extinct, it is no longer living anywhere on Earth.)

Explain Fossils

- Ask: **What are fossils?** (Fossils are traces of plants, animals, and other organisms that lived long ago.)

- Ask: **How do scientists use fossils?** (Scientists use fossils as evidence of ancient life, which they can study to learn more about ancient ecosystems like the one pictured.)

- Say: **Describe three steps that form fossils.** (1. An animal dies and is buried in mud; 2. The mud is pressed together and turns into rock; 3. The rock preserves the shape of the animal.)

- Ask: **What parts of an animal are preserved in fossils?** (Hard parts of an animal, such as its shell, bones, or teeth, can be preserved. Evidence of the animal, like footprints or wormholes can be preserved.)

ELABORATE

Research Fossils

Step 1: Have pairs of students search National Geographic websites for pictures of fossils to study.

Step 2: If time permits, have pairs draw pictures of what they think three animals looked like, based on the information they can gather from the fossil images.

EVALUATE

Have students record their answers to the Wrap It Up questions in their science notebook.

Wrap It Up!

1. **DEFINE What is a fossil?** (A fossil is a trace of an organism that lived long ago.)

2. **EXPLAIN How do fossils form?** (Fossils form when parts of organisms or traces of them are buried in mud that is pressed together and hardened into rock over a long time.)

3. **INFER Dinosaur fossils usually show their bones but not their inner organs, such as the heart and lungs. Why do you think this is so?** (Since bones are hard, they can be preserved, while softer tissue decomposes.)

READING CONNECTION

Describe the Relationship

Describe the relationship between a series of historical events, scientific ideas or concepts, or steps in technical procedures in a text, using language that pertains to time, sequence, and cause/effect.

Guide students to describe the relationship between events that result in fossilization using sequence and cause-and-effect language. For example, in the EXPLAIN section when discussing extinction and the formation of fossils, encourage students to use words such as *first, next, then,* and *finally* to summarize the process.

SCIENCE BACKGROUND

Petrification

Fossilization is a general term used to describe a myriad of preservation processes. Petrification is one type of fossilization. When something is petrified, the organic material is replaced with minerals and the material hardens like stone. The minerals can cause the material to turn shades of white, blue, purple, black, brown, red, and yellow, making petrified organisms some of the most colorful fossils. In addition, organisms that have been petrified maintain their three-dimensional shape, as opposed to just leaving behind an impression. So, like amber fossilization, petrification can preserve only the organism itself, and not evidence of the organism, like footprints or wormholes. The Petrified Forest National Monument is a forest of petrified trees in Arizona that was designated a national park in 1962.

PHYSICAL SCIENCE
Forces and Interactions

LIFE SCIENCE
Interdependent Relationships in Ecosystems
Inheritance and Variation of Traits: Life Cycles and Traits

EARTH SCIENCE
Weather and Climate

Fish in the Desert

NEXT GENERATION SCIENCE STANDARDS | DISCIPLINARY CORE IDEAS
LS4.A: Evidence of Common Ancestry and Diversity
- Some kinds of plants and animals that once lived on Earth are no longer found anywhere. (3-LS4-1)

- Fossils provide evidence about the types of organisms that lived long ago and also about the nature of their environments. (3-LS4-1)

Objective Students will be able to:
- Explain that fossils provide evidence about the types of organisms that lived long ago and the nature of their environments.

ENGAGE

Tap Prior Knowledge

- Ask students to share what they know about fish in the dessert. Say: **In the previous lesson, you learned about fossils.** Ask: **How long does it take a fossil to form?** (It can take a fossil millions of years to form.) Note that some fossils form more quickly than this.

EXPLORE

Explore Fish in the Desert

- Have students observe the picture on pages 68–69. Ask probing questions to encourage exploration. For example, ask: **What can you tell about the environment in which the fossilized animals in the picture lived? Do you think these creatures lived in a desert, sea, or forest?**

- Have students share their observations. Students may notice that, even though the fossils are in sand, the creatures are aquatic. They might conclude that these creatures must have lived in the sea, even though they were found in a desert.

Set a Purpose and Read

- Have students read in order to explain that some kinds of plants and animals that once lived on Earth are no longer found anywhere and that fossils provide evidence about them and the nature of their environments.

- Have students read pages 68–69.

EXPLAIN

Explain Fish in the Desert

- After students read pages 68–69, ask: **What can fossils provide evidence of?** (Fossils provide evidence about plants and animals that lived long ago. They also provide evidence about the habitats in which they lived.)

- Ask: **What can scientists find out about an environment by studying fossils?** (Scientists can find out what the environment in a place used to be like and how the environment has changed over time.)

- Ask: **What kinds of fossils can be found in the layer of rock called the Green River Formation?** (Fish fossils can be found in the Green River Formation.)

- Ask: **What is the Green River Formation?** (It is a layer of rock that stretches through Utah, Colorado, and Wyoming.)

- Ask: **What is the area around Utah, Colorado, and Wyoming like today?** (It is mostly desert.)

- Say: **Explain how scientists know that Utah, Colorado, and Wyoming were once covered in water.** (The fossils there are of fish, so since most fish can live only in water, scientists know that the land used to be covered in water.)

ELABORATE

Research Mammoths

Have small groups use the Internet or other resources to research mammoths. Have students in each group work together to answer the following questions in their science notebook: **What are mammoths?** (Mammoths are early relatives of elephants; they lived during the last ice age.) **Where did mammoths live, and how do scientists know?** (Scientists know that mammoths lived in North America, Asia, Europe, and North Africa because they have found their remains there.)

How do scientists know that woolly mammoths lived where it was cold? (Scientists know that woolly mammoths lived where it was cold because their remains have been found in northern latitudes, and they had thick, long fur to protect them from harsh weather.)

Find Out More About Ancient Climates

- Help students find resources to learn about redwood fossils found near the North Pole. Then, discuss questions such as: **How was the climate in this area of land different millions of years ago? How do scientists know?**

EVALUATE

Have students record their answers to the Wrap It Up questions in their science notebook.

Wrap It Up!

1. **CONTRAST How is the environment of Utah today different from the environment when the fossils in the picture formed?** (Utah used to be covered in water. Now Utah is mostly a rocky desert.)

2. **DRAW CONCLUSIONS Scientists have found fossils of clams in rocks at the top of mountains. What do these fossils suggest about the rocks?** (These rocks were underwater at one point.)

PHYSICAL SCIENCE
Forces and Interactions

LIFE SCIENCE
Interdependent Relationships in Ecosystems
Inheritance and Variation of Traits : Life Cycles and Traits

EARTH SCIENCE
Weather and Climate

READING CONNECTION

Use Photos and Text to Demonstrate Understanding

Use information gained from illustrations (e.g., maps, photographs) and the words in a text to demonstrate understanding of the text (e.g., where, when, why, and how key events occur).

Guide students in using information gained from the photos and their captions to demonstrate understanding of the text. For example, in the EXPLAIN section as you discuss the Green River Formation, direct students to the caption on page 68, Ask: **How are the Green River Formation and the state of Wyoming related?** (Part of the area that now makes up Wyoming is part of the Green River Formation.) Then direct students to the photo of the Utah canyon. Ask: **What is important about this photo?** (It shows what the area where the Green River Formation is found looks like today.) **What can you conclude from the information provided by these photos and their captions?** (The area where the Green River Formation is found was once covered by water, as evidenced by the presence of fish fossils. This area is now mostly dry desert, as shown in the picture of the Utah canyon.)

DIFFERENTIATED INSTRUCTION

Extra Support In the ELABORATE section, Research Mammoths, have students print a world map and color and label it to show where mammoths lived. Have them write a title and three facts about mammoths on the page.

Challenge In the ELABORATE section, Research Mammoths, have students research and compare the Columbian Mammoth and the Woolly Mammoth. Have students write three facts about each type of mammoth and color a world map to show where each lived.

Plants in the Antarctic

NEXT GENERATION SCIENCE STANDARDS | DISCIPLINARY CORE IDEAS
LS4.A: Evidence of Common Ancestry and Diversity
- Some kinds of plants and animals that once lived on Earth are no longer found anywhere. (3-LS4-1)

- Fossils provide evidence about the types of organisms that lived long ago and also about the nature of their environments. (3-LS4-1)

Objective Students will be able to:
- Explain that fossils provide evidence about the types of organisms that lived long ago and the nature of their environments.

ENGAGE

Tap Prior Knowledge

- Ask students to share what they know about ancient environments. Ask: **If an area is a desert today, does that mean it has always been a desert?** (No, just because an area is a desert today, it doesn't mean that it was always a desert.) **How do scientists know what an environment was like millions of years ago?** (Scientist study fossils to learn about ancient environments.)

EXPLORE

Explore Plants in the Antarctic

- Have students observe the picture on pages 70–71. Say: **Think about what you learned in the last lesson.** Ask: **What do you see in the pictures on pages 70 and 71? How do you think these pictures are related?**

- Have students share their observations. Students may notice that the bigger picture is a fossilized plant and the smaller picture is of a very cold place.

Set a Purpose and Read

- Have students read in order to explain that fossils provide evidence about the types of organisms that lived long ago and the nature of their environments.

- Have students read pages 70–71.

EXPLAIN

Explain Plants in the Antarctic

- After students read pages 70–71, ask: **Can plants be preserved in fossils?** (Yes.) Remind students that fossils can be traces of plants, animals, or other organisms that lived long ago.

- Ask: **What does it mean that the fern in the picture on pages 70–71 is extinct?** (It means that it no longer lives anywhere on Earth.)

- Ask: **What kind of environment do ferns live in?** (Ferns live in warm environments.) Show students images of modern ferns in a moist wooded or tropical environment.

- Ask: **Where was the fossil shown on pages 70–71 found?** (Antarctica) Ask: **What is the environment in Antarctica like?** (Antarctica is cold and frozen.)

- Ask: **What does the fern fossil indicate to scientists about what the environment was like in the area of land that makes up Antarctica millions of years ago?** (This area of land was once warm enough for ferns and forests to grow.)

ELABORATE

Research Plant Fossils

Have pairs of students use the Internet or library resources to find pictures of plant fossils. Have each pair print four pictures of fossils and label each one with the type of plant it is thought to be and where it was found.

Extend Your Thinking About Fossils in the Antarctic

- Have students extend their thinking about what types of living things could have lived in the area of land that makes up the Antarctic millions of years ago. Ask: **If ferns existed in this area millions of years ago, what other kinds of living things could have lived there, too?** (Other plants and trees that thrive in warmer and humid environments probably lived there, too. Also, there were probably animals that were suited to a similar environment.)

EVALUATE

Have students record their answers to the Wrap It Up questions in their science notebook.

Wrap It Up!

1. **IDENTIFY** **Where do ferns grow today?** (Today's ferns grow primarily in warm, moist places.)

2. **DESCRIBE** **Contrast the present environment of Antarctica with the environments where ferns grow today.** (The present environment of Antarctica is cold and icy. Today ferns grow in warm and humid places.)

3. **INFER** **Why do you think fossil ferns can be found in a place that is frozen all year long?** (Fossil ferns can be found in a place that is frozen all year long because the climate was different long ago.)

PHYSICAL SCIENCE
Forces and Interactions

LIFE SCIENCE
Interdependent Relationships in Ecosystems
Inheritance and Variation of Traits : Life Cycles and Traits

EARTH SCIENCE
Weather and Climate

READING CONNECTION

Ask and Answer Questions to Demonstrate Understanding

Ask and answer questions to demonstrate understanding of a text, referring explicitly to the text as the basis for the answers.

Guide students in asking and answering questions, referring to the text as the basis for the answer. For example, in the EVALUATE section when students are recording the answers to Wrap It Up, remind them to refer to the text when considering their answers. Also encourage them to share any questions they may still have and invite students to answer questions or do further research if the answers cannot be found in the text.

TEACHING WITH TECHNOLOGY

Understanding Images

Project the lesson on a whiteboard. Ask one student to circle the graphic that shows the fern fossil. Ask another to put a box around the picture that best illustrates the sentence from the text *Antarctica is so cold that the land is frozen all year long*. Have another student put a star next to the graphic that shows where Antarctica is. Have another student underline the captions of the pictures. Finally, have a student read the captions aloud, and ask the class: **How do the images add to the article?** (Possible answer: The images help readers visualize what the text says in words.)

Fossils

NEXT GENERATION SCIENCE STANDARDS | DISCIPLINARY CORE IDEAS
LS4.A: Evidence of Common Ancestry and Diversity Fossils provide evidence about the types of organisms that lived long ago and also about the nature of their environments. (3-LS4-1)

Objective Students will be able to:
- Explain how fossils provide evidence about the types of organisms that lived long ago and also about the nature of their environments.

CLASSROOM MANAGEMENT

Materials *For groups of 4:* 4 lumps of clay—green, yellow, red, tan (about ½ cup of each); 4 small objects; plastic knife; craft stick; toothpick

Time 40 minutes

Advance Preparation Make sure that clay is available in a variety of colors. Also, collect small, solid objects, such as marbles, coins, buttons, washers, paperclips, centimeter cubes, and so on. Put four different objects in a plastic bag for each group.

Teaching Tips Suggest that students keep the diameter of each layer within 3 or 4 inches, but encourage them to place objects randomly. The smaller size will help make the objects relatively easy to find, but the random placement of objects will mirror the inexact science of paleontology. If you would like to reuse the clay, provide wax paper for students to put between each layer.

What to Expect Each group will make a model of a sequence of different sedimentary rocks that formed in different environments. Each group will interpret another group's model using a chart and what they know about how sedimentary rocks form.

ENGAGE

Tap Prior Knowledge

- Ask students to recall what they learned in previous lessons about fossils. Ask probing questions to encourage exploration. For example, ask: **How is it possible for fossils of fish to be found in a desert today?** (The fossils of fish are from a long time ago when land that is a desert today was an ocean. The fossils are found under layers of rock formed over time in changing environments.)

EXPLORE

- Guide students through the investigation. Read pages 72–73 together.

  My science notebook Have students make a table in their science notebook like the one shown below. Return to the table in step 4, and remind students to use the information about fossil environments found in the chart on page 72 to describe the layers.

Example:

What the Model Means

	Color of Clay	Description of Environment
Layer 1		
Layer 2		
Layer 3		
Layer 4		

- As students begin to make their models in step 1, remind them that each layer should be thick enough that the object can leave an impression. Also remind them to keep the diameter within 4 inches, but encourage them to place objects randomly.

- As students create their second, third, and forth layers in step 2, tell them that they can add colors of clay in any order they choose. Ask: **Which rock layer in your model is the oldest? Why?** (The layer on the bottom is the oldest because it represents the first layer of sediment to be deposited.) **How is your procedure like the formation of actual sedimentary rock?** (Layers and layers of sediment pile up over time. The upper layers press down on the lower layers.)

- To keep the model fossil buried in the top layer, suggest that students put the object into the lump of clay and roll it into a ball before flattening it.

- After groups exchange models in step 3, instruct students to decide within their groups where they will make a vertical cut. Say: **Be careful to preserve any model fossils you run into.**

- Direct students to fill out the What the Model Means chart in their notebook and then draw and label each layer of their model. Suggest that students use colored pencils to represent each layer.

- Instruct students to carefully remove visible objects and draw the object in the layer it was found.

EXPLAIN

- Have students share their observations and conclusions with other groups.

- Have students compare their drawings with another group's drawings. Ask: **How are the two models different?** (Drawings will vary because each group's model was likely unique in the thickness of the layers, how the layers were ordered, and where the fossils were embedded.)

- Help students interpret their observations with probing questions such as: **What conclusions can you make about the organisms you found based on their fossils?** (The fossils give clues about the organisms' shape, size, and specific features. Fossils also provide evidence of the environments in which the rocks they are in formed.)

- Ask: **How can you tell which organisms lived the longest ago?** (by what layer they are found in; deeper layers are older.)

- **If you did not find a fossil in one or more of the layers, does that mean no organisms existed at that time?** (No, it just means we did not find any where we cut.)

ELABORATE

- Ask: **Scientists who study fossils are called paleontologists. Do you think paleontologists find fossils every time they dig? Explain.** (No. It might be easier to find fossils in some places than others, but

paleontologists are probably not finding fossils every time they dig. Fossils can be tiny and easy to miss. Also, most organisms do not leave behind a fossil. Fossils are only formed under certain conditions.)

- Ask: **Why must paleontologists dig slowly and carefully?** (They must dig slowly and carefully so that they don't harm fossils. They also want to make sure they don't miss fossils that turn up.)

- Have students use a toothpick or craft stick to dig sideways in layers in which they did not find objects in their first attempt. When an object is found, encourage students to determine the best way to recover the object without disturbing the model fossil.

EVALUATE

 Have students record their answers to the Wrap It Up Questions in their science notebook.

Wrap It Up!

1. CONCLUDE **Describe the environment of animal fossils found in the red layer of rock.** (These animals lived in warm, shallow ocean water in a warm and humid climate.)

2. INFER **What can you infer about how the environment of the area represented by these layers changed over the years?** (The changes happened slowly and over very long periods of time.)

PHYSICAL SCIENCE
Forces and Interactions

LIFE SCIENCE
Interdependent Relationships in Ecosystems
Inheritance and Variation of Traits : Life Cycles and Traits

EARTH SCIENCE
Weather and Climate

Analyze and Interpret Data

NEXT GENERATION SCIENCE STANDARDS | PERFORMANCE EXPECTATION

3-LS4-1. Analyze and interpret data from fossils to provide evidence of the organisms and the environments in which they lived long ago. [Clarification Statement: Examples of data could include type, size, and distributions of fossil organisms. Examples of fossils and environments could include marine fossils found on dry land, tropical plant fossils found in Arctic areas, and fossils of extinct organisms.] [*Assessment Boundary: Assessment does not include identification of specific fossils or present plants and animals. Assessment is limited to major fossil types and relative ages.*]

Objectives Students will be able to:
- Analyze and interpret data from pictures of fossils around the world.
- Provide evidence of the organisms and the environments in which they lived long ago.

CLASSROOM MANAGEMENT

Time 35 minutes

Teaching Tips Organize the class into groups of 2–4 students. Encourage students to work together to analyze and interpret the data from the pictures of the fossils on the map.

What to Expect Students will analyze the pictures of fossils found around the world. They will use the captions under the pictures and the map key to interpret the data and identify evidence about how the environment now is different from long ago.

ENGAGE

Set the Scene

- Remind students that they have learned about fossils and how they provide evidence of the organisms and the environments in which those organisms lived long ago.

- Ask volunteers to recall what a fossil is and how it provides evidence of the organism and the environment it lived in. (Possible answers: Fossils are traces of organisms that lived long ago. When these organisms die, they are buried. As more layers of material cover the organism, the sediment turns to rock and the rock preserves the shape of the organisms. Fossils can also be a trace of an organism, such as a footprint, that has been preserved in rock. Fossils can provide evidence of what an organism looked like and what its environment was like. Because the ancient environment of an area could be very different from the present environment, fossils are evidence that environments change.)

EXPLORE

Preview the Lesson

- Have students look at the pictures of the fossils on pages 74–75. Say: **Find the fossil of a dragonfly. Where was it found?** (Brazil, South America) **How can you tell what the environment in this area is like today?** (The map key tells what the environment is like today.)

EXPLAIN

Analyze and Interpret Fossil Data

- Have students work in small groups of 2–4 to analyze and interpret the data on the map. Have each student create a table in their science notebook like the one shown below.

Fossils Around the World

Name of Organism	Where It Was Found	What the Environment Was Like Long Ago	What the Environment Is Like Today

SCIENCE AND ENGINEERING PRACTICES

Analyzing and Interpreting Data

- Say: **Scientists use their own logic and reasoning to make sense of evidence and data.** Ask: **How did you use logical reasoning to interpret the information on the map?** (Possible answer: If a fossil was discovered that came from a sea creature, then logically that part of the map must have been an ocean, or at least close to an ocean.)

CROSSCUTTING CONCEPTS

Scale, Proportion, and Quantity

- Tell students that trilobites, one of the depicted species, went extinct over 250 million years ago. Tell them that this is nearly 200 million years before the extinction of the dinosaurs. Then ask: **What are other numbers we might see today that are this large? How does this help us understand how long ago in history this was?** (Accept reasonable answers)

Connections to Nature of Science
Scientific Knowledge Assumes an Order and Consistency in Natural Systems

- Say: **The age and location of fossils can provide information about the history of an area.** Ask: **If two fossils are found near each other, but one is found in rock that is 200 million years old and the other is found in rock that is 250 million years old, what can we infer about the fossils?** (Possible answer: One organisms lived 200 millions years ago and the other lived 250 millions years ago. The two organisms were not alive at the same time.)

75

Analyze and Interpret Data (continued)

EXPLAIN (continued)

- Say: **Fill in the table as you read about each fossil.** Suggest that students take turns reading each caption and then work as a group to fill in the table.

- After students have filled in their tables, ask questions to help them analyze and interpret the data they gathered. For example, ask:

  - **How do you know what the ancient environment of the Australian crinoid was like?** (One of the captions for the crinoids says that they were ocean creatures.)

  - **What type of environment did most of these ancient creatures live in?** (oceans or lakes)

  - **How many of the fossils shown were found in a present-day ocean?** (None were found in an ocean.)

  - **Landmasses are the dry-land parts of Earth shown on the map surrounded by the blue ocean. Given the evidence that these fossils provide, what can you infer about Earth's present-day landmasses?** (Many of Earth's current landmasses have been covered in water at some point in history.)

- Ask: **In what ways did you think like a scientist as you completed this activity?** (Possible answer: I used information provided about different fossilized organisms to infer what kind of environment each of them used to live in. I combined this with information provided in the map and key to interpret how the environment has changed over time.)

ELABORATE

Research Other Fossils

Step 1: Have students work with their groups and use the Internet to find a picture of another fossil they want to research. Have them determine where the fossil was discovered and, if possible, what the ancient environment was like compared with the present day environment.

Step 2: If time permits, project pages 74–75 on the whiteboard and have students add their fossil to the map.

EVALUATE

Have students record their answers to the Wrap It Up questions in their science notebook.

1. **INTERPRET MAPS** **What do the different colored regions on the map represent?** (The blue represents water; the other colors represent different types of environments in those present-day places.)

2. **INTERPRET DATA** **Which of the fossils shown here came from a land area that was once covered in water? How do you know?** (All of these fossils except for the dragonfly came from a land area that was once covered in water. They are all creatures that lived in oceans and lakes.)

3. **ANALYZE** **What kind of fossil was found in South America? What does this fossil show about the environment of that area a long time ago?** (A dragonfly fossil was found in South America, which shows that the environment was a warm, forested area a long time ago.)

PHYSICAL SCIENCE
Forces and Interactions

LIFE SCIENCE
Interdependent Relationships in Ecosystems
Inheritance and Variation of Traits : Life Cycles and Traits

EARTH SCIENCE
Weather and Climate

Cold or Warm?

NEXT GENERATION SCIENCE STANDARDS | DISCIPLINARY CORE IDEAS
LS4.C: Adaption For any particular environment, some kinds of organisms survive well, some survive less well, and some cannot survive at all. (3-LS4-3)

Objective Students will be able to:
- Explain how for cold and warm environments, some kinds of organisms survive well, some survive less well, and some cannot survive at all.

ENGAGE

Tap Prior Knowledge

- Ask students to share what they know about living things in cold and warm environments. Ask: **What kinds of plants and animals have you seen or do you know that live in cold environments?** (Accept any reasonable responses. Possible answers: rabbits, moose, bears, evergreen trees, etc.) Ask: **What kinds of plants and animals have you seen or do you know live in warm environments?** (Possible answers: lizards, snakes, ferns, etc.)

EXPLORE

Explore Cold or Warm

- Have students observe the pictures on pages 76–77. Ask probing questions to encourage exploration. For example, ask: **How would you contrast the picture of the polar bear with the picture of the Gila monster?**

- Have students share their observations. In the big picture, students may observe a polar bear walking through snow. They might notice that the plants aren't green. They might also notice the polar bear's size and thick fur. In the small picture, students may observe that the lizard is in the sun and the ground is dry and rocky. They may notice the cactus and that everything is brown and green.

Set a Purpose and Read

- Have students read in order to explain how, for cold and warm environments, some kinds of organisms survive well, some survive less well, and some cannot survive at all.

- Have students read pages 76–77.

EXPLAIN

Explain Cold Climate Organisms

- After students read pages 76–77, ask: **What determines where a living thing can survive?** (Whether or not a living thing can get its needs met in a place determines if it can survive there.)

- Ask: **What is the weather like where polar bears live?** (Polar bears live where it is cold.)

- Say: **Explain how polar bears' bodies are well suited to cold weather.** (Polar bears have thick fur and body fat to keep them warm.)

- Say: **Explain how polar bears, get their needs met in cold weather environments.** (Polar bears eat seals, which swim in icy waters.)

Explain Warm Climate Organisms

- Ask: **Where do Gila monsters live?** (They live where the weather is warm.)

- Say: **Explain how warmer climates help Gila monsters meet their needs.** (Gila monsters' bodies do not produce their own heat. The animals need the warm temperature to help them maintain stable body temperature. This allows the Gila monsters to move fast enough to protect themselves from predators. Gila monsters also can find plenty of insects to eat in warm climates.)

- Ask: **What are the needs that the text says the polar bear and Gila monster are both able to meet in their environments?** (They are able to meet their needs for food, safety, and warmth.)

PHYSICAL SCIENCE
Forces and Interactions

LIFE SCIENCE
Interdependent Relationships in Ecosystems
Inheritance and Variation of Traits : Life Cycles and Traits

EARTH SCIENCE
Weather and Climate

ELABORATE

Research Living Things' Needs

Have small groups of students brainstorm a list of four things that all living things need to survive. Then have each group use the Internet or library resources to research the needs of living things and compare what they find with their own lists. Discuss as a class what each group found, and direct students to understanding that all living things need food, water, air, and shelter.

Extend Your Thinking About Animal Adaptations

• Have students extend their thinking about how animals are adapted to cold or warm weather. Say: **The text says that the polar bear in the picture has thick fur and body fat that helps keep it warm in cold temperatures.** Ask: **What is another way the polar bear's fur is well suited to its environment?** If students have trouble, ask: **How would its white coat help the polar bear sneak up on its prey?** (Its white coat helps camouflage it as it hunts.) **How do you think the Gila monster's skin is suited to its environment?** (Like the polar bear's fur, the color of the lizard's skin helps camouflage it in its environment. As a result, it can hide more easily from predators.)

EVALUATE

Have students record their answers to the Wrap It Up questions in their science notebook.

Wrap It Up!

1. **DESCRIBE** **Where do polar bears live? What is the temperature like there?** (Polar bears live in cold, northern environments.)

2. **EXPLAIN** **How are polar bears able to survive in their environment?** (They have thick fur and body fat. They also eat seals, which swim in the cold water.)

3. **DRAW CONCLUSIONS** **Could a lizard survive where polar bears live? Why or why not?** (No. A lizard could not survive where polar bears live because it would not be able to stay warm enough.)

READING CONNECTION

Describe Logical Connection

Describe the logical connection between particular sentences and paragraphs in a text (e.g. comparison, cause/effect, first/second/third in a sequence).

Guide students to describe the logical connection between particular sentences and paragraphs in a text. For example, after the EXPLAIN section, ask students to describe how the second and third paragraphs in the text are related to each other. Prompt students by asking: **How are the paragraphs the same?** (They both describe an environment where a particular animal's needs are met.) **How are they different?** (They describe two different animals in two different environments.) **What is it called when you find similarities and differences?** (comparing and contrasting)

ELL SUPPORT

Comparatives and Superlatives

Beginning Provide sentence frames, such as: *Siberia is (<u>colder</u>) than Africa. Siberia is the (<u>coldest</u>) place I have been. The beach is (<u>more beautiful</u>) than the mountains. The beach is the (<u>most beautiful</u>) place I have been.* Give students a word back with the answers.

Intermediate Help students use each of these in an original sentence: *colder, coldest, more beautiful,* and *most beautiful.*

Advanced Give students the same sentence frames as above, but provide only the words *cold* and *beautiful* and have students fill in the correct form of the word.

Wet or Dry?

NEXT GENERATION SCIENCE STANDARDS | DISCIPLINARY CORE IDEAS
LS4.C: Adaption For any particular environment, some kinds of organisms survive well, some survive less well, and some cannot survive at all. (3-LS4-3)

Objective **Students will be able to:**
- Explain how, for wet and dry environments, some kinds of organisms survive well, some survive less well, and some cannot survive at all.

Science Vocabulary
tadpoles

ENGAGE

Tap Prior Knowledge

- Ask students to share what they know about where things live. Ask: **What are some animals that must live in water?** (Accept any reasonable responses. Possible answers: fish, octopi, whales) Ask: **What are some animals that live only on land?** (Possible answers: certain birds, monkeys, giraffes)

EXPLORE

Explore Wet or Dry

- Have students observe the picture on pages 78–79. Ask probing questions to encourage exploration. For example, ask: **What is the major difference between the frog's and the camel's environments? What need of the camel do you think would not be met if the camel were submerged in water for a long period?**

- Have students share their observations. Students may notice that the frog is in water, and the camel is in the desert. They might say the major difference is the presence or absence of water. They might also say that a camel would not be able to get its need for air met under water.

Set a Purpose and Read

- Have students read in order to explain how for wet and dry environments, some kinds of organisms survive well, some survive less well, and some cannot survive at all.

- Have students read pages 78–79.

EXPLAIN

Explain Organisms in Wet Environments

- After students read pages 78–79, ask: **Where do leopard frogs live?** (They live where it is wet, like ponds or moist meadows.)

- Ask: **What is a young frog called?** (A young frog is called a tadpole.)

- Say: **Explain how tadpoles, which are hatched underwater, are able to breathe.** (Tadpoles breathe underwater with gills.)

- Ask: **How do adult frogs depend on water to breathe?** (Although they have lungs, adult frogs need their skin to be wet or they will die.) Share that the reason that adult frogs need their skin to be wet is that the gases must dissolve in water before they can move through the skin.

Explain Organisms in Dry Environments

- Ask: **What kind of environment is a camel suited for living in?** (Camels are well suited to dry places.)

- Say: **Name three ways camels are suited to living in dry, desert conditions.** (1. They can survive weeks without water. 2. They have thick, tough lips for eating desert plants. 3. They can go weeks without food and use fat stored in their humps for energy.)

ELABORATE

Find Out More About Desert Animals

- Have small groups of students use the Internet or library resources to find out more about how desert animals have adapted to living in harsh conditions. Have each group find out one way that one of the following is suited to the desert: bats, owls, jackrabbits, and snakes. Have each group tell the class what they found out.

EVALUATE

Have students record their answers to the Wrap It Up questions in their science notebook.

Wrap It Up!

1. **RECALL** **Where do most frogs lay their eggs?** (Most frogs lay their eggs in water.)

2. **EXPLAIN** **How do camels survive in deserts?** (They can survive weeks without water; they have thick, tough lips for eating desert plants; they can go weeks without food and use fat stored in their humps for energy.)

3. **INFER** **Could a leopard frog survive where a camel lives? Why or why not?** (No. A leopard frog would die in the desert because it needs its skin to be moist for gases to be able to pass through it.)

READING CONNECTION

Describe the Logical Connection

Describe the logical connection between particular sentences and paragraphs in a text (e.g., comparison, cause/effect, first/second/third in a sequence).

Guide students to describe the logical connection between particular sentences and paragraphs in a text. For example, after the EXPLAIN section, ask students to describe how the paragraphs in the text are related to each other. Prompt students by asking: **How are the paragraphs similar?** (They both describe an environment in which a particular animal's needs are met.) **How are they different?** (They describe two different animals in two very different environments and the adaptations those two animals have to those environments.) **What is it called when you identify similarities and differences?** (comparing and contrasting)

SCIENCE MISCONCEPTIONS

Camel Humps

Camels store fat, not water, in their humps. This helps them survive in the harsh heat of deserts in a couple ways. First, by storing fat on their backs instead of elsewhere in their bodies, they are able to reduce the their body's overall insulation, helping them stay cool in severe temperatures. Also, such large reservoirs of fat help the camel go weeks without eating food, but still have energy. Camels have other adaptations that allow them to go without water, including being able to drink massive amounts of water in a short time. A camel can drink up to 30 gallons of water in about 13 minutes.

PHYSICAL SCIENCE
Forces and Interactions

LIFE SCIENCE
Interdependent Relationships in Ecosystems
Inheritance and Variation of Traits : Life Cycles and Traits

EARTH SCIENCE
Weather and Climate

Light or Dark?

NEXT GENERATION SCIENCE STANDARDS | DISCIPLINARY CORE IDEAS
LS4.C: Adaption For any particular environment, some kinds of organisms survive well, some survive less well, and some cannot survive at all. (3-LS4-3)

Objective **Students will be able to:**
- Explain how for light and dark environments, some kinds of organisms survive well, some survive less well, and some cannot survive at all.

ENGAGE
Tap Prior Knowledge

- Ask students to share what they know about how animals are adapted to different environments. Say: **We have learned about how animals have features that enable them to live in cold, hot, wet, and dry environments.** Ask: **What are some details that you remember about animals in each of these environments?** (Accept any reasonable responses. Possible answers: Some animals that live in cold environments have thick fur. Some animals in hot and dry environments can hold water in their bodies. Some animals in wet environments can breathe underwater.)

EXPLORE
Explore Light or Dark

- Have students observe the picture of the squid on pages 80–81. Ask probing questions to encourage exploration. For example, ask: **How do you think the squid has adapted, or is well-suited, to its dark environment? Which feature helps the squid survive without much light?**

- Have students share their observations. Students may notice the squid's large eye and say that the size of its eyes is an adaptation that allows it to see well in its dark environment.

Set a Purpose and Read

- Have students read in order to explain how, in light and dark environments, some kinds of organisms survive well, some survive less well, and some cannot survive at all.

- Have students read pages 80–81.

EXPLAIN
Explain Organisms in Light Environments

- After students read pages 80–81, ask: **What will happen to a plant without any sunlight? Explain.** (Plants depend on sunlight to make food, so without it the plant will die.)

- Ask: **Why do hawks, hummingbirds, and butterflies need light?** (These animals need light to find food.)

- Ask: **Why can bats, owls, and moths survive without much light?** (These animals can survive without much light because they do not depend on it for finding food.)

- Say: **Summarize why light is important to many plants and animals.** (Light is important to many plants and animals because they depend on it to find food.)

- Ask: **What need do seaweed and corals most likely depend on light to meet?** (These organisms most likely depend on light to meet their need for food.)

Explain Organisms in Dark Environments

- Ask: **What is the environment like 200 meters below the surface of the ocean?** (It is always dark.)

- Ask: **How is the deep sea angler adapted to living without light?** (The deep sea angler makes its own light, which lures prey close for it to more easily catch.)

- Say: **Like organisms at the surface of the ocean, the deep sea angler also depends on light for food, but in a different way. Explain.** (The deep sea angler depends on light to get food, but not to *find* the food. It makes its own light to lure shrimp and fish to its mouth.)

ELABORATE

Research Bats and Owls

Bats and owls are both animals that have adapted to low-light environments. Each animal has a unique way of finding food in the dark. Have small groups of students use the Internet or library resources to research how either bats or owls find food in the dark. Have each group present its findings to the class.

Extend Your Thinking About Glow-in-the-Dark Scorpions

- Have students investigate scorpions that give off light in the dark. Say: **Scorpions are known to glow a greenish color under certain types of light. Although many people have ideas about why, nobody knows with certainty what the purpose of the glow is.** Ask: **Thinking about what you know about how other animals need and use light, why do you think scorpions glow?** (Accept all reasonable responses. Possible answer: The light they give off attracts their prey.)

EVALUATE

Have students record their answers to the Wrap It Up questions in their science notebook.

Wrap It Up!

1. **LIST** **What are some animals that need bright sunlight to find food?** (Hawks, hummingbirds, and butterflies need bright light to find food.)

2. **EXPLAIN** **Why do plants need sunlight?** (Plants need sunlight to make food.)

3. **EVALUATE** **Could plants grow in the deep ocean? Explain.** (Some plants might be able to live in the deep ocean, but they would need uncommon adaptations to allow them to make food without light.)

An additional interactive assessment activity can be found in the Exploring Science Digital Book.

READING CONNECTION

Determine Main Idea and Details

Determine the main idea of a text; recount the key details and explain how they support the main idea.

Guide students in determining the main idea and supporting details and in recounting how key details support the main idea. For example, in the EXPLAIN section after students read the text, ask a volunteer to identify the main idea. Remind students that the main idea often is found at the beginning or end of a passage. (Just like temperature and moisture, different living things need different amounts of light to survive.) Then reread the text aloud. Have students raise their hands when they hear a detail that supports the main idea. Make a list of the details identified. Then review the list, and have volunteers tell how each detail relates to the main idea.

TEACHING WITH TECHNOLOGY

Asking and Answering Questions

Project the lesson on a whiteboard. Ask: **Which animal shown needs light to find food?** (the butterfly) Have one student circle the answer. Next, ask: **Which animal shown has large eyes that help it see in the dark?** (the squid) Have another student circle the correct picture. Finally, have a third student ask a question about the picture of the deep sea angler. Explain that one way to do this is to turn a statement in the text into a question. Have the student underline a statement that they want to turn into a question and ask the question out loud. (Possible answer: *Some of these creatures, such as the deep sea angler, make their own light.* What creature makes its own light?) Have a fourth volunteer circle the picture of the deep sea angler.

PHYSICAL SCIENCE
Forces and Interactions

LIFE SCIENCE
Interdependent Relationships in Ecosystems
Inheritance and Variation of Traits : Life Cycles and Traits

EARTH SCIENCE
Weather and Climate

Construct an Argument

NEXT GENERATION SCIENCE STANDARDS | PERFORMANCE EXPECTATION

3-LS4-3. Construct an argument with evidence that in a particular habitat some organisms can survive well, some survive less well, and some cannot survive at all. [Clarification Statement: Examples of evidence could include needs and characteristics of the organisms and habitats involved. The organisms and their habitat make up a system in which the parts depend on each other.]

Objective Students will be able to:
- Construct an argument with evidence that in a particular habitat some organisms can survive well, some survive less well, and some cannot survive at all.

CLASSROOM MANAGEMENT

Time 40 minutes

Teaching Tips Organize the class into groups of 2–4 students. Encourage students to work together to carefully follow the steps and construct an argument about where each animal lives well. Guide students through the steps one at a time, leaving time for groups to complete each step before moving on as a class to the next one.

What to Expect Students will ask the question *In what kind of habitat do the particular animals shown here survive well?* They will make a list of things each living thing pictured needs to live. Then, they will construct an argument that describes a habitat in which each animal could meet those needs and survive well. The habitats that students write about may vary, but should allow for the animals to meet the needs described in the captions.

ENGAGE

Set the scene.

- Remind students that they have learned about how some living things can survive better than others in a particular environment. Ask: **Would a camel or a polar bear survive better in a hot desert environment? Explain.** (A camel would survive better in a hot desert environment because it has traits that help it cope with hot, dry weather—traits that a polar bear does not have.) **In what kind of environment do polar bears survive well? Explain.** (Possible answer: Polar bears survive well in cold, snowy environments because they have traits that allow them to deal with harsh winter weather, such as thick layers of fur and fat.)

EXPLORE

- Have students look at the pictures of the animals on pages 82–83. Ask: **What can you observe about each animal's environment from the picture?** (Accept all reasonable responses. Possible answer: The duck is in water, the muskox is in snow, and the star-nosed mole is in an area with moss and mud.)

EXPLAIN

Ask a question.

- After reading the introductory paragraph on page 82, ask: **What is one step for constructing an argument?** (One step is to ask a question.)

- Have a volunteer read the question in step 1. Then, say: **You will work in small groups to construct an argument that answers this question.**

Read and observe.

- Ask: **What is the next step for constructing an argument?** (The second step is to read and observe in order to get information.)

- Have a volunteer read the text in step 2. Then, ask: **What information will you prepare a list of as you read the captions under the pictures?** (Students will prepare a list of the kinds of things each animal needs to survive well.)

- Say: **Tables can help you organize your observations so that you can easily use them as evidence later.** Ask: **How can you use a table to organize your observations about the needs of these organisms?** (Accept reasonable solutions. See below for an example table.) Guide students to draw their tables in their science notebook.

Animal Needs

Organism	What It Needs

- Have students take turns reading the captions on pages 82–83 in their groups. Have them record their observations in their tables.

- After students have read the captions and filled in their charts, ask questions to help them think about other characteristics that make each animal suited to a particular habitat. Ask: **What characteristics do mallard ducks have that help them get what they need?** (Mallard ducks have webbed feet that help them move through water and wide bills to help them get food.)

- Ask: **What are some characteristics that a muskox has that help it get what it needs?** (Possible answer: A muskox has long, shaggy hair to keep it warm and sharp hooves to help it find food.)

- Ask: **What are some characteristics that a star-nosed mole has that help it get what it needs?** (Possible answer: A star-nosed mole has a highly sensitive nose and clawed feet to help it find food and dig tunnels.)

SCIENCE AND ENGINEERING PRACTICES

Engaging in Argument from Evidence

- Tell students that when scientists construct an argument, they gather lots of evidence. Ask: **Besides looking at pictures and reading the captions, how else could you gather evidence about what these animals need to survive?** (Possible answers: I could do research on the animal. I could observe the animal in its natural habitat.)

CROSSCUTTING CONCEPTS

Cause and Effect

- Remind students that they have learned that environments can change over very long periods of time. Say: **It is possible that the muskox's environment might warm or the duck's environment might become very dry over time. What effects might these changes cause?** (Possible answers: The muskox and duck might not be able to survive as well or at all in their changed environments. The changes might cause the animals to move to more suitable environments or might cause them to become extinct.)

- Encourage students to link concepts of cause and effect, as well as varying environments, to other areas of science. For example, in earth science, the formation of particular landforms, rock formations, or even different weather phenomena are often entirely dependent on environmental factors such as rainfall, proximity to an ocean, and longitude and latitude.

PHYSICAL SCIENCE
Forces and Interactions

LIFE SCIENCE
Interdependent Relationships in Ecosystems
Inheritance and Variation of Traits : Life Cycles and Traits

EARTH SCIENCE
Weather and Climate

Construct an Argument (continued)

EXPLAIN (continued)

Construct an Argument

- Ask: **What is the final step?** (The final step is to construct an argument.)

- Have a volunteer read the text in step 3. Then, ask: **What will you use as evidence for your arguments describing the particular habitat in which each animal can survive well?** (Students will use the information they collected in their tables as evidence for their arguments.)

- Remind students to also consider what they can see in the photographs and the characteristics that help each animal get what it needs as they construct their arguments.

- Have students present their arguments to the class. Allow students to give each other constructive feedback. Encourage students to rebut challenges to their arguments using data from their research. As necessary, have students redraft their arguments to address flaws in logic and reasoning or misinterpretation of data.

- When students finish presenting, tell them that when constructing an argument they do not always need to follow this specific order of steps. At any stage, students and scientists may choose to redefine the question or generate arguments to replace an idea that isn't working out.

- Ask: **In what ways did you think like a scientist as you completed this activity?** (Possible answer: I used evidence from the photos and captions about these animals to argue what kinds of environments they would survive best in.)

ELABORATE

Construct an Argument for Other Animals' Habitats

My science notebook Have each group use the Internet or other resources to find a picture of an animal that is not addressed in this lesson. Instruct each group to print the picture and write a caption similar to the ones on pages 82–83. Then, have groups exchange pictures and construct an argument that describes a particular habitat in which the animal can survive well.

EVALUATE

My science notebook Check to make sure students have used their charts to organize evidence and recorded their arguments that describe habitats in which the animals pictured on pages 82–83 can survive well. Then ask students these questions. Have them record the answers in their science notebook.

1. **INFER How does the star-nosed mole use its big, clawed feet?** (The star-nosed mole uses its feet to dig through the soil as it searches for food.)

2. **CONCLUDE Do you think a muskox lives in a hot or cold environment? Explain.** (A muskox lives in a cold environment; it has thick fur and hooves that help it dig in snow.)

3. **ANALYZE How do a mallard duck's webbed feet and wide bill help it find food?** (A mallard eats plants and small animals that live in water. It's feet help it swim, and its bill helps it catch the small animals or pull up plants from underwater.)

RUBRICS

Teacher Rubric Use the scale descriptions to guide your assessment of the student's work. Assess each item separately, and then decide on one overall score, using the following scale:

4: Student performs with thorough understanding.

3: Student performs with adequate understanding.

2: Student performs with basic understanding.

1: Student performs with limited understanding.

Rubric	Scale			
The student worked with a group to read and make observations about the needs of organisms.	4	3	2	1
The student worked with a group to successfully organize their observations in a table.	4	3	2	1
The student constructed an argument with evidence describing particular habitats in which animals can survive well.	4	3	2	1
The student presented their argument and rebutted challenges using data from research.	4	3	2	1
If warranted, the student revised their argument to address lapses in logic or factual errors.	4	3	2	1
Overall Score	4	3	2	1

Student Rubric Have students complete a self-evaluation similar to that shown below.

Rubric	Yes	Not Yet
1. I can work with a group to read and make observations about the needs of organisms.		
2. I can work with a group to organize my observations in a table.		
3. I can construct an argument with evidence describing particular habitats in which animals can survive well.		
4. I can present my argument and rebut challenges using data from my research.		
5. I can revise my argument to address misunderstandings or errors.		

SCIENCE BACKGROUND

Mallard Ducks, Muskoxen, and Star-Nosed Moles

Mallard Ducks Mallards are omnivorous birds that generally weigh about two to three pounds (about 1 to 1.3 kg) and can live to be about 10 years old in the wild. Male mallards are easily recognized by their green head and yellow bill. Female mallards are light brown and have a noticeable blue stripe on their wings. Mallards can be found in freshwater, saltwater, and wetlands all across the Northern Hemisphere.

Muskoxen These Arctic herbivores weigh up to 800 pounds (about 360 kg) and stand four or five feet (about 1–1.5m) from ground to shoulder. Their long, shaggy hair has two layers to help protect them from the severe cold of their habitat, and their hooves are effective for finding plants that are buried beneath inches of snow. They also have two curved horns used for defense in the event of an attack. As herd animals, muskoxen also rely on safety in numbers, traveling in groups of two or three dozen. When threatened, the herd will surround their young to keep predators at bay.

Star-Nosed Moles The star-nosed mole is most notable for its impressive nose, which has 22 feelers that radiate from it like fingers. These appendages are covered in receptors that make the mole's nose so sensitive to touch that it can detect a grain of salt in a pile of sand. The star-nosed mole lives underground and relies on its nose to find worms and insects to feed on. Although this mole is nearly blind, its nose can also transmit three-dimensional pictures to the mole's brain, effectively giving it a way to "see" without using light.

PHYSICAL SCIENCE
Forces and Interactions

LIFE SCIENCE
Interdependent Relationships in Ecosystems
Inheritance and Variation of Traits : Life Cycles and Traits

EARTH SCIENCE
Weather and Climate

Life Cycles

NEXT GENERATION SCIENCE STANDARDS | DISCIPLINARY CORE IDEAS
LS1.B: Growth and Development of Organisms Reproduction is essential to the continued existence of every kind of organism. Plants and animals have unique and diverse life cycles. (3-LS1-1)

Objectives **Students will be able to:**
- Explain that reproduction is essential to the continued existence of every kind of organism.
- Explain that living things have unique and diverse life cycles.

Science Vocabulary
reproduce, life cycle

ENGAGE

Tap Prior Knowledge

- Ask students to share what they know about words that start with *re–*. Ask: **What does it mean if you have to redo something?** (It means you have to do it again.) Ask: **How are rechargeable batteries different from regular batteries?** (Rechargeable batteries can be charged again.) **What do you do if your friend asks you to retell a story?** (You tell it again.) **What do you think the letters *re–*mean at the beginning of a word?** (They mean to do something again.)

EXPLORE

Explore Populations and Ecosystems

- Have students observe the picture on pages 84–85. Ask probing questions to encourage exploration. For example, ask: **What do you see in the picture? Which animal is at the beginning of its life? Which animal is likely to be closer to the end of its life?**

- Have students share their observations. Students may say that the picture shows a mother with her baby. They may say that the baby is at the beginning of its life and the mother is likely to be closer to the end of her life.

Set a Purpose and Read

- Have students read in order to explain life cycles and reproduction.

- Have students read pages 84–85.

EXPLAIN

Explain Reproduction

- After students read pages 84–85, ask: **Is a baby orangutan similar to or different from its mother?** (A baby orangutan is both similar to and different from its mother.)

- Ask: **After the orangutan is born, what happens?** (After birth, the orangutan will grow.)

- Ask: **What does the orangutan grow into over 10 or 15 years?** (The orangutan grows into an adult.)

- Ask: **What happens after the orangutan becomes an adult?** (After the orangutan becomes an adult, it can reproduce.)

- Remind students that the letters *re–* at the beginning of a word means to do something again.

- Ask: **What does reproduce mean?** (It means to produce again, or to give birth to young.)

- Ask: **What happens at the end of an individual orangutan's life?** (The orangutan grows old and dies.)

Explain Life Cycles

- Say: **Define *life cycle*.** (A life cycle is a series of changes a living thing goes through during its lifetime.)

- Ask: **Do different organisms have different life cycles?** (Yes. Each kind of organism has its own particular life cycle.)

- Ask: **If living things die at the end of their life cycles, how do plants and animals continue to live on Earth?** (Reproduction allows each kind of plant and animal to continue to have some living individuals on Earth.)

PHYSICAL SCIENCE
Forces and Interactions

LIFE SCIENCE
Interdependent Relationships in Ecosystems
Inheritance and Variation of Traits : Life Cycles and Traits

EARTH SCIENCE
Weather and Climate

ELABORATE

Extend Your Thinking About Life Cycles

Have students extend their thinking about life cycles. Say: **Remember that each kind of organism has its own particular life cycle. However, the stages of most organisms' life cycles can be compared. Think about the changes the orangutan in the text went through.** Ask: **Can you summarize the changes?** (The stages for the orangutan are birth, growth and development, reproduction, and death of individual organism. Although individual organisms die, reproduction allows the kind of organism to continue living on earth.) As students come up with the answers, write the stages birth, growth and development, and reproduction on the board in a circular pattern and connect the stages with arrows. Be sure students understand that although an individual organism's life ends in death, the cycle for the particular kind of organism continues through reproduction.

EVALUATE

Have students record their answers to the Wrap It Up questions in their science notebook.

Wrap It Up!

1. **DEFINE What is a life cycle?** (A life cycle is a series of changes a living thing goes through during its lifetime.)

2. **COMPARE AND CONTRAST How are a baby orangutan and its mother alike? How are they different?** (A baby orangutan looks like its mother. They are different because of their stage of life and their individual traits.)

3. **APPLY What are the stages in the life cycle of a cat?** (birth, growth and development, reproduction, and death of individual cat)

READING CONNECTION

Describe Logical Connection

Describe the logical connection between particular sentences and paragraphs in a text (e.g., comparison, cause/effect, first/second/ third in a sequence).

Guide students to describe the logical connection between particular sentences and paragraphs in a text (e.g., comparison, cause/effect, first/second/third in a sequence). Encourage them to refer explicitly to the text. For example, after completing the first section in the EXPLAIN section, point out that that the sentences in the first paragraph describe a sequence—a life cycle. Ask volunteers to retell the sequence described. Then ask students to point out any words or phrases that are clues that you are reading a sequence. (Then, After, finally)

ELL SUPPORT

Prefixes *re–, un–, non–*

Beginning Have students circle the prefix and then match the word with its meaning.

reusable	not happy
unhappy	able to be used again
nonstop	without stopping

Intermediate Have students match the above words and meanings, and then write definitions for the prefixes *re–, un–,* and *non–*.

Advanced Have students write definitions of the words *reusable, unhappy,* and *nonstop.* Then, have them write definitions for the prefixes *re–, un–,* and *non–*. Lastly, have them combine the prefixes with the stems *–sense, –fair,* and *–appear* to create three new words. (nonsense, unfair, and reappear)

Life Cycle of a Jalapeño Pepper Plant

NEXT GENERATION SCIENCE STANDARDS | DISCIPLINARY CORE IDEAS
LS1.B: Growth and Development of Organisms Reproduction is essential to the continued existence of every kind of organism. Plants and animals have unique and diverse life cycles. (3-LS1-1)

Objectives **Students will be able to:**
- Explain life cycle diagrams.
- Describe the unique life cycle of a jalapeño pepper plant.

ENGAGE

Tap Prior Knowledge

- Ask students to share what they know about life cycles. Ask: **How do plants change as they grow?** (Accept any reasonable responses. Possible answers: Plants get bigger as they grow. Sometimes they change shape or color. They also might grow leaves, trunks, or fruit.)

EXPLORE

Explore the Life Cycle of a Jalapeño Pepper Plant

- Have students read the lesson title and observe the pictures on pages 86–87. Ask probing questions to encourage exploration. For example, ask: **What do the photos and the term *life cycle* lead you to think this lesson will be about?**
- Have students share their observations. Students may say that the lesson will be about changes in plants during their lives, in particular the jalapeño plant.

Set a Purpose and Read

- Have students read in order to explain how a jalapeño pepper plant has its own characteristic life cycle and that reproduction is essential to its continued existence.
- Have students read pages 86–87.

EXPLAIN

Explain Life Cycle Diagrams

- After students read pages 86–87, ask: **What does the diagram on page 87 show?** (The diagram shows the life stages of a jalapeño pepper plant.)
- Ask: **What do the arrows show?** (The arrows show the order in which the life stages occur.)
- Remind students that things arranged in a particular order are called a sequence.
- Ask: **How does the diagram help you understand a jalapeño pepper plant's life cycle?** (The diagram shows what a jalapeño pepper plant looks like at each stage and puts the stages in a sequence.)

Describe the Life Cycle of a Jalapeño Pepper Plant

- Ask: **What does the seed of the jalapeño pepper grow into?** (The seed grows into a seedling.)
- Have students point to the jalapeño seed and then trace the diagram as you move through the different stages.
- Ask: **What does the seedling grow into?** (The seedling grows into a young plant.)
- Say: **The next stage is the adult plant.** Ask: **What happens during this stage?** (Flowers can grow, and the flowers may produce fruit called jalapeño peppers. Each individual plant eventually dies.)
- Ask: **How does the life cycle continue?** (There are seeds in jalapeño pepper fruits. These seeds can grow into new seedlings, and the life cycle repeats.)

PHYSICAL SCIENCE
Forces and Interactions

LIFE SCIENCE
Interdependent Relationships in Ecosystems
Inheritance and Variation of Traits : Life Cycles and Traits

EARTH SCIENCE
Weather and Climate

ELABORATE

Find Out More About Plant Life Cycles

 All plants go through a life cycle as they grow. Life cycles of different plants may look similar, but they have some differences. Have pairs of students choose another type of plant and research its life cycle. Have students draw the life cycle and write labels that describe the life stages. If time permits, have volunteers discuss the differences between the life cycle of the plant they researched and the life cycle of a jalapeño pepper plant.

Research Seed Dispersal

- Remind students that for seeds to grow into seedlings, they must be located in a place with the proper soil temperature and moisture. Explain to students that different plants have different ways of dispersing seeds. Have small groups of students use the Internet or library resources to research how the seeds of the dandelions, coconuts, and raspberries are dispersed.

EVALUATE

 Have students record their answers to the Wrap It Up questions in their science notebook.

Wrap It Up!

1. IDENTIFY **Which parts of a pepper plant produce fruit?** (The flowers may produce fruit.)

2. SEQUENCE **Put these life cycle stages in order: young plant, seedling, seed, adult plant. Start with a seed.** (seed, seedling, young plant, adult plant)

3. ANALYZE **In which stage of its life cycle does a pepper plant reproduce?** (A pepper plant reproduces in its adult stage.)

An additional interactive assessment activity can be found in the Exploring Science Digital Book.

READING CONNECTION

Describe Logical Connection

Describe the logical connection between particular sentences and paragraphs in a text (e.g. comparison, cause/effect, first/second/third in a sequence).

Guide students to describe the logical connection between particular sentences and paragraphs in a text. For example, in the EXPLAIN section, remind students that something that shows or tells an order of events is a sequence. Then guide students to describe the life cycle diagram on page 87 as a sequence. Ask students to point out where in the text they are drawing their answers from.

DIFFERENTIATED INSTRUCTION

Extra Support Write the following parts of the plant life cycle on separate index cards: *seed, seedling, young plant,* and *adult plant*. Shuffle the cards, and help students place them in order to make a complete life cycle.

Challenge Have students place the above index cards in order and write captions for each stage in the life cycle of a plant.

Life Cycle of a Ladybug

NEXT GENERATION SCIENCE STANDARDS | DISCIPLINARY CORE IDEAS
LS1.B: Growth and Development of Organisms Reproduction is essential to the continued existence of every kind of organism. Plants and animals have unique and diverse life cycles. (3-LS1-1)

Objective Students will be able to:
- Describe the unique life cycle of a ladybug.

Science Vocabulary
larva, pupa

ENGAGE

Tap Prior Knowledge

- Ask students to share their personal observations of ladybugs. Ask: **What do you know about ladybugs?** (Accept any reasonable responses. Possible answers: They are small insects with six legs. They are red with black spots. They are good to have in a garden.) Ask: **How do you think you can tell an adult ladybug from a much younger one?** (Accept all answers at this point. Students may know ladybugs go through life stages, i.e., pupa and larva, which look nothing like an adult ladybug.)

EXPLORE

Explore Life Cycle of a Ladybug

- Have students observe the picture on pages 88–89. Ask probing questions to encourage exploration. For example, ask: **How is this diagram similar to the diagram we studied in the previous lesson? How is it different?**

- Have students share their observations. Students may notice that the diagram shows a sequence like the diagram of the jalapeño plant on page 87 does. They may notice that the diagram shows the same number of stages, but that this diagram shows pictures of an insect's life cycle instead of a plant's.

Set a Purpose and Read

- Have students read in order to describe the life cycle of a ladybug.
- Have students read pages 88–89.

EXPLAIN

Describe the Life Cycle of a Ladybug

- After students read pages 88–89, ask: **As what does a ladybug begin its life?** (A ladybug begins its life as an egg.)

- Have students point to the ladybug eggs and then trace the diagram as you move through the different stages.

- Ask: **What is the ladybug called in the stage of life after the egg?** (A ladybug is called a larva in the stage after the egg.)

- Ask: **How does the larva grow?** (It grows by eating small insects.)

- Ask: **What happens to the larva's outer covering as it grows?** (It sheds its outer covering as it grows.)

- Ask: **What is the next stage of life for a ladybug after the larva stage?** (After the larva stage comes the pupa stage.)

- Ask: **What does the pupa turn into?** (The pupa turns into an adult ladybug.)

- Ask: **How does an adult ladybug differ from the other stages?** (It has wings and spots. Also, it can fly.)

- Explain that the adult ladybug has a pair of wings that are red with black spots, and a pair of inner wings that it can use to fly. The life of each individual ladybug ends in death.

- Ask: **How does the life cycle continue?** (The adult female ladybug lays eggs on a leaf.)

ELABORATE

Research Ladybug Life Cycle Time Line

 Have pairs of students use the Internet or library resources to research the length of each stage in a ladybug's life cycle, including how long ladybugs usually live as adults. Have students make a life cycle drawing and write captions that include the length of each stage.

Find Out More About Ladybugs

- Have students find out more about how ladybugs can be helpful to humans. Say: **Ladybugs can be helpful to humans. In fact, many gardeners put ladybugs in their gardens.** Have students use the Internet or library resources to research how ladybugs are used to eliminate various garden pests. Tell students to summarize their finding with one or two drawings that show ladybugs in various stages of their lives and being used to control aphids, mealybugs, and other garden pests.

EVALUATE

 Have students record their answers to the Wrap It Up questions in their science notebook.

Wrap It Up!

1. **LIST** **What are the stages of a ladybug's life cycle?** (The stages of a ladybug's life cycle are: egg, larva, pupa, and adult.)

2. **CONTRAST** **List some differences between the pupa and the adult stages in the ladybug life cycle.** (The adult ladybug has wings and can fly. The pupa doesn't have a hard shell yet and cannot fly. The pupa does not have wings and has different coloring from the adult ladybug.)

An additional interactive assessment activity can be found in the Exploring Science Digital Book.

PHYSICAL SCIENCE
Forces and Interactions

LIFE SCIENCE
Interdependent Relationships in Ecosystems
Inheritance and Variation of Traits : Life Cycles and Traits

EARTH SCIENCE
Weather and Climate

READING CONNECTION

Use Photos and Text to Demonstrate Understanding

Use information gained from illustrations (e.g., maps, photographs) and the words in a text to demonstrate understanding of the text (e.g., where, when, why, and how key events occur.)

Guide students to use information gained from the diagram on page 89 to demonstrate understanding of the text. For example, when asking questions in the EXPLAIN section, ask how the photos and captions in the diagram help them understand the sequence of the stages in the life cycle of a ladybug.

SCIENCE BACKGROUND

Complete and Incomplete Metamorphosis

Ladybugs and other insects, such as butterflies and moths, undergo complete metamorphosis, which includes four stages: egg, larva, pupa, and adult. In the pupa stage, the insect's body undergoes many changes. The pupa stage may last several days to a week or more. The insect emerges when it has finished changing into an adult. Other insects, such as dragonflies, progress through only three stages: egg, nymph, and adult. The nymph generally looks like a smaller version of the adult but usually lacks wings. This transformation is known as incomplete metamorphosis.

Life Cycle of a Leopard Frog

NEXT GENERATION SCIENCE STANDARDS | DISCIPLINARY CORE IDEAS
LS1.B: Growth and Development of Organisms Reproduction is essential to the continued existence of every kind of organism. Plants and animals have unique and diverse life cycles. (3-LS1-1)

Objective Students will be able to:
- Describe the life cycle of a leopard frog.

ENGAGE
Tap Prior Knowledge

- Ask students to share what they know about frogs. Ask: **What does a frog look like?** (Accept all reasonable answers. Possible answers: A frog has long back legs and short front legs. It usually has big eyes on the sides of its head and a long tongue to catch insects. Frogs can be different colors, but they often have smooth, moist skin.)

EXPLORE
Explore the Life Cycle of a Leopard Frog

- Have students observe the picture on pages 90–91. Ask probing questions to encourage exploration. For example, ask: **Which picture on page 91 looks most like the frog jumping out of the water on page 90? How do the two pictures look alike? What do you think the diagram on page 91 shows?**

- Have students share their observations. Students may notice that the frog on page 90 looks the most like the adult frog in the diagram on page 91. They may say that the eyes, body, legs, and skin look the same. They may also say that the diagram on page 91 shows the life cycle of a leopard frog.

Set a Purpose and Read

- Have students read in order to describe the life cycle of a leopard frog.

- Have students read pages 90–91.

EXPLAIN
Describe the Life Cycle of a Leopard Frog

- After students read pages 90–91, ask: **In what stage does a frog begin its life?** (A frog begins its life as an egg.)

- Have students point to the frog eggs and then trace the diagram as you move through the different stages.

- Ask: **Where does an adult female frog lay its eggs?** (An adult female frog lays its eggs in a pond or swamp.)

- Ask: **What do the eggs grow into?** (The eggs grow into tadpoles.)

- Say: **Describe a tadpole and where it lives.** (A tadpole has a tail and no legs. It lives underwater and breathes through gills.)

- Say: **A tadpole grows into a young frog.** Ask: **How does the young frog change as it grows?** (It begins to grow legs, and its tail begins to shorten.)

- Ask: **How is an adult frog different from a young frog?** (An adult frog breathes air. It has no tail, long legs, and smooth, slick skin.)

- Explain that adult frogs can live on land because they breathe air, but they still spend a lot of time in water. The life of each individual frog ends in death.)

- Ask: **How does the life cycle continue?** (An adult female frog lays eggs.)

ELABORATE

Research Amphibians and Metamorphosis

Have pairs of students look up the definitions of *amphibians* and *metamorphosis* and write them in their science notebook. Have pairs discuss the following questions: **Is the process of a frog's life cycle a metamorphosis? Explain.** (Yes. The process of a frog's life cycle is a metamorphosis because the frog changes shape as it grows.) **Is a frog an amphibian? Explain.** (Yes, a frog is an amphibian. It can live on water and on land. It spends the first stages of its life in water, and then later uses its lungs to breathe as an adult.) After a few minutes, have students share their answers and discuss them as a class.

Extend Your Thinking About How a Leopard Frog Changes

- **Step 1:** Have students extend their thinking about the changes a leopard frog goes through as it grows. Say: **The leopard frog changes form during its life cycle.** Ask: **How do you think these changes affect what the frog eats at each stage? Do you think they eat the same food or different food at each stage?** (Possible answer: When a frog is in its early stages it is smaller and lives underwater. As an adult it is larger and can breathe outside of water. Because its size and environment change, what it eats probably changes, too.)

- **Step 2:** If time permits, have pairs of students use the Internet or library resources to find out what a frog eats at each stage in its life cycle.

EVALUATE

Have students record their answers to the Wrap It Up questions in their science notebook.

Wrap It Up!

1. RECALL **What are the stages in the life cycle of a frog?** (egg, tadpole, young frog, and adult)

2. CONTRAST **Describe some differences between the tadpole stage and the adult stage of the frog.** (An adult frog breathes air and has full-grown legs and no tail. A tadpole has a tail and no legs. It breathes through gills.)

An additional interactive assessment activity can be found in the Exploring Science Digital Book.

READING CONNECTION

Describe the Relationship

Describe the relationship between a series of historical events, scientific ideas or concepts, or steps in technical procedures in a text, using language that pertains to time, sequence, and cause/effect.

Guide students to describe the relationship between the series of stages in the life cycle of a leopard frog using language that pertains to sequence. Prompt students to use words such as *first, then, next,* and *finally* as they answer questions during the EXPLAIN discussion.

DIFFERENTIATED INSTRUCTION

Extra Support Write words and phrases on the board that describe either the tadpole or adult stage of the frog, such as: *legs, no legs, tail, no tail, gills, lives in water,* and *lives on land.* Have students match these words and phrases to either the tadpole or adult frog.

Challenge Have partners plan, write, and perform a short skit that shows the life cycle of a frog. One partner should be the narrator while the other acts out the changes in the frog's life cycle.

PHYSICAL SCIENCE
Forces and Interactions

LIFE SCIENCE
Interdependent Relationships in Ecosystems
Inheritance and Variation of Traits : Life Cycles and Traits

EARTH SCIENCE
Weather and Climate

Life Cycles

NEXT GENERATION SCIENCE STANDARDS | DISCIPLINARY CORE IDEAS
LS1.B: Growth and Development of Organisms Reproduction is essential to the continued existence of every kind of organism. Plants and animals have unique and diverse life cycles. (3-LS1-1)

Objective **Students will be able to:**
- Describe the sequence of stages in the life cycle of a spotted salamander.

CLASSROOM MANAGEMENT

Materials *For groups of 4:* 4 Stages in the Life Cycle of a Salamander charts, 2 scissors, 4 pieces of construction paper, 2 glue stick, 4 markers

Time 35 minutes

Advance Preparation Make copies of the Stages in the Life Cycle of a Salamander blackline master (English or Spanish), which can be found at the end of this Teacher Guide.

Teaching Tips You may want to project page 91 of the previous lesson, "Life Cycle of a Leopard Frog" onto a whiteboard for students to reference during the activity.

What to Expect Each student will make a life cycle diagram showing the sequence of stages in a salamander's life.

ENGAGE

Tap Prior Knowledge

- Ask students to recall what they learned in previous lessons about life cycles. Ask probing questions to encourage exploration. For example, ask: **What does a life cycle diagram show?** (A life cycle diagram shows the sequence of stages that an animal or plant goes through as it grows.)
- Have students recall details about the specific stages a leopard frog passes through as it matures. Tell them that in this activity they will be learning about the spotted salamander, an animal closely related to frogs that goes through similar stages.

EXPLORE

- Guide students through the investigation. Read pages 92–93 together.

 Have students make a table for recording their observations in their science notebook.

Example:

Stages in Life Cycle of a Leopard Frog

	Name of Stage	Notes
Stage 1		
Stage 2		
Stage 3		
Stage 4		

- Have students use the internet or library resources to research the stages in a the life cycle of a spotted salamander, including how long each stage can last (The life stages of the spotted salamander can vary depending on environmental conditions such as temperature. Typical life stages: eggs hatch after 4–7 weeks, larvae live in water for 2–4 months, juveniles live on land for 2–7 years before the reproductive adult stage. A spotted salamander typically lives about 20 years in the wild.) Tell students to record this data in the Notes column of their chart.
- Then, have students use their notes to help them determine the proper sequence of the pictures of the salamander life cycle.
- Suggest that students cut out one stage at a time and place it in the correct position on the construction paper. Remind students to wait until all the stages are positioned correctly before making the commitment to glue them down.

- Make sure students understand that it does not matter where they start their diagrams as long as the stages follow the correct sequence.

- Before students begin Step 4, ask: **How will you show the order of stages?** (Students should draw arrows pointing from one stage to the next.) Have students use arrows to show the sequence of stages in a salamander's life cycle and write a title about the diagram.

EXPLAIN

- Have students share their observations and conclusions with other students in their group.

- Help students interpret their observations with probing questions such as: **What are the stages of a salamander's life cycle?** (egg, larva, young salamander (juvenile) adult salamander)

- Guide students to realize that, though frogs and salamanders have similar life cycles, they are ultimately different. Say: **The life cycles of salamanders and frogs are similar, but they are also unique. Explain.** (Both salamanders and frogs begin life as eggs, develop into aquatic larvae, and grow to be able to live on land. However, their life cycles ultimately are unique because they are different animals. Students may notice that the larval salamander has external gills.)

- Lead students to realize that reproduction is essential to the continuance of a species. Ask: **How do you think the life cycle of a salamander continues?** (An adult female salamander lays eggs.)

- Now have students within a group make generalizations about their observations. Explain that a generalization is a general conclusion drawn from specific observations. For example, after observing a variety of ducks, a student might generalize that all ducks have webbed feet, bills, and feathers. Then ask: **What generalizations can you make about the life cycles of animals?** (All animals go through stages of growth and changes, but each animal has a life cycle that is unique to its species, and each animal depends on reproduction for the continuance of its species.)

ELABORATE

- Have students write captions for each stage shown in their diagram of the salamander's life cycle.

- Tell students that both frogs and salamanders are amphibians. Remind students that, in general, amphibians can live on water and on land, they spend the first stages of life in water, and they use lungs to breathe as adults. Ask: **Do you think the life cycle of a frog or salamander would more resemble another amphibian or the life cycle of an animal that is not an amphibian? Explain.** (The life cycles of amphibians will most likely be more similar to other amphibians than they would be to non-amphibian. Amphibians share similarities that affect how they grow and develop.)

EVALUATE

Have students record their answers to the Wrap It Up questions in their science notebook.

Wrap It Up!

1. DESCRIBE **Where does the larva of a spotted salamander live?** (The larva of a spotted salamander lives in the water.)

2. COMPARE **How are the life stages of the spotted salamander similar to the life stages of a frog?** (Both begin life in a mass of eggs, grow into larvae that live in water, develop lungs and live on land, and develop into adult organisms that can reproduce.)

3. CONTRAST **How are the life stages of a spotted salamander different from those of a frog?** (A spotted salamander is not called a tadpole in the larva stage. Salamander larvae have external gills.)

READING CONNECTION

Use Photos and Text to Demonstrate Understanding

Use information gained from illustrations (e.g., maps, photographs) and the words in a text to demonstrate understanding of the text (e.g., where, when, why, and how key events occur).

Guide students to use information gained from photos and the words in the text to demonstrate understanding of the text. For example, when students are constructing their diagrams, encourage them to use the information they gain from the photos to help them understand what they are supposed to do in each step.

PHYSICAL SCIENCE
Forces and Interactions

LIFE SCIENCE
Interdependent Relationships in Ecosystems
Inheritance and Variation of Traits : Life Cycles and Traits

EARTH SCIENCE
Weather and Climate

Develop a Model

NEXT GENERATION SCIENCE STANDARDS | PERFORMANCE EXPECTATION
3-LS1-1. Develop models to describe that organisms have unique and diverse life cycles but all have in common birth, growth, reproduction, and death. [Clarification Statement: Changes organisms go through during their life form a pattern.] [*Assessment Boundary: Assessment of plant life cycles is limited to those of flowering plants. Assessment does not include details of human reproduction.*]

Objective **Students will be able to:**
- Develop two models to describe that organisms have unique and diverse life cycles but all have in common birth, growth, reproduction, and death.

CLASSROOM MANAGEMENT

Materials construction paper; markers; scissors; clay

Time 30 minutes for research; 40 minutes to develop and present models

Advance Preparation To save time later, have materials out before you begin the lesson. Also, you may want to collect library books with information about the living things listed on page 94 for students to use in their research.

Teaching Tips Although students will make their own models, you may want to organize the class into groups of 4 or 5 students who can share materials such as markers and scissors. If time is short, instead of having each student explain their models to the class, have students post their models around the room, grouped with similar organisms. Then, allow time for students to circulate and observe all the models. As a class, discuss any similarities and differences they noticed.

What to Expect Students will choose two living things from the list in the text. Then they will research, design, and construct explanatory models of the living things' life cycles. They will analyze their models with the help of a classmate, make revisions, and share the final model with the class.

ENGAGE

Set the scene.

- Ask a volunteer to read the introductory paragraph on page 94. Tell students that an explanatory model is a representation of something that explains how the real thing works. When students viewed the life cycle diagrams in the previous lessons, they were looking at simple explanatory models of life cycles that allowed them to compare and contrast the life cycles of different organisms. Explanatory models can use two-dimensional images or three-dimensional materials to represent objects and concepts.

Research the models.

- Say: **One step in developing a model is to conduct research.** Then have a volunteer read the text in step 1.

- Guide students through the research process. First, direct students' attention to the list of living things. Say: **Choose two living things from the list. You will research and construct models of each living thing's life cycle.** Allow students time to choose the organisms they want to research.

  My science notebook Next, help students use library books or the Internet to find out about the life cycles of the organisms they chose. Remind them to record their findings in their science notebook.

EXPLORE

Construct explanatory models.

- When all students have completed their research, say: **The next step is to design models that use your research.** Then, have a volunteer read step 2.

- Guide students through the design process. Ask: **Which life stages will you include in your model? How will you organize them and show them as a sequence? What information will you include as captions?** Say: **List any materials you will use to build your models.** Allow students time to consider each question and write the answers in their science notebook.

- Encourage students to use sketches to explain how they will design their models.

Construct your models.

- When all students have completed their research, say: **Now you will construct your models.** Then have a volunteer read step 3.

- Guide students through the construction process. Say: **Collect the materials you listed in your science notebook. Then use your materials to construct your models.**

- Remind students to include captions. For examples of captions, refer students to the previous four lessons.

EXPLAIN

Analyze and revise your models.

- When all students have completed their models, say: **The next step is to analyze and revise your models.** Tell students they may use the internet or other resources to fill in any gaps or missing information from their models.

- Guide students through the analysis and revision process. Have students trade models with a classmate and explain what happens in each stage. Say: **Ask your classmate for his or her feedback. Was there anything he or she didn't understand? Is there something he or she would add or would like to know?**

- Say: **Review the information you used to develop your models. Then do new research to confirm or add to your information. Analyze your models and make any necessary changes.** Allow time for students to revise their models.

SCIENCE AND ENGINEERING PRACTICES

Developing and Using Models

- Say: **Scientists use models, data, and evidence to describe phenomena.** Ask: **Why are models appropriate to use to examine these organisms' life cycles?** (Possible answer: Models are better than graphs or tables because they are more visual. You can see the different stages of the animal's life.)

CROSSCUTTING CONCEPTS

Patterns

- After the class has presented all of their models, ask students to discuss the patterns they can pick out in these life cycles. Emphasize that these organisms are all very different from each other, but can share certain similar stages in their life cycles (all have egg, juvenile, and adult stages), and certain organisms have multiple stages in common. (Possible answer: Toads and butterflies have young forms that are very different from their adult forms.)

- Encourage students to link concepts of patterns, as well as life cycles, to other disciplines of science. For example, in physical science and engineering, the manufacturing of different goods is often called the "product life cycle," in which raw materials are gathered and processed, shaped into a final form, used by people, and finally recycled or disposed of.

PHYSICAL SCIENCE
Forces and Interactions

LIFE SCIENCE
Interdependent Relationships in Ecosystems
Inheritance and Variation of Traits : Life Cycles and Traits

EARTH SCIENCE
Weather and Climate

Develop a Model (continued)

EXPLAIN (continued)

Share and explain your models.

- When all students have completed their research, say: **Finally, share with your classmates your completed models.** Then have a volunteer read step 5.

- Guide students through the sharing process. Allow time for students to explain their models to the class. Ask each student to describe how their models are similar and how they are different.

- After all students have shared and explained their models, ask: **What similarities and differences did you notice between your models and your classmates' models? How are the life cycles of these living things alike? How are the different?** Guide students to recognize that the life cycles have birth (or hatching from an egg or sprouting from a seed), growth, and reproduction in common. The life of each individual organism ends in death. Also guide them to recognize some of the differences between the life cycles of the living things that were explored in this lesson.

- Ask: **In what ways did you think like a scientist as you completed this activity?** (Possible answer: I conducted research to construct a model of different organisms' life cycles, and used my findings and models to explain what I learned to my peers.)

ELABORATE

Extend Your Thinking About How Life Cycles Compare

My science notebook Have small groups of students choose two life cycles models from the class to compare and contrast. Have each group create a Venn diagram to describe how the life cycles are similar and how they are different. Remind students to label each circle and to write differences in the areas that don't overlap and similarities in the area that does overlap.

EVALUATE

My science notebook Check to make sure students have recorded the plans for their models in their science notebook. Then ask students these questions. Have them record the answers in their science notebook.

1. RECALL **What was the purpose of creating two life cycle models?** (The purpose was to use the models to explain how different living things have different life cycles.)

2. APPLY **What steps would you follow to make a life cycle model of another organism?** (1. Research the life cycle; 2. Plan an explanatory model; 3. Construct the model; 4. Analyze and revise the model; and 5. Share and explain the model.)

3. GERNERALIZE **What do the organisms' life cycles have in common?** (The organisms' life cycles include birth [or hatching from an egg or sprouting from a seed], growth, and reproduction. The life of each individual organism ends in death.)

RUBRICS

Teacher Rubric Use the scale descriptions to guide your assessment of the student's work. Assess each item separately, and then decide on one overall score, using the following scale:

4: Student performs with thorough understanding.

3: Student performs with adequate understanding.

2: Student performs with basic understanding.

1: Student performs with limited understanding.

Rubric	Scale			
The student conducted research on the life cycles of two living things.	4	3	2	1
The student used research to plan and design two models.	4	3	2	1
The student successfully constructed models showing the life cycles of two living things.	4	3	2	1
The student shared his or her models with a classmate and gave and received feedback.	4	3	2	1
The student analyzed his or her models and made revisions.	4	3	2	1
The student compared and contrasted his or her models with other students' models in the class.	4	3	2	1
Overall Score	4	3	2	1

Student Rubric Have students complete a self-evaluation similar to that shown below.

Rubric	Yes	Not Yet
1. I can conduct research on an organism's life cycle.		
2. I can use my research to design a model of an organism's life cycle.		
3. I can construct a model of an organism's life cycle.		
4. I can analyze and revise my model.		
5. I can share and explain my model.		

SCIENCE BACKGROUND

Life Cycles

Gray Whales Newborn gray whales are called calves. They are usually born in December through February in the shallow waters off the Mexican coast. They are dark grey or black with dimples all over their skin, about 15–16 feet (almost 5m) long, and weigh about 1,500–2,000 pounds (680–900 kg). They grow quickly and in the spring migrate up the North American Pacific Coast to feed in northern waters. Adult gray whales are 40–50 feet (12–15 m) long and weigh 30–40 tons (13,600–18,100 kg).

Toads The life cycle of a toad is similar to a frog's. Toads, however, lay their eggs in long strands instead of in a cluster. Toads emerge from their eggs as dark black tadpoles, which then grow legs and become young toads. Adult toads have bumpy, dry skin, a wide body, short back legs, and a poison gland behind their eyes.

Monarch Butterflies Monarch butterflies begin life as eggs. Adult female monarchs lay the eggs in the spring on milkweed plants. The eggs hatch into larvae, called caterpillars, and eat the milkweed to grow. After about two weeks, they enter the pupa, or chrysalis, stage. During this stage, the larva transitions to an adult butterfly. Adult monarch butterflies emerge from their chrysalis with distinctive orange and black markings.

Tomatoes A tomato plant begins life when a seed from the fruit of an adult plant is buried in fertile soil. With water and sun, the seed grows roots and a stem that pushes through the soil. As the young plant transitions into a mature plant, it grows more leaves and flowers. The flowers turn into tomatoes, which have seeds so that the life cycle can repeat itself.

Dandelions Seeds from an adult dandelion usually find their way to fertile soil by means of the wind. These seeds sprout roots, leaves and a flower bud, which blooms into a yellow flower. The flower eventually sheds its yellow petals and its flower head transforms into

Inherited Traits: Looks

NEXT GENERATION SCIENCE STANDARDS | DISCIPLINARY CORE IDEAS
LS3.A: Inheritance of Traits Many characteristics of organisms are inherited from their parents. (3-LS1-1)
LS3.B: Variation of Traits Different organisms vary in how they look and function because they have different inherited information. (3-LS1-1)

NEXT GENERATION SCIENCE STANDARDS | PERFORMANCE EXPECTATIONS
3-LS3-1. Analyze and interpret data to provide evidence that plans and animals have traits inherited from parents and that variation of these traits exists in a group of similar organisms. [Clarification Statement: Patterns are the similarities and differences in traits shared between offspring and their parents, or among siblings. Emphasis is on organisms other than humans.]
[Assessment Boundary: Assessment does not include genetic mechanisms of inheritance and prediction of traits. Assessment is limited to non-human examples.]

Objectives Students will be able to:
- Explain how many characteristics of organisms are inherited from their parents.
- Explain that different organisms vary in how they look and function because they have different inherited information.

Science Vocabulary
trait, inherited traits

ENGAGE

Tap Prior Knowledge

- Ask students to share what they know about inherited traits. Ask: **In what ways do you look like your parents?** (Accept any reasonable responses. Possible answers will include hair color, eye color, face shape, height, the shape of certain features, and so on.)

EXPLORE

Explore Inherited Traits

- Have students observe the pictures on pages 96–97. Ask probing questions to encourage exploration. For example, ask: **What vegetables are shown in the pictures on pages 96–97? Do all the vegetables of one kind look alike? How do they look different?**

- Have students share their observations. Students may see corn, tomatoes, and potatoes. They may notice that all the vegetables of a particular kind have a variety of colors and shapes.

Set a Purpose and Read

- Have students read in order to explain how many characteristics of organisms are inherited from their parents and different organisms vary in how they look and function because they have different inherited information.

- Have students read page 96.

EXPLAIN

Explain Inherited Traits

- After students read page 96, ask: **What is another word for *trait*?** (Another word for trait is *characteristic*.) Explain that characteristics include the physical appearances of a living thing, or how it looks.

- Direct students to the large photo of the potatoes on pages 96–97. Discuss how the traits of these potatoes compare with potatoes students may regularly eat. Ask: **Before you saw this photograph, how would you have described potatoes?** Encourage students to list traits including size (large, small), shape (round, oval), and color (brown, red, golden). Then ask: **How would you describe the traits of the potatoes pictured here?** (Possible answers: The potatoes are long and thin, like fingers. They are brightly colored. They have bumps, and some of their ends are pointed.) Ask: **Where did the traits of each potato come from?** (The traits came from the parent plants.)

- Now direct students to the small photos of corn and tomatoes on page 96. Repeat the series of questions and comparisons using the visible traits of these plants and the traits of the common varieties students are probably familiar with.

PHYSICAL SCIENCE
Forces and Interactions

LIFE SCIENCE
Interdependent Relationships in Ecosystems
Inheritance and Variation of Traits: Life Cycles and Traits

EARTH SCIENCE
Weather and Climate

Think Like a Scientist: Analyze and Interpret Data

- Direct students to read the white text box on page 97 and to examine the pictures.

- Ask students what differences they notice between the two parent plants, if any. Then ask them to compare and contrast the parents with the offspring. Ask: **How are the parents and alike and different? How are the offspring alike and different from each other?** How do the different snapdragon offspring compare to their parents, and to each other? (The parents are both, but the offspring are pink, red, and white).

- Ask students to talk about the two discussion questions with their groups. Then ask: **What evidence can you provide to show that the offspring have inherited traits from their parents?** (the plants have the same types of stems, flowers, height, and shape.) What evidence can you provide to show that the offspring have traits that vary from each other? (Some offspring are pink like the parents, but one is red and another is white.

- Ask: **In what ways did you think like a scientist as you completed this activity?** (Possible answer: I used pictures of snapdragons, as well as what I know about variation and inherited traits, to interpret how snapdragon offspring can resemble their parents, differ from them, and how offspring can vary among themselves.)

ELABORATE

Research Inherited Traits in Humans

Step 1: Have pairs of students use the Internet or other resources to research traits that humans inherit. Have each pair make a list of three inherited traits and their variations.

Step 2: If time permits, have each pair draw or print examples of each trait and its variations in a chart as shown below. Then have pairs share their charts with the class.

Trait	Variation Examples

EVALUATE

Have students record their answers to the Wrap It Up questions in their science notebook.

Wrap It Up!

1. **DEFINE What is an inherited trait?** (An inherited trait is a trait, or characteristic, passed down from parents to offspring.)

2. **LIST List some inherited traits of potatoes.** (size, shape, and color)

3. **GENERALIZE List two other traits of tomatoes and corn besides color.** (size and shape)

SCIENCE AND ENGINEERING PRACTICES

Analyzing and Interpreting Data

- Say: **Scientists use logical reasoning to explain phenomena.** Ask: **What logical explanation can you give for a blond haired child from two brown haired parents?** (Possible answer: The child must have inherited the blond genes from her parents. The child may have been adopted.)

CROSSCUTTING CONCEPTS

Patterns

- Students may be intrigued by how some variations, such as color, can vary so much from parents to offspring. Ask them to think about and discuss traits they or their friends might have that are very different from either of their parents. (Possible answers: eye color, hair color, skin tone, freckles, color-blindness.)

Inherited Traits: Functions

NEXT GENERATION SCIENCE STANDARDS | DISCIPLINARY CORE IDEAS
LS3.A: Inheritance of Traits Many characteristics of organisms are inherited from their parents. (3-LS3-1)
LS3.B: Variation of Traits Different organisms vary in how they look and function because they have different inherited information. (3-LS3-1)

NEXT GENERATION SCIENCE STANDARDS | PERFORMANCE EXPECTATIONS
3-LS3-1. Analyze and interpret data to provide evidence that plans and animals have traits inherited from parents and that variation of these traits exists in a group of similar organisms. [Clarification Statement: Patterns are the similarities and differences in traits shared between offspring and their parents, or among siblings. Emphasis is on organisms other than humans.] [*Assessment Boundary: Assessment does not include genetic mechanisms of inheritance and prediction of traits. Assessment is limited to non-human examples.*]

Objectives Students will be able to:
- Explain how many characteristics of organisms are inherited from their parents.
- Explain that different organisms vary in how they function because they have different inherited information.

ENGAGE
Tap Prior Knowledge
- Ask students to think about the differences between a lion and an eagle. Ask: **What did the lion inherit that the eagle did not that allows it to hunt and eat other large animals?** (Possible answer: The lion has large teeth and claws that allow it to hunt and eat other large animals.) **What did the eagle inherit that the lion did not that allows it to fly?** (Possible answer: The eagle has wings that allow it to fly.)

EXPLORE
Explore Inherited Traits: Functions
- Have students observe the pictures on pages 98–99. Ask probing questions to encourage exploration. For example, ask: **What trait do the three birds have in common? What is a trait that they do not have in common? Why do you think some of their traits are the same and some are different?**
- Have students share their observations. Students may notice that all the birds have feathers and similar eyes. They might also notice that while the birds all have beaks, their beaks are different shapes and sizes. They might say that the birds all have feathers to help them fly, but their beaks are different shapes and sizes because they use them differently.

Set a Purpose and Read
- Have students read in order to explain how many characteristics of organisms are inherited from their parents, and different organisms vary in how they function because they have different inherited information.
- Have students read page 98.

EXPLAIN
Explain Inherited Traits
- After students read page 98, ask: What determines the shape of a bird's beak (a bird's beak is an inherited trait.). Then ask: **What function does a bird's beak serve?** (The size and shape of a bird's beak help the bird catch and eat different foods.)
- Say: **Explain how a whooping crane uses its long beak.** (A whooping crane uses its long beak to find food in shallow water.)
- Ask: **Which bird shown on pages 98–99 tears meat from its prey? Explain how you know.** (The caption states that the eagle uses its pointy, hooked beak to tear meat from its prey.
- Say: **Explain how different organisms inherit different traits.** (Organisms inherit traits from their parents that help them get what they need from their ecosystems. They inherit these traits from their parents.)

Think Like a Scientist: Analyze and Interpret Data

- Direct students to read the white text box on page 97 and to examine the pictures.

- Ask students what differences they notice between the two parents, if any. Then ask them to compare the parents to the offspring. Then ask: **How do the different parakeet offspring compare to their parents, and to each other?** (The two offspring on the left have the similar coloring to the parents, while the two on the right are more blue and green. All the offspring are about the same size and have similar patterns.)

- Ask students to talk about the two discussion questions with their groups. Then ask: **What evidence can you provide to show that the offspring have inherited traits from their parents?** (The birds have similar eyes, beaks, feet, feather patterns, body shape, and body size.) What evidence can you provide to show that the offspring have traits that vary from each other? (Some offspring are the same color as the parents, while the others are different colors.)

- Ask: **In what ways did you think like a scientist as you completed this activity?** (Possible answer: I used pictures of parakeets, as well as what I know about variation and inherited traits, to interpret how parakeet offspring can resemble their parents, differ from them, and how the offspring can vary among themselves.)

ELABORATE

Extend Your Thinking About Inherited Traits and Function

- Have students extend their thinking about inherited traits and function by considering the following questions. Say: **Look at the difference in the whooping crane's legs and the hawfinch's legs on pages 98–99. Think about each bird's ecosystem.** Ask: **What function do you think each bird's legs serve? Explain.** (Possible answer: The whooping crane needs long legs to wade through the water, and the hawfinch needs short legs for steady perching on branches and plants.)

EVALUATE

 Have students record their answers to the Wrap It Up questions in their science notebook.

Wrap It Up!

1. **RECALL** **What makes beak shape an example of an inherited trait?** (Beak shape is an example of an inherited trait because it is passed down from parent to offspring.)

2. **EXPLAIN** **How does the shape of the whooping crane's beak affect the way the beak functions?** (The whooping crane's long beak is able to reach into shallow water and allows the crane to find food.)

SCIENCE AND ENGINEERING PRACTICES

Analyzing and Interpreting Data

- Say: **Scientists can use logical reasoning to understand the function of an organisms' traits.** Ask: **If you had never seen a hummingbird but knew that it drank nectar from flowers, what type of beak do you think it might have?** (Possible answer: Long and slender to get inside the flowers.)

CROSSCUTTING CONCEPTS

Patterns

- Say: **A pair of sisters or brothers can sometimes look very different from each other, even though they have the same parents.** Ask: **Can you explain why this might be?** (Possible answer: Even though brothers and sisters have the same parents, they won't inherit exactly the same traits. For example, one brother might inherit his mom's dark hair and brown eyes, while the other might inherit his dad's blond hair and freckles.)

Acquired Traits

NEXT GENERATION SCIENCE STANDARDS | DISCIPLINARY CORE IDEAS

LS3.A: Inheritance of Traits
- Many characteristics of organisms are inherited from their parents. (3-LS3-1)
- Other characteristics result from individuals' interactions with the environment, which can range from diet to learning. Many characteristics involve both inheritance and environment. (3-LS3-2)

LS3.B: Variation of Traits
- Different organisms vary in how they look and function because they have different inherited information. (3-LS3-1)
- The environment also affects the traits that an organism develops. (3-LS3-2)

Objectives Students will be able to:
- Explain how some characteristics of organisms result from individuals' interactions with the environment.
- Explain that different organisms vary in how they look and function because environmental factors, like diet, affect the traits that an organism develops.

Science Vocabulary
acquired traits

ENGAGE

Tap Prior Knowledge

- Ask students to share what they learned about traits in previous lessons. Ask: **What is a trait?** (A trait is a characteristic.) Ask: **What is an inherited trait?** (An inherited trait is a trait that is passed down from parents to offspring.)

EXPLORE

Preview Acquired Traits

- Have students read the title of the lesson and observe the pictures on pages 100–101. Ask: **What do you think the title means? Can you tell from the pictures what acquired trait of the flamingos the text might tell about?**

- Have students share their observations. Students may say the title means a characteristic that is not inherited, but picked up somewhere else. They may say they think the color of the flamingos' feathers might be the acquired trait the text tells about.

Set a Purpose and Read

- Have students read in order to explain how some characteristics of organisms result from individuals' interactions with the environment, and different organisms vary in how they look and function because environment factors, like diet, affect the traits that an organism develops.

- Have students read pages 100–101.

EXPLAIN

Describe Acquired Traits

- After students read pages 100–101, ask: **What are traits that are not inherited called?** (Traits that are not inherited are called acquired traits.) Remind students that inherited traits are characteristics passed down from parents to offspring.

- Ask: **What is an acquired trait?** (An acquired trait is a characteristic gained from the environment.)

- Say: **Diet is an environmental factor that can affect an organism's traits.** Ask: **What traits can diet affect?** (Diet can affect an animal's body size, weight, and health.)

- Ask: **What color feathers are flamingos born with?** (Flamingos are born with white feathers.)

- Ask: **What makes some flamingos' feathers turn pink?** (Some foods in their diets make some flamingos' feathers turn pink.)

- Ask: **Why are pink feathers an acquired trait for flamingos?** (Pink feathers are an acquired trait because they are acquired through diet, not inherited.)

PHYSICAL SCIENCE
Forces and Interactions

LIFE SCIENCE
Interdependent Relationships in Ecosystems
Inheritance and Variation of Traits : Life Cycles and Traits

EARTH SCIENCE
Weather and Climate

ELABORATE

Research Acquired Traits in Humans

Step 1: Have pairs of students use the Internet or other resources to research examples of traits that humans acquire. Then have each pair make a list of three traits they have each acquired (a total of six traits per pair).

Step 2: If time permits, have each student share their acquired traits with the class. Make a master list of the class's acquired traits on the board.

Extend Your Thinking About Acquired Traits From Diet

• Diet can affect other traits of animals besides their color. Ask: **What other ways can you think of that diet can affect an animal's traits? Explain.** (Diet could affect an animal's size and health. Animals that have more fat in their diet or more food available to them may be larger and weigh more. They may also be able to build more muscle mass and fight disease more efficiently. Animals that don't have proper nutrition during their developing years might be smaller or underdeveloped physically and mentally.)

EVALUATE

 Have students record their answers to the Wrap It Up questions in their science notebook.

Wrap It Up!

1. **CONTRAST What is the difference between an inherited trait and an acquired trait?** (An inherited trait is a characteristic passed down from parents to offspring. An acquired trait is a characteristic gained from the environment.)

2. **IDENTIFY What is the evidence that pinkness in flamingos is an acquired trait?** (Flamingos with a certain diet have pink feathers.)

3. **EXPLAIN How might diet affect an animal's body weight?** (Animals that have more food available might weight more than those with leaner diets.)

READING CONNECTION

Determine the Main Idea and Key Details

Determine the main idea of a text; recount the key details and explain how they support the main idea.

Guide students to determine the main idea of a text, recount the key details, and explain how those details support the main idea. For example, when previewing the lesson in the EXPLORE section, remind students that titles and photos can give clues that will help them determine the main idea. Also have them read the first three sentences. Ask students to state the main idea in their own words. Then, before beginning the EXPLAIN section, say: **Now let's reread to determine the key details of the text**. After finishing the EXPLAIN section, ask: **How did the key details of the text support the main idea?** (The key details supported the main idea by giving an example of and explaining an acquired trait in flamingoes.)

SCIENCE BACKGROUND

Why Diet Affects Color

The color-changing agent in an animal's diet can usually be traced back to plants or algae that produce pigments that animals don't naturally produce. One pigment called a carotenoid impacts the color of several species. For example, flamingos turn pink when carotenoids appear in large quantities in their food source. In particular, flamingos that eat more shrimp are pinker, not because the shrimp produce carotenoids, but because the algae the shrimp feast on do. Carotenoid-producing algae is also responsible for the pink color of salmon and the deep yellow or red that canaries can turn when they eat a lot of paprika, cayenne, or red pepper. Humans that consume large amounts carotenoids through carrots, squash, pumpkin or sweet potatoes also can take on a yellowish tone.

More Acquired Traits

NEXT GENERATION SCIENCE STANDARDS | DISCIPLINARY CORE IDEAS

LS3.A: Inheritance of Traits
- Many characteristics of organisms are inherited from their parents. (3-LS3-1)
- Other characteristics result from individuals' interactions with the environment, which can range from diet to learning. Many characteristics involve both inheritance and environment. (3-LS3-2)

LS3.B: Variation of Traits
- Different organisms vary in how they look and function because they have different inherited information. (3-LS3-1)
- The environment also affects the traits that an organism develops. (3-LS3-2)

Objectives **Students will be able to:**
- Explain how some characteristics of organisms result from individuals' interactions with the environment.
- Explain that different organisms vary in how they look and function because environmental factors, like the weather, affect the traits that an organism develops.

ENGAGE

Tap Prior Knowledge

- Ask students to share what they learned about acquired traits in the previous lessons. Ask: **What is an acquired trait?** (An acquired trait is a characteristic that is gained from the environment.) Ask: **What are some examples of an acquired trait?** (Possible answers: knowledge, skills, memories, behaviors, etc.)

EXPLORE

Explore More Acquired Traits

- Have students observe the picture on pages 102–103. Ask probing questions to encourage exploration. For example, ask: **What do you notice about the tree in the picture? Why do you think this tree grew like this?**
- Have students share their observations. Students may notice that the tree is growing at an odd angle. They might say that it may have grown this way because of factors in its environment, like wind. Others might say it grew this way because of traits it inherited from its parents.

Set a Purpose and Read

- Have students read in order to explain how some characteristics of organisms result from individuals' interactions with the environment, and different organisms vary in how they look and function because environmental factors, like weather, affect the traits that an organism develops.
- Have students read pages 102–103.

EXPLAIN

Describe More Acquired Traits

- After students read pages 102–103, ask: **Other than diet, what is one way that traits can be acquired from the environment?** (Traits can also be acquired from factors in the environment like the weather.)
- Ask: **How does weather affect how tall a sunflower grows?** (A sunflower that gets a lot of sunlight will grow taller than a sunflower that gets only a little sunlight.)
- Say: **Explain how traits can be both inherited and acquired.** (Traits can be both inherited and acquired when the environment affects a trait that was passed down from parents.) **Explain how the shape of the tree in the picture on pages 102–103 is both inherited and acquired.** (The general shape of the tree and its limbs are inherited traits. The tree's drastic bend in one direction is an acquired trait because it became that way as a result of strong winds.)

ELABORATE

Research Plant Galls

A gall is an outgrowth on a plant caused by insects, parasites, fungi, or bacteria. Have pairs of students use the Internet or library resources to find pictures of three different plant galls. Have pairs label each picture with information about what caused the gall. Discuss as a class why galls are an acquired trait.

Extend Your Thinking About Inherited and Acquired Traits

- Have students extend their thinking about traits that are both inherited and acquired by discussing the following question. Ask: **Is the texture of your hair an example of an inherited or acquired trait? Why?** (Possible answer: Hair texture is an example of a trait that is both inherited and acquired because you inherit a certain texture from your parents, but it can change depending on environmental factors, like what kind of shampoo you use, if you dye it, if you perm it, how much you are in the sun, etc.)

EVALUATE

Have students record their answers to the Wrap It Up questions in their science notebook.

Wrap It Up!

1. ANALYZE **Which part of the shape of the tree shown on this page is inherited? Which part is acquired?** (The general shape of the tree and its limbs are inherited. The way the branches have been bent by the wind is acquired.)

2. IDENTIFY **What factor in the environment affects this tree's shape?** (The wind affects the tree's shape. Students may also be aware of the plant's natural growth responses to light and gravity.)

3. INFER **Describe how you think this tree might look if it were growing in a place with little wind.** (The tree would probably be more upright and evenly extended in all directions.)

PHYSICAL SCIENCE
Forces and Interactions

LIFE SCIENCE
Interdependent Relationships in Ecosystems
Inheritance and Variation of Traits: Life Cycles and Traits

EARTH SCIENCE
Weather and Climate

READING CONNECTION

Ask and Answer Questions to Demonstrate Understanding

Ask and answer questions to demonstrate understanding of a text, referring explicitly to the text as the basis for the answers.

Guide students to ask and answer questions to demonstrate understanding of the text. Encourage them to refer explicitly to the text as the basis for answers. For example, in the EVALUATE section when students are recording their answers to the Wrap It Up, remind them to refer to the text when considering their answers. Also encourage them to share any questions they may still have, and invite students to answer those questions or do further research if the answers cannot be found in the text.

DIFFERENTIATED INSTRUCTION

Extra Support Have students make a set of 15 study cards with traits on the front and either "acquired" or "inherited" on the back. Have pairs of students work together to quiz each other using the study cards.

Challenge Have students make a list of five inherited traits and five acquired traits. Then have students circle the traits that could be considered both inherited and acquired. Have them explain the ones they circled to a partner.

Learning

NEXT GENERATION SCIENCE STANDARDS | DISCIPLINARY CORE IDEAS
LS3.A: Inheritance of Traits Other characteristics result from individuals' interactions with the environment, which can range from diet to learning. (3-LS3-2)
LS3.B: Variation of Traits The environment also affects the traits that an organism develops. (3-LS3-2)

Objectives Students will be able to:
- Explain how some characteristics of organisms result from individuals' interactions with the environment.
- Explain that different organisms vary in how they look and function because environmental factors, like learned behaviors, affect the traits that an organism develops.

ENGAGE

Tap Prior Knowledge

- Ask students to share what they know about acquired traits from previous lessons. Ask: **What are two ways you have read that animals acquire traits?** (We have learned that animals acquire traits from environmental factors, like diet and weather.)

EXPLORE

Explore Learning

- Have students observe the picture on pages 104–105. Ask probing questions to encourage exploration. For example, ask: **What is the chimpanzee in the picture doing? How is he using the stick?**
- Have students share their observations. Students may notice that the chimpanzee is poking the stick into a termite mound in the small picture and eating termites off the stick in the big picture. They may say that the chimpanzee is using the stick like a spoon to get termites out of the mound.

Set a Purpose and Read

- Have students read in order to explain how some characteristics of organisms result from individuals' interactions with the environment and different organisms vary in how they look and function because the environment affects the traits that an organism develops.
- Have students read pages 104–105.

EXPLAIN

Describe Learning

- After students read pages 104–105, ask: **What is another kind of trait besides physical characteristics?** (Besides physical characteristics, traits can be actions or behaviors.) Remind students that a behavior is an action taken by animals to satisfy a particular need.
- Ask: **For what reasons do animals act in certain ways?** (Animals act to get food and meet other needs.) Say: **Explain how an animal might learn to behave differently.** (An animal interacts with its environment and learns to behave based on its experience.)
- Ask: **How have chimpanzees learned to find food in a way that is different from most other types of animals?** (Chimpanzees have learned to use tools to find food.) Ask: **How do you know using tools is an acquired trait for a chimpanzee?** (Using tools is an acquired trait because it is not a skill a chimpanzee is born with.) Ask: **How do chimpanzees acquire the skill of using tools?** (Chimpanzees acquire the skill of using tools through learning.)

ELABORATE

Extend Your Thinking About Acquired Traits From Learning

- Learned behaviors are acquired traits. For example, dog tricks are learned, so they are considered acquired, not inherited, traits. Say: **Suppose you want to teach your dog to sit on command.** Ask: **How do you know sitting on command is an acquired trait?** (Sitting on command is an acquired trait because it is a learned behavior.) **Why do you think saying the same word, using the same motion, and giving your dog a treat after it sits are important for teaching this behavior?** (The dog learns that every time it sees you do the certain motion and hears a certain word, it will get a treat if it sits down.)

EVALUATE

 Have students record their answers to the Wrap It Up questions in their science notebook.

Wrap It Up!

1. **RECALL What is behavior?** (behaviors are action taken by animals to satisfy particular needs.)

2. **EXPLAIN What is something a chimpanzee can learn?** (A chimpanzee can learn to use tools.)

3. **SUMMARIZE How can the environment affect the way an animal behaves?** (As an animal interacts with its environment, it learns to behave based on its experience.)

READING CONNECTION

Determine the Main Idea and Key Details

Determine the main idea of a text; recount the key details and explain how they support the main idea.

Guide students to determine the main idea of a text, recount the key details, and explain how those details support the main idea. For example, after students initially read the text, remind them that titles and photos can give clues that will help them determine the main idea. Also point out that the main idea often is found at the beginning or end of a passage. Ask students to state the main idea in their own words. Then, before beginning the EXPLAIN section, say: **Now let's reread to determine the key details of the text.** After finishing the EXPLAIN section, ask: **How did the key details of the text support the main idea?** (Key details supported the main idea by giving an example of and explaining a learned behavior in chimpanzees.)

SCIENCE BACKGROUND

Jane Goodall

Jane Goodall is a British scientist known worldwide for her extensive study of and discoveries regarding chimpanzee behavior. Among Goodall's most profound discoveries was chimpanzees' use of tools. Before her observation of a chimpanzee using a stick to eat termites, it was thought humans were the only animals to use tools. Other significant discoveries were that chimpanzees hunt and eat meat and that they act as families. Goodall observed familial relationships among chimpanzees that lasted throughout their lives. Many of these behaviors mimic what we see in human families and continue to be of great interest to researchers of chimpanzee behavior today.

PHYSICAL SCIENCE
Forces and Interactions

LIFE SCIENCE
Interdependent Relationships in Ecosystems
Inheritance and Variation of Traits : Life Cycles and Traits

EARTH SCIENCE
Weather and Climate

Environment and Traits

NEXT GENERATION SCIENCE STANDARDS | PERFORMANCE EXPECTATION

3-LS3-2: Use evidence to support the explanation that traits can be influenced by the environment. [Clarification Statement: Examples of the environment affecting a trait could include normally tall plants grown with insufficient water are stunted; and, a pet dog that is given too much food and little exercise may become overweight.]

Objective Students will be able to:
- Explain how traits can be influenced by the environment.

CLASSROOM MANAGEMENT

Materials *For groups of 4:* 2 wheatgrass seedlings; masking tape; marker; ruler; spray bottle

Time 25 minutes for setup and observation; 15 minutes a day for the next three days; 30 minutes for observation and discussion on the fifth day

Advance Preparation Plant seeds a few days before the experiment begins so that there is some growth to start. Put soil in small plastic cups, cut bottles, or waxed paper cups. Spread seeds on top and dampen soil. Cover with plastic wrap and set in a sunny spot. Dampen soil as necessary. Also, clear enough space for all the cups in a sunny part of the classroom.

Teaching Tips Make sure the cups are stored in a place where they will not be disturbed during the week. Ideally, all the cups would receive the same amount of sunlight. If that is not possible, make sure each group's pair of cups receives the same amount of light so that it is a constant. Begin project on a Monday.

What to Expect Students will observe how whether a plant gets water influences its traits. They should find that the plant that receives water grows taller and is healthier than the one that does not.

ENGAGE

Tap Prior Knowledge

- Ask students to recall what they learned in previous lessons about how environment affects traits. Ask: **What are two ways you have learned that an organism's traits can be influenced by its environment?** (diet and other environmental factors, such as the weather)

EXPLORE

- Guide students through the investigation. Read pages 106–107 together.

  My science notebook Have students make a table for recording their observations in their science notebook.

- Example:

Wheatgrass Observation Table

Day	__ Sprays of Water/Day (height in cm)	No Water (height in cm)
Day 1		
Day 2		
Day 3		
Day 4		
Day 5		

- After students have labeled their cups, have them record their predictions in their notebook. Ask: **What do you think will happen if you water one seedling and not the other? How will this environmental difference affect each plant's height?** (Possible answer: The plant that receives water will grow faster and taller than the one that does not.)

- Have students measure the height of each plant in centimeters and record their observations in the "Day 1" row of the Wheatgrass Observation Table.

- As students complete Step 3, remind them to make the soil damp, but not too wet. Have them record the number of sprays they use in the second column of the chart.

- Make time for students to measure any growth, record their observations, and water their plants every day for a week or more if needed for observable results. On the last day, after students measure their plants and record their observations, leave time for discussion. Ask: **What were the final heights of your plants? Was your prediction supported by your data?**

EXPLAIN

- Have students share their observations and conclusions. Ask: **Do your results differ from other groups? If so, can you explain why?** In general, students should find that the watered plant grew faster and taller. If a group severely over- or under-watered a plant, that group's results might vary drastically from other groups'.

- Help students interpret their observations with probing questions such as: **What can you infer about how a plant's height is influenced by the amount of water in its environment?** (Since plants need water to grow and survive, the amount of water in an environment can affect traits such as height.)

ELABORATE

- Ask: **How would your investigation have differed if you had used cacti that require very little water? Explain.** (Students may realize that there may have been very little observable difference between a cactus that received a few sprays of water a day and a cactus that received no water. The experiment would need to be carried out over a longer period or the variables would need to be changed if the subject were cacti because the plants have different water requirements.)

- Ask: **Did you notice any other traits that were influenced by the amount of water in the environment? If not, what other traits might be affected if a plant consistently received less water than it needed?** (Students may have noticed or concluded that a plant's color and firmness might also be influenced by the amount of water in its environment.)

EVALUATE

 Have students record their answers to the Wrap It Up questions in their science notebook.

Wrap It Up!

1. **PREDICT Did your results support your predictions? Explain.** (Answers will vary based on students' predictions. Possible answer: Yes. My results supported my prediction that the plant that received water would grow taller than the one that did not.)

2. **INTERPRET Explain whether your results provide evidence that traits can be affected by the environment.** (Possible answer: Yes. My results provide evidence that traits can be affected by the environment because the plant that received water grew taller.)

3. **CONCLUDE Is seedling height an inherited trait, an acquired trait, or both? Explain.** (Each kind of plant inherits its general height, but the amount of water it receives can affect its height. So, plant height is both inherited and acquired.)

SCIENCE AND ENGINEERING PRACTICES

Constructing Explanations and Designing Solutions

- Discuss with students the different types of evidence that scientists might use to support explanations. Then ask: **What type of evidence did you use?** (Possible answers: Data and observations.)

CROSSCUTTING CONCEPTS

Cause and Effect

- Say: **Cause-and-effect relationships can be used to describe change.** Ask: **Phrase your argument as a cause-and-effect relationship statement.** (Possible answer: Watering the plant caused it to grow taller.)

PHYSICAL SCIENCE
Forces and Interactions

LIFE SCIENCE
Interdependent Relationships in Ecosystems
Inheritance and Variation of Traits · Life Cycles and Traits

EARTH SCIENCE
Weather and Climate

Variation and Survival

NEXT GENERATION SCIENCE STANDARDS | DISCIPLINARY CORE IDEAS
LS4.B: Natural Selection Sometimes the difference in characteristics between individuals of the same species provide advantages in surviving, finding mates, and reproducing. (3-LS4-2)

Objective **Students will be able to:**
- Explain how sometimes the difference in characteristics between individuals of the same species provide advantages in surviving.

Science Vocabulary
variations

ENGAGE

Tap Prior Knowledge

- Ask students to share what they know about the benefits of variation. Ask: **Which basketball team do you think will win more games: a team with a strong defensive player, a strong inside shooter, a strong rebounder, a strong outside shooter, and a strong dribbler or a team with 5 strong inside shooters? Why?** (Accept any reasonable responses. Possible answer: The team with a variety of strengths probably wins more games because its players can adapt to a variety of situations.)

EXPLORE

Explore Variation and Survival

- Have students observe the pictures on pages 108–109. Ask probing questions to encourage exploration. For example, ask: **If the seaweed in the sea dragon's environment were replaced with a species that is redder, would the sea dragon shown or one that is slightly redder have a better chance of surviving? Why?**

- Have students share their observations. Students may notice that the animals in the pictures blend in with their environments so well that they are camouflaged. They may say that if the seaweed were replaced with a redder species, a sea dragon that is slightly redder would have a better chance of surviving because it would be less visible to predators.

Set a Purpose and Read

- Have students read in order to explain how sometimes the difference in characteristics between individuals of the same species provides advantages in surviving.

- Have students read pages 108–109.

EXPLAIN

Explain Variation and Survival

- After students read pages 108–109, remind them that a trait is a characteristic that is either inherited or acquired. Ask: **What is one trait that sea dragons have that helps them blend in with their environment?** (Sea dragons have leaf-shaped structures all over their bodies.)

- Ask: **Which sea dragons are the least likely to get eaten? Why?** (The sea dragons that blend in best with their environments are least likely to be eaten because they are least likely to be seen by predators.) Remind students that predators are animals that hunt and eat other animals.

- Say: **Why don't all sea dragons have the same traits as the pictured sea dragon?** (All sea dragons don't have the same traits as the pictured sea dragon because environments can change, and different environments require different traits for survival.)

- Ask: **What are variations?** (Variations are differences between individuals of the same type of organism.) Ask: **Why is a species more likely to survive with variations than without?** (A species is more likely to survive with variations because as environments change, some individuals will be able to survive better than others. If all the individuals had the exact same traits, when their environment changed, they all would be at risk.)

ELABORATE

Find Out More About Variation and Disease Resistance

 Cut small squares of paper, marking four with a black "X." Have students draw squares from a bowl and then stand up. Say: **Imagine our class is a population of ferrets. A deadly disease has arrived in our community. If you have an "X" on your square you are a ferret that is immune to the disease.** Begin the spread of the disease by tapping a student on the shoulder. If her square is blank, she now has the disease. She must go tap another student and then sit down. If the student tapped has an "X" on his square, he can tell the infected student that he can't get sick, and the infected student must go tap another student and then sit down. Play until only the immune ferrets are left standing. Ask: **How is variation important for resisting disease? What would have happened if none of the ferrets were immune to the disease?** (Variation is important for resisting disease because if none of a population is immune to a disease, it could wipe out the whole population.)

Extend Your Thinking About Variation and Survival

- Have students extend their thinking about variation and survival by discussing the following example. Say: **A Florida population of panthers was on the verge of becoming extinct, or dying out. Scientists introduced panthers with different traits to the population and the population grew.** Ask: **Why do you think this approach worked?** (Introducing panthers with different traits worked because it introduced variations into the population. The variations made the panthers better able to adapt to changing environments and fight disease.)

EVALUATE

 Have students record their answers to the Wrap It Up questions in their science notebook.

Wrap It Up!

1. **EXPLAIN Describe how traits of the sea dragon shown here help it survive.** (The leaf-shaped structures on the sea dragon and its coloring help it survive. These traits help it blend in with its environment and hide from predators.)

2. **INFER Suppose a few of the thorn bugs in the photo above were orange. What could you infer about the variation in thorn bug color?** (You could infer that the orange thorn bugs would survive best in a different environment than the green thorn bugs.)

READING CONNECTION

Use Photos and Text to Demonstrate Understanding

Use information gained from illustrations (e.g., maps, photographs) and the words in a text to demonstrate understanding of the text (e.g., where, when, why, and how key events occur).

Guide students to use information gained from illustrations and the words to demonstrate understanding of the text. For example, in the EXPLORE section, guide students to support their answers with information gained from the photo. In the EXPLAIN section, encourage students to use information in the photos as well as the text to answer questions.

TEACHING WITH TECHNOLOGY

Text Support

Project the lesson on a whiteboard. As you ask questions in the EXPLAIN section, have volunteers underline information in the text that helps them answer the question. (Answers in order: *Sea dragons have leaf-shaped structures all over their bodies; The sea dragons that blend in best with seaweed are less likely to be seen and eaten; The best traits in one place and time may not be best in another place and time; Variations are differences between individuals of the same type of organisms; Variations help some of a type of living thing survive over time as things change.*)

PHYSICAL SCIENCE
Forces and Interactions

LIFE SCIENCE
Interdependent Relationships in Ecosystems
Inheritance and Variation of Traits : Life Cycles and Traits

EARTH SCIENCE
Weather and Climate

Variation and Mates

NEXT GENERATION SCIENCE STANDARDS | DISCIPLINARY CORE IDEAS
LS4.B: Natural Selection Sometimes the difference in characteristics between individuals of the same species provide advantages in surviving, finding mates, and reproducing. (3-LS4-2)

Objective Students will be able to:
- Explain how sometimes the difference in characteristics between individuals of the same species provide advantages in finding mates and reproducing.

ENGAGE
Tap Prior Knowledge

- Ask students to share what they know about variation from the previous lesson. Ask: **What are variations?** (Variations are differences between individuals of the same type of organism.) Ask: **What is one way variations can help a species survive?** (Possible answer: As environments change, variations can make sure that a population will survive the changes because some traits are more useful, depending on the environment.)

EXPLORE
Explore Variation and Mates

- Have students observe the title of the lesson and picture on pages 110–111. Ask probing questions to encourage exploration. For example, ask: **What is the first thing you see when you look at this picture? What do you think is happening in this picture?**

- Have students share their observations. Students may say the first thing they notice is the bird's big red throat. They may also say that the bird is trying to attract a mate with its red throat and that it seems to have worked.

Set a Purpose and Read

- Have students read in order to explain how differences in characteristics between individuals of the same species may provide advantages in finding mates and reproducing.

- Have students read pages 110–111.

EXPLAIN
Describe Variation and Mates

- After students read pages 110–111, have students identify the male great frigatebird. Ask: **How can you tell which bird is the male great frigatebird?** (You can tell which bird is the male because male great frigatebirds have bright red pouches on their throat that they can fill with air.) Ask: **Why does a male great frigatebird have this trait?** (He has this trait so that he can blow up the pouch like a balloon and get the attention of female great frigatebirds.)

- Ask: **Besides blowing up the red pouch on his throat, what else does a male great frigatebird do to attract a mate?** (He opens his wings wide and shakes his head like a dance.)

- Ask: **How do the female great frigatebirds choose a mate?** (They choose the male with the most impressive display.) Point out that the female great frigatebird does not have bright colors. Ask: **Why is it important that the female great frigatebirds do not have bright colors?** (It is important because she needs to blend in with the environment so that she can protect her young.)

- Ask: **How does the variation of color between male and female frigatebirds help the species survive?** (The male's bright colors helps attract a mate and ensures reproduction. The female's muted colors help ensure the safety of the young.)

ELABORATE

Research Variation and Mates in Birds

 Have small groups of students use the Internet or library resources to find pictures of both male and female bluebirds, peacocks, robins, and hummingbirds. Have them summarize and draw a conclusion about their findings.

Extend Your Thinking About Variation and Mates

- Have students extend their thinking about variation and mates by discussing this example. Say: **Scientists debate the function of a lion's mane. Some scientists think manes play a role in attracting a mate. Some do not. Either way, healthier males seem to have thicker, darker manes.** Ask: **If manes do help lions attract mates, what traits do you think female lions would be attracted to? Explain.** (Females would probably be attracted to thick, dark manes because they would indicate that the male is healthy and able to fight and reproduce.)

EVALUATE

 Have students record their answers to the Wrap It Up questions in their science notebook.

Wrap It Up!

1. EXPLAIN **What advantage does the trait of a bright red pouch give a male great frigatebird?** (The bright red pouch helps the male birds attract mates.)

2. INFER **What is the disadvantage of having the bright pouch?** (The bright color makes it easier for predator to see the birds.)

READING CONNECTION

Determine the Main Idea and Key Details

Determine the main idea of a text; recount the key details and explain how they support the main idea.

Guide students to determine the main idea of a text, recount the key details, and explain how those details support the main idea. For example, when previewing the lesson in the EXPLORE section, remind students that titles and photos can give clues that will help them determine the main idea. Also remind them that the main idea can often be found near the beginning or end of a passage. Ask students to state the main idea in their own words. Then, before beginning the EXPLAIN section, say: **Now let's reread to determine the key details of the text.** After finishing the EXPLAIN section, ask: **How did the key details of the text support the main idea?** (The key details supported the main idea by giving an example of how the traits of the male frigatebird help it attract a mate, and how the traits of the female frigatebird help her hide from predators and keep her young safe.)

ELL SUPPORT

Noun/Verb/Adjective Forms of Words

Beginning Provide sentence frames, such as: *(Variation) is important for a species' survival. Please (vary) your response. The (varied) color of the birds was interesting.*

Intermediate Have students complete the above sentence frames, and then identify each word as a noun, verb, or adjective.

Advanced Have students identify the following terms as noun, verb, or adjective, and then use each one in an original sentence: *variation, vary,* and *varied.*

PHYSICAL SCIENCE
Forces and Interactions

LIFE SCIENCE
Interdependent Relationships in Ecosystems
Inheritance and Variation of Traits : Life Cycles and Traits

EARTH SCIENCE
Weather and Climate

Construct an Explanation

NEXT GENERATION SCIENCE STANDARDS | PERFORMANCE EXPECTATION
3-LS4-2. Use evidence to construct an explanation for how the variations in characteristics among individuals of the same species may provide advantages in surviving, finding mates, and reproducing. [Clarification Statement: Examples of cause and effect relationships could be plants that have larger thorns than other plants may be less likely to be eaten by predators; and, animals that have better camouflage coloration than other animals may be more likely to survive and therefore more likely to leave offspring.]

Objective Students will be able to:
- Construct an explanation for why the pink form of katydids is less common in adults than in hatchlings.

CLASSROOM MANAGEMENT

Time 40 minutes

Teaching Tips Organize the class into groups of 2–4 students. Encourage students to work together to construct an explanation.

What to Expect Students will observe and discuss the pictures of katydids in groups. They will consider what they learned in previous lessons, and construct an explanation for why the pink form of katydid is less common in adults than in hatchlings.

ENGAGE

Set the Scene

- Remind students that they have learned how variation can provide advantages. Say: **Recall the thorn bugs on page 109. Which thorn bugs were most likely to survive? Explain.** (The thorn bugs that looked more like thorns were most likely to survive because predators could see them less easily.)

EXPLORE

Preview the Lesson

- Have students look at the pictures on pages 112–113. Say: **Describe the insects you see in these pictures. How many types of insects do you see? How are they similar? Different?** (The pictures show three of the same type of insect. They are of similar shapes and sizes and have a similar vein pattern, but they are different colors.)

EXPLAIN

Make Observations

- After reading the introductory paragraph on page 112, instruct students to take turns reading the captions under the photographs in their groups. Then, guide students to make observations about what they see. Allow time for groups to discuss each question. Ask:

  - **What are some inherited traits these katydids share?** (Possible answers: the shape of their wings, six legs, long back legs, a vein pattern that looks like a leaf, and so on)
  - **What inherited trait do they not share? How do they vary?** (They vary in color.)
  - **How do katydids look like leaves?** (The vein pattern on their wings and shape of their wings resemble leaves.)
  - **Which katydid looks the least like a leaf? Explain.** (The pink katydid looks the least like a leaf because of its color.)
  - **Which katydid best blends in to the environment in the photograph? Explain.** (The green katydid because it is almost exactly the same color as the leaf it is on.)

Construct an Explanation

- Ask students to recall how variation can provide advantages in surviving, finding mates, and reproducing. Ask: **Which katydid do you think has the greatest chance of surviving in its current environment? Explain.** (The green katydid; it is best camouflaged from predators.)
- Ask: **Which katydid has the least chance of surviving as a hatchling? Explain.** (The pink katydid; it is the only one that does not start out green, which means it doesn't blend in with the environment.)
- Ask: **Why might the pink form of katydid be less common in adults than in hatchlings?**

(The color of the pink hatchlings makes them visible to predators. The longer the pink form of katydid is alive, the more opportunity these insects have to be seen and eaten.)

- Have students write their explanations in their science notebook.

- Ask: **In what ways did you think like a scientist as you completed this activity?** (Possible answer: I used observations of katydids from photos, and used what I know about variations and survival, to come up with an explanation for why the pink form of katydid is less common in adults than in hatchlings.)

ELABORATE

Support Your Explanation

 Have students write three facts that support their explanations for why the pink form of katydid is less common in adults than in hatchlings.

Extend Your Thinking About Variation and Survival

- **Step 1:** Ask: **How does the color variation of katydids provide advantages for survival of the species?** (The color variation ensures that different katydids will survive better in different environments. So, if the environment changes, at least some of the katydids will have a good chance of surviving.)

Step 2: If time permits, have groups discuss environments in which each of the katydids pictured would have an advantage over the others. Ask: **Can you think of an environment in which all three colors of katydids would have a fair chance of surviving?** (Perhaps a fall forest or someplace with both green and yellow vegetation and pink flowers would provide the katydids with equal opportunity to survive.)

EVALUATE

 Have students record their answers to the Wrap It Up questions in their science notebook.

Wrap It Up!

1. **CONSTRUCT AN EXPLANATION** **Why might the pink form of katydid be less common in adults than in hatchlings?** (As hatchlings grow, they might become less and less common because their color makes them visible to predators. Pink hatchlings may be more common than adults because they were just born, but the longer they are alive, the more opportunity they have to be eaten.)

2. **CAUSE AND EFFECT** **How does the trait of color help katydids survive?** (The color variation ensures that different katydids will survive in different environments.)

SCIENCE AND ENGINEERING PRACTICES

Constructing Explanations and Designing Solutions

- Discuss with students the difference between using evidence to support an explanation and using evidence to construct an explanation. Then ask which they did in this activity and why they chose that answer. (Possible answer: I used evidence to construct an explanation because I was given information but not an explanation of why some katydids change color.)

CROSSCUTTING CONCEPTS

Cause and Effect

- Explain to students that certain tropic plant species can have bright pink leaves. Have students discuss with their groups what might happen if, after a long period of time, a population of katydids were to live in an area where only these pink-leafed plants grew. Ask: **What do you think the most common katydid color would be then? Why?** (Possible answer: I think pink katydids would become more common because their color would help them blend in and avoid being eaten.)

PHYSICAL SCIENCE
Forces and Interactions

LIFE SCIENCE
Interdependent Relationships in Ecosystems
Inheritance and Variation of Traits : Life Cycles and Traits

EARTH SCIENCE
Weather and Climate

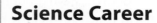

Marine Ecologist

NEXT GENERATION SCIENCE STANDARDS | CONNECTION TO THE NATURE OF SCIENCE
Scientific Knowledge Assumes an Order and Consistency in Natural Systems Science assumes consistent patterns in natural systems.

Objective Students will be able to:
- Connect the concepts of consistent patterns and natural systems with the career of a marine ecologist.

ENGAGE

Tap Prior Knowledge

- Ask students to share some of their personal experiences with the ocean. Encourage students who have not been to the ocean to think about pictures of the ocean they have seen. Ask: **What living things did you see?** Possible answers: fish, stingray, crabs, algae, jellyfish, etc.) **What nonliving things did you see?** Possible answers: water, sand, rocks, trash, etc.) Remind students that all the living and nonliving things in an area and the way they interact is called an ecosystem.

EXPLORE

Preview the Lesson

- Have students look at the title and pictures on pages 114–115. Say: **The title of this lesson is Marine Ecologist. An ecologist is a type of scientist.** Ask: **What word does "ecologist" remind you of? What do you think an ecologist studies? What do you think a marine ecologist studies?**

- Have students share their thoughts. Students may say that "ecologist" reminds them of "ecology" or "ecosystem." Students may that an ecologist studies ecosystems. They may use the pictures to realize that a marine ecologist studies ocean ecosystems.

Set a Purpose and Read

- Have students read in order to learn about the work of a marine ecologist.

- Have students read pages 114–115.

EXPLAIN

Describe the Work of a Marine Ecologist

- After students read pages 114–115, ask: **What made Enric Sala want to spend his life working to save the health of the ocean?** (Growing up, he saw people polluting the water and taking too many fish.) **What kind of scientist is Enric?** (He is a marine ecologist.) **What is a marine ecosystem?** (Marine ecosystems are the communities of living things in the ocean.)

- Say: **Describe what Enric does and some of his discoveries as a marine ecologist.** (Enric leads explorations to some of the most unspoiled parts of the ocean. He and his team have discovered crystal clear water, a deep-sea coral reef, new kinds of fish, and sharks.)

- Ask: **How does Enric's work help save the health of the ocean?** (Possible answer: His work has influenced world leaders to protect certain areas of the ocean.)

Connect Science Topics to the Career of a Marine Ecologist

- Say: **Explain how Enric is "show[ing] the world what the ocean was like hundreds of years ago."** (Enric visits areas of the ocean that are unspoiled by human activity. He takes pictures of these areas to study them and show people how living things interact in these areas.)

- Ask: **Why do you think it is important for marine ecologists to study the natural patterns and systems of the ocean?** (The natural patterns and systems of the ocean show how living things interact in a balanced way. By studying this balance, marine ecologists can help create solutions for increasing the health of areas with unbalanced ecosystems.)

Find Out More

- Ask: **Is this a career you would find interesting? Why or why not?** Accept all positive and negative responses.) For students who find this to be an interesting career, ask: **Why would you like to be a marine ecologist?** (Possible answer: I would like to be a marine ecologist because all my favorite animals live in the ocean, and I would like to study where they live and how they interact.)

ELABORATE

Research Enric Sala's Work

 Enric Sala is one of National Geographic's Explorers-in-Residence, and National Geographic has an extensive collection of information, photographs, articles, interviews, and videos about Sala's work. Have groups of students visit National Geographic websites to explore these resources.

EVALUATE

 Have students record the answers to the questions below in their science notebook.

1. DESCRIBE **What does a marine ecologist do?** (A marine ecologist studies the communities of living things in the ocean.)

2. INFER **Why does Enric visit unspoiled areas of the ocean?** (He visits unspoiled areas to study what ocean ecosystems are like in their natural state.)

3. INTREPRET **When Enric says, "I want to show the world what the ocean was like hundreds of years ago and why we have to preserve it," what does he mean?** (He means that he wants people to understand how different the ocean is now than it was hundreds of years ago and that is important to restore some of the natural balance.)

PHYSICAL SCIENCE
Forces and Interactions

LIFE SCIENCE
Interdependent Relationships in Ecosystems
Inheritance and Variation of Traits : Life Cycles and Traits

EARTH SCIENCE
Weather and Climate

READING CONNECTION

Use Photos and Text to Demonstrate Understanding

Use information gained from illustrations (e.g., maps, photographs) and the words in a text to demonstrate understanding of the text (e.g., where, when, why, and how key events occur).

Guide students to use information gained from photos and the words in the text to demonstrate understanding of the text. For example, after students have read through the text, ask: **How do the words in the text help you understand what is occurring in the pictures?** (The text helps me understand that the man in the picture is a marine ecologist named Enric Sala. I can infer from the text that Enric is studying the ducky grouper on page 115.) **How do the pictures help you understand what you read in the text?** (The pictures help me understand that a marine ecologist is someone who studies living things in the ocean. They also give me an idea of what it might be like to be a marine ecologist.)

ELL SUPPORT

Suffixes –ology and –ist

Beginning Provide students with the definition of the prefixes *bio–* (connected with life or living things) and *geo–* (connected with Earth). Have students add endings onto the words.

Biology	the study of living things
Biologist	someone who studies living things
Geology	the study of Earth
Geologist	someone who studies Earth

Intermediate Provide students with the definition of the prefixes *bio–* (connected with life or living things) and *geo–* (connected with Earth) and the suffixes *–ist* (someone who studies something) and *–ology* (the scientific study of something). Then, have students write definitions for *biology, biologist, geology,* and *geologist*.

Advanced Give students definitions for *biology, biologist, geology,* and *geologist*. Then have them write definitions for the prefixes *bio–* and *geo–* and the suffixes *–ist* and *–ology*.

Earth Science

Grade 3. Weather and Climate

Performance Expectations

Students who demonstrate understanding can:

3-ESS2-1. Represent data in tables and graphical displays to describe typical weather conditions expected during a particular season. [Clarification Statement: Examples of data could include average temperature, precipitation, and wind direction.] [*Assessment Boundary: Assessment of graphical displays is limited to pictographs and bar graphs. Assessment does not include climate change.*]

3-ESS2-2. Obtain and combine information to describe climates in different regions of the world.

3-ESS3-1. Make a claim about the merit of a design solution that reduces the impacts of a weather-related hazard. [Clarification Statement: Examples of design solutions to weather-related hazards could include barriers to prevent flooding, wind resistant roofs, and lightning rods.]

Disciplinary Core Ideas

ESS2.D: Weather and Climate
* Scientists record patterns of the weather across different times and areas so that they can make predictions about what kind of weather might happen next. (3-ESS2-1)
* Climate describes a range of an area's typical weather conditions and the extent to which those conditions vary over years. (3-ESS2-2)

ESS3.B: Natural Hazards
* A variety of natural hazards result from natural processes. Humans cannot eliminate natural hazards but can take steps to reduce their impacts. (3-ESS3-1) (Note: This Disciplinary Core Idea is also addressed by 4-ESS3-2.)

Science and Engineering Practices

Analyzing and Interpreting Data
Analyzing data in 3–5 builds on K–2 experiences and progresses to introducing quantitative approaches to collecting data and conducting multiple trials of qualitative observations. When possible and feasible, digital tools should be used.
* Represent data in tables and various graphical displays (bar graphs and pictographs) to reveal patterns that indicate relationships. (3-ESS2-1)

Obtaining, Evaluating, and Communicating Information

Obtaining, evaluating, and communicating information in 3–5 builds on K–2 experiences and progresses to evaluating the merit and accuracy of ideas and methods.

- Obtain and combine information from books and other reliable media to explain phenomena. (3-ESS2-2)

Engaging in Argument from Evidence

Engaging in argument from evidence in 3–5 builds on K–2 experiences and progresses to critiquing the scientific explanations or solutions proposed by peers by citing relevant evidence about the natural and designed world(s).

- Make a claim about the merit of a solution to a problem by citing relevant evidence about how it meets the criteria and constraints of the problem. (3-ESS3-1)

Crosscutting Concepts

Patterns

- Patterns of change can be used to make predictions. (3-ESS2-1), (3-ESS2-2)

Cause and Effect

- Cause and effect relationships are routinely identified, tested, and used to explain change. (3-ESS3-1)

Connections to Engineering, Technology, and Applications of Science
Influence of Engineering, Technology, and Science on Society and the Natural World

- Engineers improve existing technologies or develop new ones to increase their benefits (e.g., better artificial limbs), decrease known risks (e.g., seatbelts in cars), and meet societal demands (e.g., cell phones). (3-ESS3-1)

Connections to Nature of Science
Science is a Human Endeavor

- Science affects everyday life. (3-ESS3-1)

PHYSICAL SCIENCE
Forces and Interactions

LIFE SCIENCE
Structure, Function, and Information Processing

EARTH SCIENCE
Weather and Climate

Weather

NEXT GENERATION SCIENCE STANDARDS | DISCIPLINARY CORE IDEAS
ESS2.D: Weather and Climate Scientists record patterns of the weather across different time zones and areas so they can make predictions about what kind of weather might happen next. (3-ESS2-1)

Objectives Students will be able to:
- Define and describe weather.
- Explain that weather changes over time.

Science Vocabulary
weather

ENGAGE

Tap Prior Knowledge

- Have students share some of their favorite or memorable weather experiences, such as a bad thunderstorm, a breezy summer day, a heavy snowfall, a crisp autumn day, or a hailstorm. Then initiate a discussion about how weather affects their day-to-day lives and activities.

EXPLORE

Explore Weather

- Have students look at the photos on pages 118–119. Ask probing questions to encourage exploration. For example, ask: **What are some words that can be used to describe weather?** (Possible answers: rainy, snowy, cold, hot, humid, stormy, cloudy, and rainy) **Without looking at the caption, what one word would you use to describe the weather in the large photo?** (Students may suggest stormy or cloudy.)

Set a Purpose and Read

- Have students read in order to describe weather and explain how it changes.
- Have students read pages 118–119.

EXPLAIN

Define Weather

- Point out the vocabulary word *weather*. Ask a volunteer to read the definition aloud. Explain that the word *condition* means "the state that something is in." For example, a weather forecaster might describe weather conditions as sunny or cloudy. Also, point out that weather is specific to a certain place and time, and can change quickly.

- You may wish to point out that *weather* and *climate* are not the same things. Students will learn in the lesson on pages 132–133 that climate is the general pattern of weather in an area over a long period of time. Climate changes generally occur slowly. Weather changes from day to day, hour to hour, or even minute to minute.

Describe Weather and Explain How It Changes

- Have students look outside and describe the current weather. If your classroom doesn't have windows, have students recall the weather conditions they saw on the way to school. If your students will be recalling earlier weather conditions, ask: **Do you think the weather is exactly the same now as it was earlier? Explain.** (Answers will vary. Discuss any obvious changes in the day's weather. If students state that the weather did not change, point out that some properties of the air, such as wind speed, temperature, and humidity, likely did.)

- Ask: **How quickly does weather change?** (Weather can change from minute to minute, hour to hour, day to day, and season to season.)

ELABORATE

Find Out More About Weather

 Have students use the Internet or your local paper to record high and low temperatures, wind speed, precipitation, cloud cover, and humidity for five consecutive days. Have students use the data to write a short paragraph to explain the weather of the week. Encourage students to include drawings that depict one or more days of the observed weather.

Research Weather Adages

- Have students conduct research to find some common weather adages and write them in their science notebook. Examples include "Cold is the night when the stars shine bright" and "The higher the clouds, the finer the weather." If possible, have students research how accurately the adages reflect or predict the weather. Have students choose one or two of the sayings and explain in their own words

what they mean. Have interested students extend this activity by using the weather data they collected for two consecutive days to write their own sayings.

EVALUATE

 Have students record their answers to the Wrap It Up questions in their science notebook.

Wrap It Up!

1. **DEFINE** **What is weather?** (Weather is the set of conditions in the air outside at a certain time and place.)

2. **EXPLAIN** **Tell three ways in which weather can change.** (Weather can change from day to day, hour to hour, and season to season.)

3. **DESCRIBE** **What is the weather like in the large photo on these two pages?** (Possible answer: The weather is stormy. The sky is cloudy. It might also be cool.)

ELL SUPPORT

Describe Weather

Beginning Provide students with sentence frames to help them describe weather. For example: *Weather is the state of the atmosphere at a certain (time) and (place). Scientists can measure (changes) in weather. Weather can change (quickly).*

Intermediate Help students make a picture dictionary page that includes a variety of weather terms. Have students add to the dictionary as they work through this section.

Advanced Have students write new, single-sentence captions in their own words for each of the photos shown in this lesson.

READING CONNECTION

Determine Main Idea and Details

Determine the main idea of a text; recount the key details and explain how they support the main idea.

Guide students in determining the main idea of the text and the key details that support the main idea. For example, in the EXPLORE section, remind students that the main heading and boldfaced words on a page are often clues to the main idea. Say: **Use these clues to determine the main idea.** (weather) As you move onto the EXPLAIN section, invite students to find key details in the text about the topic of weather. For example, the words *sunny, cloudy, hot, cold, windy, calm, dry,* and *wet* are all words that describe weather. Prompt students to explain how these details support the main idea. Then have students determine the main idea of the paragraph on page 119. Remind them that the main idea is often found at the beginning of the paragraph. After students have identified "weather changes" as the main idea, have volunteers point out details and explain how they support the main idea.

Weather Measurements

NEXT GENERATION SCIENCE STANDARDS | DISCIPLINARY CORE IDEAS
ESS2.D: Weather and Climate Scientists record patterns of the weather across different time zones and areas so they can make predictions about what kind of weather might happen next. (3-ESS2-1)

Objectives Students will be able to:
- Identify and describe instruments that are used to measure weather.
- Describe the weather data that these instruments measure.

Science Vocabulary
thermometer, wind vane, barometer, rain gauge, wind, precipitation, air pressure

ENGAGE
Tap Prior Knowledge

- Ask: **How does weather change from day to day?** (Possible answers: Some days are hotter than others; sometimes it rains or snows; some days it is windy or cloudy.) Then ask students if they can think of any ways in which scientists measure the weather conditions they just described. Students may say that scientists use thermometers to measure temperature.

EXPLORE
Explore Weather Instruments

- Have students look at the photos of weather instruments on page 120. Ask probing questions to encourage exploration. For example, ask: **Have you ever seen any of these instruments? What do you think they are used for?**

- Have students share their answers. Some students may be familiar with thermometers from reading them at home or using them in science investigations to measure temperature. Students may also be familiar with a wind vane and the compass directions that are represented by N, S, E, and W.

Set a Purpose and Read

- Have students read in order to identify weather instruments and how they are used to take weather measurements.

- Have students read pages 120–121.

EXPLAIN
Identify Weather Instruments

- Direct students' attention to the weather instruments on page 120. Tells students that scientists use tools, or instruments, to make weather measurements. Read the names of the instruments and the captions aloud. Ask: **How does a thermometer measure temperature?** (The liquid inside the thermometer rises when it gets warmer and falls when it gets cooler.)

- **Which instrument is used to measure wind direction?** (a wind vane) **What do the letters on the wind vane stand for?** (north, south, east, west) **In this photo, what direction is the wind blowing? How do you know?** (It is blowing from the south. The wind vane shows the direction from which the wind is blowing.)

- **Which instrument is used to measure rainfall?** (a rain gauge) **How does a rain gauge measure rainfall?** (The rain gauge is marked with numbers to show how much rain has fallen.)

Describe Weather Measurements

- Direct students' attention to the boldfaced vocabulary word *precipitation*, and have students pronounce the word aloud. Ask: **What are some different kinds of precipitation?** (rain and snow). Say: **Name other kinds of precipitation that are not listed in your book.** (hail, sleet, freezing rain) **What do all types of precipitation have in common?** (They fall from clouds.)

- Ask: **What instrument is used to measure air pressure?** (a barometer) **What can we expect when the air pressure in our area rises?** (The weather will be fair.) **What can we expect when the air pressure in our area falls?** (The weather will be cloudy or stormy.) **How do you think scientists use these patterns to predict the weather?** (Changes in air pressure cause changes in weather. Scientists know that if air pressure is falling, stormy weather is likely on the way. If it is rising, the weather is turning fair.)

Note: The scientist in the large photograph is using a weather instrument that includes an anemometer. An anemometer is used to measure wind speed. Students will be making anemometers in the *Investigate* on pages 122–123.

ELABORATE

Find Out More About Weather Instruments

 Invite students to use a thermometer to measure the temperature each day for one week and record their observations in their science notebook. Explain to students that they should make each measurement in a shaded area at the same time and place each day. Place a milliliter measuring cup outdoors, and have students measure and record any precipitation that falls. If a barometer is available, show students how to read it and record the barometric pressure each day. Challenge students to identify patterns in their weather measurements and to use these patterns to make predictions about the weather.

- To demonstrate the importance of taking consistent measurements and controlling variables in a scientific observation, have students take temperature measurements in a shady and a sunny location during the observation period for the exercise above.

These two locations should be the same place throughout the exercise. Ask students to summarize how the measurements differ and why the readings from the shaded location provide better data. (If the day is very sunny, the readings from the unshaded location may be significantly warmer. By taking all readings in the shade across time, students know they are measuring the air temperature without regard to additional warming by the sun in certain areas.)

EVALUATE

 Have students record their answers to the Wrap It Up questions in their science notebook.

Wrap It Up!

1. EXPLAIN **Tell why scientists record patterns of weather across different times and areas.** (Possible answer: Because patterns repeat, scientists can use past patterns of weather that they have studied to predict future weather.)

2. CAUSE AND EFFECT **How do changes in temperature affect air?** (Changes in temperature cause air to move.)

An additional interactive assessment activity can be found in the Exploring Science Digital Book.

ELL SUPPORT

Measure Weather Factors

Beginning Help students identify tools for measuring weather by asking either/or questions, such as: *Does a thermometer measure temperature or humidity? Does a barometer measure air pressure or wind speed?*

Intermediate Have students use sentence frames to identify and compare tools for measuring weather. For example:
A (thermometer) measures temperature.
A (barometer) measures air pressure.

Advanced Have students use sentence stems to identify and compare tools for measuring weather. For example:
With a barometer, you can . . .
To measure wind speed, you can . . .

READING CONNECTION

Determine Word Meaning

Determine the meaning of general academic and domain-specific words and phrases in a text relevant to *a grade 3 topic or subject area.*

Guide students in determining the meaning of domain-specific words in the text. For example, in the EXPLAIN section as you examine each photo of the weather instruments, have students read the boldfaced vocabulary word and then describe each instrument and explain what it does and how it is used. When describing vocabulary related to weather measurements, have students pair the measurement with the instrument it is measured with, for example: *temperature/thermometer; wind/wind vane; precipitation/rain gauge; air pressure/barometer.*

PHYSICAL SCIENCE
Forces and Interactions

LIFE SCIENCE
Structure, Function, and Information Processing

EARTH SCIENCE
Weather and Climate

Weather

NEXT GENERATION SCIENCE STANDARDS | DISCIPLINARY CORE IDEAS

ESS2.D: Weather and Climate Scientist record patterns of weather across different times and areas so that they can make predictions about what kind of weather might happen next. (3-ESS2-1)

Objectives **Students will be able to:**
- Measure and record two types of changes in weather—wind speed and air temperature.
- Analyze weather data and interpret patterns to construct reasonable explanations from the data.

CLASSROOM MANAGEMENT

Materials *For groups of 4:* heavy paper plate; golf-ball-sized lump of clay; unsharpened pencil; 2 sturdy drinking straws; masking tape; 4 small, identical paper cups (3 oz.); marker; straight pin; stopwatch or timer; Celsius thermometer

Time 40 minutes on the first day; 10 minutes each day for 1 week

Advance Preparation Use the photo on page 123 as a guide to build a sample anemometer.

1. Tape the straws together intersecting at right angles.

2. Push the straight pin through the center of the straws, and twist it a little to enlarge the hole.

3. Use the marker to draw an "X" on one of the cups.

4. Use pieces of clay and tape to secure the cups to the straws. Make sure that the "X" on the one cup is facing outward.

5. Use clay to affix the pencil to the paper plate to form a stand.

6. Poke the pin into the pencil eraser to join the cup assembly to the stand.

Test the instrument with an electric fan or hair dryer on low to make sure that the pencil is mounted correctly and that the cups are secure and spin freely. Display the instrument you made so that students can refer to it as they build their own.

Teaching Tips For the anemometers to function properly, the clay must securely anchor the pencil, and the hole in the straws must be large enough so that the cups can spin freely.

What to Expect Students will build simple anemometers and use those and thermometers to measure wind speed and air temperature. They will also observe general weather conditions as they collect data to look for any patterns or relationships among wind speed, temperature, and general weather conditions.

ENGAGE

Tap Prior Knowledge

- Say: **Describe air.** (Answers will vary. Possible answers: a mix of gases; invisible; surrounds Earth; called "wind" when it moves.)

EXPLORE

- Caution students to take care with the pin so that they do not stick their fingers.

- Guide students through the investigation. Read pages 122–123 together.

My science notebook Have students make a table for recording their measurements and observations in their science notebook.

Example:

Date and Time	Air Temperature	Wind Speed (Number of Revolutions per Minute)					Other Weather Observations (clouds, precipitation, wind direction)
		1	2	3	4	Avg.	

- In step 1, use the Advance Preparation note to guide students in making their anemometers.
- Before starting step 2, ask: **Why do the anemometers need to be in open areas?** (Putting them near a building or tree might prevent wind from reaching them, resulting in inaccurate speeds.) **Is the number of times the X on the cup passes a certain point an actual wind speed? Explain.** (No. Actual wind speed is measured in kilometers per hour. These instruments measure only relative speeds.) Tell each student to measure and record the relative wind speed and then average the results when they return to the classroom.
- In step 3, coach students to read the thermometer at the proper angle to avoid a distorted reading.
- After students have measured and recorded wind speed and temperature, have them record other observable weather factors, such as cloud cover and any precipitation.
- Have students measure and observe weather data at the same time of day for four consecutive days and record the data in their science notebook.

EXPLAIN

- Have two groups combine and share their data and observations. Say: **Study the weather data and observations in your data tables.** Ask: **What patterns do you see in your data?** (Answers will vary depending on the data they recorded.)

ELABORATE

- Invite interested students to design and make a wind vane. Ask students how they could use their anemometers as models for making a wind vane. Students may suggest that instead of using cups they use two flat pieces of cardboard on a single straw. Students can mark the paper plate base with the compass directions north, south, east, and west. Point out that the wind vane will point into the wind. Encourage students to add the data about wind directions to their weather data tables.

EVALUATE

 Have students record their answers to the Wrap It Up questions in their science notebook.

Wrap It Up!

1. **SUMMARIZE How did the data for wind speed and temperature change during the week?** (Answers will depend on actual weather. Encourage students to look for patterns.)

2. **EXPLAIN How did your weather tools help you measure the weather conditions?** (I used the anemometer to measure relative wind speed by counting the number of turns it made per minute. I used the thermometer to measure temperature by determining the level of the liquid in the tube.)

3. **COMPARE AND CONTRAST How were the data collected at different areas alike and different?** (Answers will depend on actual weather.)

READING CONNECTION
Describe the Relationship

Describe the relationship between a series of historical events, scientific ideas or concepts, or steps in technical procedures in a text, using language that pertains to time, sequence, and cause/effect.

Remind students that all *Investigates* are set up to show a procedure. Ask: **What is the relationship among the steps in the procedure?** Guide students to understand that the steps follow a sequence, which is indicated by the numbers in the green boxes. Ask: **Why is it important to carry out the steps in the sequence indicated by the numbers?** (Possible answer: The activity won't work if you don't follow the sequence. For example, you can't use the anemometer until you have correctly assembled it.)

PHYSICAL SCIENCE
Forces and Interactions

LIFE SCIENCE
Structure, Function, and Information Processing

EARTH SCIENCE
Weather and Climate

Patterns and Predictions

NEXT GENERATION SCIENCE STANDARDS | DISCIPLINARY CORE IDEAS
ESS2.D: Weather and Climate Scientists record patterns of the weather across different time zones and areas so they can make predictions about what kind of weather might happen next. (3-ESS2-1)

Objectives **Students will be able to:**
- Use a map key to interpret the symbols and colors used on a weather map.
- Make weather predictions using weather maps.

Science Vocabulary
front

ENGAGE

Tap Prior Knowledge

- Ask: **How did you decide what to wear today? Did the weather have anything to do with it?** (Some students may say that they did choose the clothes they have on because of the current weather or because of how the weather is expected to change later in the day.) Use students' responses to initiate a discussion about weather, how it changes, and how it might be predicted.

EXPLORE

Explore Weather Maps

- Ask students to examine pages 124–125. Ask probing questions to encourage exploration. For example, ask: **What types of information are shown on these maps? What are the boxes on the right sides of the maps? Why do you think the maps are labeled *Day 1* and *Day 2*? How could you figure out what a map for *Day 3* might look like?**

- Have students share their answers. Some students may say that weather data are shown on these maps and that the boxes are map keys. Others may say that the maps show the weather on different days and that a third map could be made by observing differences between the two maps shown.

Set a Purpose and Read

- Have students read in order to learn how to interpret weather maps and to predict weather using maps.

- Have students read pages 124–125.

EXPLAIN

Define Weather

- Remind students that weather is the state of the atmosphere at a certain place and time. Say: **Think about a weather report you have heard, seen, or read about.** Ask: **What types of data were included in the report?** (Possible answers: temperature, air pressure, precipitation) **Did the report include any maps?** (Answers will vary.)

Understand the Information on Weather Maps

- Direct students' attention to the weather maps on page 125. Explain that the small box in the lower right corner of the map is called a map key. Say: **A map key explains the colors and symbols that are used on a map.** Ask: **How is color used on these weather maps?** (Color is used to show temperature.) **What do the blue and red curving lines represent?** (These lines represent cold and warm fronts.) **What is a weather front?** (A weather front is a boundary where two different large air masses meet.) **How is rain shown on the map?** (dashed lines) **How is snow shown?** (dots)

Explain How Maps Can Be Used to Observe How Weather Changes

- Say: **Compare the two maps. Describe how the cold front in the western United States moved from Day 1 to Day 2.** (It moved south and east.) Say: **Explain how this affected the temperature of Los Angeles.** (As the cold front moved closer to the city, the temperature dropped.) Ask: **How did the warm front north and east of Chicago change from Day 1 to Day 2?** (It moved farther north and got smaller.) Say: **Predict how this cold front may affect weather in New York on Day 3.** (Possible answer: The temperature may drop.)

Predict Weather Using Weather Maps, Weather Symbols, and a Map Key

- Say: **Imagine that these maps show the current weather. Also imagine that the cold front west of Denver will continue to move in the same direction. Predict what the weather in this city will be like in a day or two.** (Possible answer: Temperatures will drop and rain will fall.)

ELABORATE

Extend Your Thinking About Predicting Weather

 Say: **Imagine again that the weather map on page 125 is today's map. Use the map and its key to predict what our weather will be like for the next few days.** Have students record their predictions in their science notebook. They should include a range of temperatures and any possible precipitation. If necessary, help students

locate your town or city on the map. You might want to challenge students to trace the base map in their science notebook and use colored pencils to translate their predictions from words into symbols on the base maps. Remind students to include a map key.

EVALUATE

 Have students record their answers to the Wrap It Up questions in their science notebook.

Wrap It Up!

1. **DESCRIBE** **In general, how did the fronts move from Day 1 to Day 2?** (The fronts generally moved from west to east.)

2. **INTERPRET MAPS** **Look at the Day 1 map. Describe the weather in Chicago on that day.** (It's raining in Chicago. The temperature is between 60°F and 70°F.)

3. **PREDICT** **Study both maps. Tell what the you think weather will be like in Chicago on the day after Day 2.** (A cold front is moving away from Chicago. The rainy weather will move on, and it should stop raining in Chicago.)

PHYSICAL SCIENCE
Forces and Interactions

LIFE SCIENCE
Structure, Function, and Information Processing

EARTH SCIENCE
Weather and Climate

SCIENCE BACKGROUND

Air Masses and Fronts

An air mass is a large volume of air that essentially has the same temperature and moisture throughout. Weather in the continental United States is governed by four major air masses—cold, dry air masses; cold, wet air masses; warm, dry air masses; and warm, wet air masses. When any of these air masses meet, a front is formed. A cold front forms where the leading edge of a cold air mass meets a warm air mass. Cold fronts can produce stormy weather. As a cold front passes through an area, winds change, skies clear, and temperatures drop. A warm front forms where the leading edge of a warm air mass meets a cold air mass. Warm fronts can cause light precipitation in the form of rain or snow, but as they pass, air pressure rises, skies clear, and temperatures increase.

READING CONNECTION

Use Maps to Demonstrate Understanding

Use information gained from illustrations (e.g., maps, photographs) and the words in a text to demonstrate understanding of the text (e.g., where, when, why, and how key events occur).

Guide students in determining how the maps in the text help them understand patterns of weather and how to predict weather. For example, in the EXPLAIN section as you examine how maps can be used to observe weather changes, make sure students understand the meaning of all of the symbols in the key. Have them relate the symbols to the maps, asking detailed questions about where fronts occur; where temperatures are hot, cold, or in between; or where precipitation is taking place. In the EXPLAIN section when using the maps to predict weather, ask students to describe how they use the key and information on the map to predict the patterns of weather.

The Pattern of the Seasons

NEXT GENERATION SCIENCE STANDARDS | DISCIPLINARY CORE IDEAS
ESS2.D: Weather and Climate Scientists record patterns of the weather across different time zones and areas so they can make predictions about what kind of weather might happen next. (3-ESS2-1)

Objective(s) Students will be able to:
- Identify the sequence of seasons.
- Describe patterns of change in the seasons over time.

ENGAGE

Tap Prior Knowledge

- Ask each student to name his or her favorite season and explain in a short phrase why it is his or her favorite. Tally the results in a table. Have each season listed across the top of the table in a different color. In the first row of the table, put the number of students who prefer this season by using tally marks. In the second row record a list of the reasons this season is preferred.

EXPLORE

Explore Seasons

- Have students look at pages 126–127. Ask probing questions to encourage exploration. For example, ask: **How are the photos alike? How are they different? Do you notice any similarities or differences in the colors in the photographs for each season?**

- Have students share their answers. Most students should notice that the photos are of the same mountain scene from different angles and that the colors of vegetation for each season differ. The tops of the mountains remain white.

Set a Purpose and Read

- Have students read in order to identify the seasons and patterns of change over time.

- Have students read pages 126–127.

EXPLAIN

Sequence the Seasons

- Say: **Look at the photos on pages 126–127. Describe what you see in the winter photo.** (Possible answer: Snow is covering the ground and the mountains. It appears to be cold.) Ask: **How is the spring photo different from the winter one? Use information from the text and what you know about the seasons to explain what caused these changes.** (Possible answer: The snow in low-lying areas has melted because of warmer temperatures. Flowers have bloomed because temperatures are warmer and there are more hours of daylight.)

- Ask: **Which season is the hottest?** (Most students will say that summer is hottest.) **Now use the captions and text to describe the changes that take place as summer changes to fall.** (Possible answer: Length of daylight decreases, amount of precipitation decreases, average temperatures decrease, and the leaves on the trees change colors.) Say: **The seasons repeat in the same pattern every year. Sequence the seasons starting with summer.** (summer, fall, winter, spring)

Identify the Seasons

- Display an annual calendar. Invite a student to find the first day of spring on the calendar. Ask: **During which months of the year do we have spring?** (March, April, May, June) Then have a student note the first day of summer. Ask: **During which months of the year do we have summer?** (June, July, August, September) Repeat for the first day of fall and the first day of winter.

Predict Patterns of Change

- Ask: **What do you predict the weather will be like in January?** (Answers will vary with location. Possible answer: It will most likely be cool or cold; it may snow or sleet.) Ask: **What** do you predict the weather will be like in July? (Answers will vary with location. Possible answer: It will be hot and sunny. It might be dry.) Note that high in the mountains temperatures are cold and snow often remains throughout the seasons.

ELABORATE

Extend Your Thinking About the Seasons

 Provide students with pictures of the seasons in your state. Have students choose one picture, such as a scene of a farm in winter. Ask students to draw pictures of what the same scene in the picture will look like in spring, summer, and fall, showing a pattern of seasonal changes. Invite students to share and discuss their drawings.

Find Out More About the Seasons

 Ask students what they notice about the number of hours of daylight in the summer and winter months. Most students will notice that there are more hour of daylight in summer than in winter. Invite students to conduct research to find out how the average number of daylight hours changes from season to season. Challenge students to present their findings in a graph.

EVALUATE

 Have students record their answers to the Wrap It Up questions in their science notebook.

Wrap It Up!

1. SEQUENCE **Name the seasons in order, starting with winter.** (winter, spring, summer, fall)

2. CONTRAST **Tell how weather differs in spring and summer.** (Spring weather is cooler and often rainier than summer weather.)

3. ESTIMATE **The average temperature of a city is 9°C (48°F) in winter and 29°C (83°F) in summer. Estimate what its average spring temperature might be.** (An average spring temperature for this city will be much warmer than in winter, but cooler than in summer. It might be about 20°C (70°F).)

An additional interactive assessment activity can be found in the Exploring Science Digital Book.

PHYSICAL SCIENCE
Forces and Interactions

LIFE SCIENCE
Structure, Function, and Information Processing

EARTH SCIENCE
Weather and Climate

SCIENCE BACKGROUND

Daylight Hours

The sun's apparent course across the sky changes with the seasons. It appears to travel higher in the sky in summer. Because the part of Earth that is experiencing summer is tilted more directly toward the sun, to observers on Earth the sun is visible in the sky longer. As a result, in summer there are more hours of daylight. The reverse is true in winter. In the northern hemisphere, the sun appears to cross low in the southern sky, resulting in fewer hours of daylight.

READING CONNECTION

Use Photos and Text to Demonstrate Understanding

Use information gained from illustrations (e.g., maps, photographs) and the words in a text to demonstrate understanding of the text (e.g., where, when, why, and how key events occur).

Guide students in determining how the photos and their captions help them understand how the seasons change. For example, in the EXPLAIN section after students describe what they see in the photos, ask them how the captions relate to the photos and the concept of changing seasons.

Seasonal Changes

NEXT GENERATION SCIENCE STANDARDS | DISCIPLINARY CORE IDEAS
ESS2.D: Weather and Climate Scientists record patterns of the weather across different time zones and areas so they can make predictions about what kind of weather might happen next. (3-ESS2-1)

Objective(s) Students will be able to:
- Analyze data to identify sequences of seasons over time.
- Analyze data to predict patterns of change in seasons over time.

ENGAGE

Tap Prior Knowledge

- Ask students to recall the sequence of seasons from the previous lesson, and write the names of the seasons on the board. Ask: **What kind of weather happens in each season?** (Students may suggest that in many areas it is hot in summer, cooler in springtime and fall, and cold in winter. Answers will vary depending on location.) Record their responses on the board.

EXPLORE

Explore Seasonal Changes

- Have students look at pages 128–129. Ask probing questions to encourage exploration. For example, ask: **What season do you think is shown in the photo? Explain why you think so. What kind of changes in weather do you expect to occur in the fall? Why do you expect those changes?**

- Have students share their answers. Most students will suggest that the photo shows fall because the trees are changing colors. Students may say that it will be getting colder because fall follows summer. Some students may add that they expect these changes because they have seen the same pattern of seasonal changes year after year.

Set a Purpose and Read

- Have students read in order to analyze data to identify sequences and predict patterns of change in seasons over time.

- Have students read pages 128–129.

EXPLAIN

Describe Data in Tables and Graphs

- Say: **Look at the data on pages 128 and 129. Describe what you see.** (Possible answers: The data table on page 128 shows seasonal patterns in Charlottesville, Virginia. The table shows average high and low temperatures, and precipitation for the four seasons. The two bar graphs also show average high and low temperatures, and precipitation for the four seasons for Charlottesville, Virginia.) **How are the data alike? How do they differ?** Both show the same data for Charlottesville. The table shows the data in numbers. The graphs use bars to show the data.) **How are the data in the table organized?** (All of the data for each season are in a different column.) **What types of data are being compared?** (the average high and low temperatures, and average precipitation) **How are the data in the first bar graph organized?** (The high and low temperatures are shown by two bars with a different color for each season.) **How are the data in the second bar graph organized?** (The average precipitation is shown by bars with a different color for each season.)

Analyze Seasonal Data for Charlottesville, Virginia

- Call students' attention to the data table on page 128. Ask: **What is the average high temperature for Charlottesville in the fall?** (16°C, which is 61°F) **What is the city's springtime average low temperature?** (9.5°C, or 49°F) Then call attention to the bar graphs. Ask: **How does the average low temperature of summer compare to the average high temperature of fall? Explain how you know.** (The temperatures are nearly the same. The bars on the graph are nearly the same height.) **During which season does this city get most of its precipitation?** (summer)

Predict Patterns of Change in Seasons

- Say: **Look at the data table. Predict what the average low temperature might be in Charlottesville in July.** (The average low temperature in July in this city might be about 17°C, or 63°F.) **Look at the bars on the graph for average precipitation. Predict how much precipitation Charlottesville might get on average next winter.** (It might average a little more than 20 cm.)

ELABORATE

Find Out More About the Seasons in Your State

Have students conduct research to find out the average high and low temperatures, and the average amount of precipitation for each season in your area. Have them organize their findings in a data table in their science notebook. They may use the data table or bar graphs on pages 128–129 as examples for ways to organize their data. Then have students use their data to make predictions about the weather for your current season. They may answer questions such as: **How much precipitation do you predict your area might average this season? What do you predict might be the average high temperature? The average low temperature? How much precipitation do you predict your area might get next July? Next December?**

EVALUATE

Have students record their answers to the Wrap It Up questions in their science notebook.

Wrap It Up!

1. INTERPRET GRAPHS **What is the difference between the average high and low fall temperatures in Charlottesville?** (11°C)

2. PREDICT **What might the average amount of precipitation be in Charlottesville next summer?** (about 34 cm)

PHYSICAL SCIENCE
Forces and Interactions

LIFE SCIENCE
Structure, Function, and Information Processing

EARTH SCIENCE
Weather and Climate

SCIENCE MISCONCEPTIONS

Reasons for Seasons

Some students might incorrectly think that the warmer temperatures and greater number of daylight hours during summer are the result of Earth being closer to the sun in summer and farther from the sun in winter. However, Earth is actually slightly closer to the sun when it is winter in the Northern Hemisphere. The seasonal patterns of change we experience are the result of Earth's tilt on its axis and its revolution around the sun.

READING CONNECTION

Use Illustrations to Demonstrate Understanding

Use information gained from illustrations (e.g., maps, photographs) and the words in a text to demonstrate understanding of the text (e.g., where, when, why, and how key events occur).

Guide students in determining how the graphs along with the text help them understand the seasonal changes in weather. In the EXPLAIN section as you compare and contrast the data, make sure students understand why scientists collect this kind of data. (so that they are able to describe average weather for an area during each season) Ask: **What do the charts tell you about the seasonal weather changes in Charlottesville, Virginia?**

Represent Data

NEXT GENERATION SCIENCE STANDARD | PERFORMANCE EXPECTATION
3-ESS2-1. Represent data in tables and graphical displays to describe typical weather conditions expected during a particular season. [Clarification Statement: Examples of data could include average temperature, precipitation, and wind direction.]
[*Assessment Boundary: Assessment of graphical displays is limited to pictographs and bar graphs. Assessment does not include climate change.*]

Objective(s) Students will be able to:

- Represent data in graphical displays to describe typical weather conditions during a particular season.

- Compare and contrast data to find patterns of change for different seasons.

CLASSROOM MANAGEMENT

Time 40 minutes

Advance Preparation Prior to the activity, gather data for students to use from almanacs or Internet weather sources. Data should include information about average low and high temperatures, average precipitation, and average wind speed for each of the four seasons.

Teaching Tips Organize the class into groups of 3 or 4. Assign each group a season. Be sure that all seasons are represented among the various groups.

What to Expect Students' graphical displays should show the average low and high temperatures, average precipitation, and average wind speed for each of the four seasons. Students should represent their graphical data in tables and bar graphs. Their graphic displays should also incorporate the concepts they have studied in earlier lessons in this unit.

ENGAGE

Set the scene.

- Ask students to think about the weather in your area. Ask: **How is weather in winter where we live different from weather in summer?** (Possible answers: In winter it is cold, with ice and snow, similar to the photo on p. 131. There is even ice and snow on the thermometer shown in the photo. Summer is warmer, with rain; in winter it is cooler, with lots of rain, but summer is very hot and dry.)

- Choose a season with variable weather in your area, and ask students questions about what they know about it. For example: **During summer, is the weather the same every day? What changes have you observed?** (Possible answer: Some days are warmer than others. Sometimes it rains steadily all day, and sometimes there are big storms. Other times there are no clouds or rain, and the air feels dry.)

Ask a question.

Tell students that now they do their own work to answer the following question:

What is the weather like for one season in your area? Make it clear that students are not answering the question at this time. They will work in groups and use real weather data to answer the question. Have students record the question in their science notebook. Then assign students to groups, and guide them as they plan their investigations by asking the following questions:

- **Which of the four seasons will you research?**

- **What will you research about your season?** Have students record in their science notebook what kind of data they will collect for their chosen season.

- **How will you organize your data?** Ask students to describe the different ways in which they have recorded data from other science investigations or ways they have seen data displayed in their science text. Write students' suggestions on the board. Students may suggest that they can record data in tables, charts, and graphs such as picture graphs or bar graphs.

- After students have agreed upon a plan with the members of their group, direct them to record their plan in their science notebook.

Example:

1. Our group will research data about winter in our area.
2. We will use reference materials to research data about high and low average temperature, average precipitation, and average wind speed.
3. We will display the data in tables.
4. From the tables, we will make bar graphs to compare the different data.

EXPLORE

Research and organize data.

- Guide students in collecting and organizing their data. Discuss with them ways in which they can record their data. Point out that scientists often use tables and bar graphs to help them organize their data. Suggest that students look at the tables and bar graphs on pages 128–129 as examples. Remind students that tables use rows and columns to display numerical data. Tables are useful for comparing data such as high and low temperatures.

Example:

Average Temperatures for Summer Months

Month	June	July	August
average high temperature	72°F	84°F	78°F
average low temperature	56°F	65°F	60°F

- Review with students the different ways they can display data in a bar graph. Remind them that the bars are used to represent the numerical data found in tables and charts. Bars can be horizontal or vertical and are useful for comparing quantities. Students can use double bar graphs to compare numerical data such as high and low temperatures.

Example:

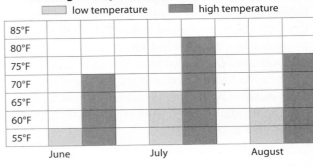

Average Temperatures for Summer Months

low temperature   high temperature

SCIENCE AND ENGINEERING PRACTICES

Analyzing and Interpreting Data

- Review different types of tables and graphical displays, such as bar graphs and pictographs, with students. Ask: **What other types of graphs could you have used to represent your data? What types of graphs or tables would not work well?** (Possible answer: A line graph could have displayed the temperatures well but a pie chart would not have.)

CROSSCUTTING CONCEPTS

Patterns

- Say: **Scientists recognize and identify patterns to make predictions about future changes.** Ask: **What predictions can you make after analyzing the weather patterns in your graphs?** (Answers will vary depending on what seasons students chose. accept responses supported by evidence.)

- Encourage students to link concepts of patterns and graphing data over time to other disciplines of science. For example, in life science, organisms will grow at different rates throughout their lives and depending on the season. This can be observed in tree rings, which indicate more growth of the trunk in summer and little or no growth in winter. Measuring the thickness of these rings can provide information about the weather from previous seasons.

PHYSICAL SCIENCE
Forces and Interactions

LIFE SCIENCE
Structure, Function, and Information Processing

EARTH SCIENCE
Weather and Climate

Represent Data (continued)

EXPLAIN

Analyze and interpret data.

- Remind students that the numbers they have recorded are data. When they look at their data and think about what they mean, it prepares them to answer the question they have been investigating: *How can you represent some weather data for one season in your area?*

- Ask: **How can you use your results to answer the question?** Ask students to explain how they organized their data. Ask: **Did you use different tables to represent the data for temperature, precipitation, and wind speed? How did you organize the data? What kinds of bar graphs did you use? Do the data in the tables and bar graphs help you compare and analyze your data?** Have students record the results of their investigations and their conclusions in their science notebook.

  Example: We organized the data for temperature, precipitation, and wind speed in three different tables. For each table, we recorded data for each month of the season. Then we used the data in the tables to make three bar graphs. For high and low temperature, we used a double bar graph to compare the temperatures. For precipitation, we collected data for both average amounts of rain and snowfall. For wind speed, we collected monthly averages and plotted them on a bar graph.

Present and explain.

- Have groups with the same season compare and contrast their tables and graphs. Ask them to note the similarities and differences among the data. Ask: **Did you use the same reference materials? Is one source more reliable than another?** Encourage students to revisit any differences in data and conduct additional research to explore any discrepancies.

- Ask: **How did you think like a scientist while you completed this activity?** (I created graphs to analyze data to see the patterns in the weather, just like a scientist would do.)

ELABORATE

- Extend the investigation by having students collaborate in comparing their data with the data from a different season. For example, have students compare data for winter and summer, for spring and fall, for spring and summer, or for fall and winter. Have students note and describe the different patterns for temperature, wind speed, and precipitation.

- Ask students to use their data to make predictions about weather for the upcoming seasons. Ask: **Based on data, what do you predict the weather might be like in June? About how much rain do you expect there will be? How many inches of snow might you predict there will be in January? What month of the year do you expect will be the coldest? The warmest?**

EVALUATE

Check to make sure students have organized their data into tables and bar graphs in their science notebook. Then ask students these questions. Have them record the answers in their science notebook.

1. **APPLY** **What is the temperature range for your chosen season? How can you find out?** (Answers will vary depending on the data collected. Students should subtract the highest average temperature from the lowest average temperature to find the range.)

2. **EXPLAIN** **Did you find any patterns between temperature and precipitation? Explain.** (Answers will vary depending on the data students collect.)

3. **COMPARE** **When comparing your data to those of other seasons, did you notice any patterns of change from season to season?** (Answers will vary depending on the data students collect. Patterns of change should generally show warmer temperatures in summer and cooler temperatures in winter. Patterns of precipitation will vary depending on the climate of your area. Some areas may experience rainy or dry seasons.)

RUBRICS

Teacher Rubric Use the scale descriptions to guide your assessment of the student's work. Assess each item separately, and then decide on one overall score, using the following scale:

4: Student performs with thorough understanding.

3: Student performs with adequate understanding.

2: Student performs with basic understanding.

1: Student performs with limited understanding.

Rubric	Scale			
The student planned and conducted an investigation to organize data that could serve as the basis to answer the question.	4	3	2	1
The student collected data for average temperatures, precipitation, and wind speed.	4	3	2	1
The student constructed tables and bar graphs to display the different weather data.	4	3	2	1
The student compared weather data with other groups and presented their data, describing the typical weather patterns.	4	3	2	1
Overall Score	4	3	2	1

Student Rubric Have students complete a self-evaluation similar to that shown below.

Rubric	Yes	Not Yet
1. I can plan an investigation and carry out the steps.		
2. I can gather data and organize my findings in tables and bar graphs.		
3. I can analyze my results and compare my data with other groups.		
4. I can communicate my results, using evidence from my investigation to describe weather conditions.		

PHYSICAL SCIENCE
Forces and Interactions

LIFE SCIENCE
Structure, Function, and Information Processing

EARTH SCIENCE
Weather and Climate

Climate

NEXT GENERATION SCIENCE STANDARDS | DISCIPLINARY CORE IDEAS

ESS2.D: Weather and Climate Climate describes a range of an area's typical weather conditions and the extent to which those conditions vary over years. (3-ESS2-2)

Objectives **Students will be able to:**
- Define *climate*.
- Differentiate between weather and climate.
- Explore the different climate zones of the United States.

Science Vocabulary
climate

ENGAGE
Tap Prior Knowledge

- To introduce the concept of climate zones, display a map of the United States. Say: **Imagine that you will be visiting three different friends in the middle of December. Your friends live in Texas, southern Florida, and Ohio.** Then have a volunteer point to each state on the map. Ask: **What type of outdoor clothing should you pack to visit each friend?** (Most students will realize that December will be a colder month in each location. However, guide students to conclude that they would need to pack much warmer, heavier clothes for their visit to Ohio than for their trips to Florida and Texas.)

EXPLORE
Preview the Lesson

- Have students study the map and the locations of the cities on pages 132–133. Ask: **What do you think you will be learning in this lesson?** (Students may say that they will be learning about climate and climate zones in the United States.)

Set a Purpose and Read

- Have students read in order to explain what climate is and to describe differences in climate in the United States.
- Have students read pages 132–133.

EXPLAIN
Differentiate Between Weather and Climate

- Point out the vocabulary term *climate*. Ask: **Are weather and climate the same things?** (No.) **What is weather?** (Weather describes what the conditions of the air outside are like at a certain time and place.) **What is climate?** (Climate is the general pattern of the weather in an area over a long period of time.) Ask: **In your own words, what is the difference between weather and climate?** (Possible answer: Weather can change quickly over hours, days, and weeks. Climate is the cycle of similar weather patterns year after year.) **Use an example to explain the difference between weather and climate.** (Possible answer: The weather today is cold and rainy. Many clouds are in the sky. However, rain is rare where we live and most days are clear. So, although the current weather is cold and rainy, we live in a dry climate.)

Describe Four Climate Zones in the United States

- Point out the map key on page 133. Ask: **What does this map key show?** (different climate regions in the United States) Point out the different colors on the map key and what type of climate they stand for. Explain that when a climate is humid, it means there is a lot of moisture in the air. Ask: **What type of weather might you expect when it is humid out?** (Possible answer: rain, sleet, hail, snow, fog; some students may suggest that humid air can feel thick and wet against the skin.)
- Call students' attention to the information and map on page 132. Ask: **How would you describe the average high and low temperatures for Portland, Oregon? Are the temperatures hot, cold, or warm?** (Students may say the temperatures range between warm and cold.) **How much rain does the city get?** (about 92 centimeters, or 36 inches) **How would you describe Portland's climate?** (It is mild and rainy, or humid.)

- Say: **Now study the climate information for Yuma, Arizona.** Ask: **Based on the average temperatures and precipitation, how does the climate compare with the climate in Portland?** (It is warmer, and there is much less rain.) **How would you describe the climate of Yuma?** (It is a hot and dry climate.)

- Say: **Study the climate information for Syracuse, New York.** Ask: **According to the map key, what kind of climate does this city have?** (warm summers and no dry season) Say: **Study the climate information for St. Petersburg, Florida.** Ask: **What kind of climate does this city have?** (humid and mild) Ask: **Which city gets more precipitation?** (St. Petersburg) **Why do you think that St. Petersburg gets more precipitation?** (Possible answer: St. Petersburg is along the Gulf Coast. Water evaporating from the ocean may make the weather much more humid and cause more precipitation than what Syracuse experiences.)

ELABORATE

Extend Your Thinking About Climate

Have students locate your area on the map and use the map key to identify the climate region. Ask students to write a description of the climate of your area based on their own experiences. Students should consider whether temperatures are hot, mild, or cold and the amount of precipitation your state gets, including rain and snow. Encourage students to draw pictures that illustrate their climate descriptions. Invite students to share and discuss their descriptions.

Find Out More About Climate

Step 1: Tell students that many different kinds of climate zones, such as tropical wet, tropical dry, tundra, semiarid, arid, subarctic, and ice, exist all over the world. Have students use a dictionary to learn about these terms.

Step 2: If time permits, have them choose a climate zone and conduct research to describe the temperatures, average precipitation, and where in the world the climate zone is found.

EVALUATE

Have students record their answers to the Wrap It Up questions in their science notebook.

Wrap It Up!

1. **DEFINE** **What is climate?** (Climate is the general weather pattern in an area over a long period of time.)

2. **DESCRIBE** **What is the climate like in much of Florida?** (Florida has a humid climate with hot summers and warm winters.)

3. **INTERPRET MAPS** **What is the climate like in your area?** (Answers will depend on your location. Help students locate your area on the map.)

PHYSICAL SCIENCE
Forces and Interactions

LIFE SCIENCE
Structure, Function, and Information Processing

EARTH SCIENCE
Weather and Climate

DIFFERENTIATED INSTRUCTION

Extra Support Provide students with a word bank that includes the following terms and phrases: *clouds, humidity, precipitation, wind speed, temperature, lightning, fog, changes quickly,* and *repeats year after year.* Have students use the terms and phrases to complete a Venn diagram that differentiates between weather and climate.

Challenge Ask students to do the same activity as described above, but do not provide a word bank and let students determine the type of graphic organizer they will use.

READING CONNECTION

Use Maps, Photos, and Text

Use information gained from illustrations (e.g., maps, photographs) and the words in a text to demonstrate understanding of the text (e.g., where, when, why, and how key events occur).

Guide students in determining how the map, photos, and text on pages 132–133 help them understand the different climate zones in the United States. For example, in the EXPLAIN section as you compare and contrast the different climate zones, make sure students use information gained from the main text, map, photos, and captions to demonstrate understanding of climate regions in the United States.

NATIONAL GEOGRAPHIC LEARNING | **Think Like a Scientist**

Obtain and Combine Information

NEXT GENERATION SCIENCE STANDARDS | PERFORMANCE EXPECTATION
3-ESS2-2. Obtain and combine information to describe climates in different regions of the world.

Objectives **Students will be able to:**
- Obtain and combine information to describe climates in different regions of the world.
- Analyze the information to draw conclusions about climates.

CLASSROOM MANAGEMENT

Time 40 minutes

Teaching Tips Organize the class into pairs or groups of 3. Encourage students to work together to identify patterns shown on the map.

What to Expect Students will analyze the map and accompanying information to identify and describe climate patterns in different regions around the world. Students should note that each box pertains to a different country with data that describe its average temperature patterns and precipitation.

ENGAGE
Tap Prior Knowledge

Ask students to think about the lessons they have read so far in this unit. Ask: **In what ways does weather change from day to day?** (Weather changes include changes in temperature, wind speed and direction, air pressure, and amount of precipitation.) **What is the difference between weather and climate?** (Weather describes the conditions in the air at a certain time and place. Climate is the pattern of weather in an area over a long period of time.) **What is the climate like in our area?** (Answers will vary but should reflect general seasonal weather patterns of temperature and precipitation.)

EXPLORE
Preview the Lesson

- Call attention to the main heading on page 134. Ask: **What are some different ways you have learned to obtain and combine information?** (Possible answers: by looking information up in reference materials such as almanacs and on the Internet, by combining data in charts and tables, and by representing data in graphs such as bar graphs) Tell students that in this lesson, they will apply what they have learned in order to compare the climates of different countries around the world.

EXPLAIN
Analyze the Map

- After students have read through pages 134–135, call attention to the map. Ask: **What does the map illustrate?** (the world) Then point out the map key, and ask: **What does the map key show?** (It shows the different climate regions of the world.) Engage students in using the map key by asking questions such as, **What climate region is represented by the light green color?** (humid mild climate) **What is represented by the dark green color?** (humid warm climate)

- Next, call attention to the various boxes surrounding the map, and point out that they represent cities in different countries around the world. Ask: **How can you tell the climate for each of these cities?** (Each picture has a line that leads to that city's location on the map. Each location falls within a colored zone, which indicates the type of climate there.) Point out that the colors of the caption boxes for each city match the climate region colors identified in the map key. Ask: **What is the climate of Oulu, Finland? Explain.** (It has a climate with cool summers and a dry season. The line from the box leads to the purple area on the world map. The key for purple tells the climate.) **What other city has a similar climate?** (Magadan, Russia)

- Have groups work independently to compare and contrast the different climates represented on the map. Suggest that they write a description of the climate of each city. Then aid students in making comparisons. Ask: **Which two cities have a very dry climate?** (Giza, Egypt, and Alice Springs, Australia) **How is the climate of Buenos Aires, Argentina, different from the climate of Kinshasa, DR Congo?** (Buenos Aires has a humid, mild climate, while Kinshasa has a humid, warm climate.)

- Finally, have groups analyze the data found in the boxes for each city. Ask questions such as: **Which city has the lowest average January temperature?** (Oulu, Finland) **Which city has the highest average July temperature?** (Giza, Egypt) **Which city has the highest average annual precipitation?** (Kinshasa, DR Congo) **Which city has the lowest average annual precipitation?** (Giza, Egypt)

- Ask: **How did you think like a scientist as you completed this activity?** (Possible answer: I used a map to obtain and combine information about climates around the world.)

ELABORATE

Have students further explore climate zones using Internet resources such as the NOAA (National Oceanic and Atmospheric Administration) and National Geographic websites. Have students research and write a summary in their science notebook about Earth's most extreme climates.

EVALUATE

1. **INTERPRET MAPS** **Use the map key to describe the climate of Minneapolis, Minnesota.** (It has warm summers and no dry season.)

2. **IDENTIFY** **Name two cities with similar climates. How do you know they have similar climates?** (Possible answer: Oulu and Magadan have similar climates because both are the same color on the map. The photos of these two cities also show similarities in climate.)

3. **CONTRAST** **How are climates near the equator different from climates closer to the poles?** (Climates near the equator are warmer than climates closer to the poles.)

SCIENCE AND ENGINEERING PRACTICES

Obtaining, Evaluating, and Communicating Information

- Explain to students that many scientists get information from multiple sources. Ask: **If you wanted to get more, reliable information about one of these cities, where would you look?** (Answers will vary, but consider the reliability of the source in the students' answers.)

CROSSCUTTING CONCEPTS

Patterns

- Say: **Patterns of change can be used to make predictions.** Ask: **What patterns of change did you notice as you moved from the cities in the north and south parts of the map toward the equator?** (Possible answer: The temperature appears to change from cool to warm as you get closer to the equator.)

PHYSICAL SCIENCE
Forces and Interactions

LIFE SCIENCE
Structure, Function, and Information Processing

EARTH SCIENCE
Weather and Climate

Weather Hazards

NEXT GENERATION SCIENCE STANDARDS | DISCIPLINARY CORE IDEAS
ESS3.B: Natural Hazards A variety of natural hazards result from natural processes. Humans cannot eliminate natural hazards but can take steps to reduce their impacts. (3-ESS3-1)

Objectives **Students will be able to:**
- Identify and describe a variety of natural hazards such as thunderstorms, hurricanes, and floods.
- Describe some of the impacts of natural hazards.

ENGAGE

Tap Prior Knowledge

- Ask students who have experienced a severe weather event such as a thunderstorm to describe what happened during the weather event and how the weather changed. Use students' responses to initiate a discussion about severe or hazardous weather.

EXPLORE

Preview the Lesson

- Have students read the main heading and view the photographs on pages 136–137. Ask: **What do you think you will be learning about in this lesson?** (Students may say that they will be learning about different kinds of weather hazards and how they affect the environment and people.)

Set a Purpose and Read

- Have students read in order to identify weather hazards and their impact on humans.
- Have students read pages 136–137.

EXPLAIN

Define Weather Hazards

- Write the word *hazard* on the board, and ask students what it means. Explain that a hazard is something that might be dangerous or pose a risk to people's safety. Ask: **What are two types of storms that can cause hazards to property and harm people?** (thunderstorms and hurricanes)

Describe Weather Hazards from Hurricanes and Thunderstorms

- Write the word *thunderstorm* on the board, and draw a line to separate the two words that make up the compound word. Ask: **Why do we call this kind of storm a thunderstorm?** (Loud noises called thunder caused by lightning occur during this kind of storm.) **What other kinds of hazards can occur during thunderstorms?** (Possible answer: flooding from heavy rain during the storm) **What makes lightning and floods hazardous to people?** (Possible answer: Lightning can strike a person causing injury; it can start fires if it strikes a house or trees. Floods can wash away homes and cause other kinds of damage to property and land.)

- Ask: **What kinds of hazards occur during a hurricane?** (Possible answer: strong winds, heavy rains, flooding) Tell students that a hurricane is a storm that forms over oceans and has winds over 119 kilometers per hour (74 mph). Hurricanes are categorized by their wind speed. The faster the wind speed, the more dangerous is the storm. Then, call attention to the photo of the roller coaster on page 135. Explain to students that in October 2012, one of the most powerful hurricanes to hit the United States struck the Northeast Coast. Hurricane Sandy was the largest Atlantic Ocean storm on record, causing massive flooding and widespread destruction of homes and beachfront properties. Ask: **How can people protect themselves from such a storm?** (Possible answer: They can evacuate, or leave the area.)

ELABORATE

Research Hurricane Sandy

 Invite interested students to find out more about Hurricane Sandy. Encourage students to find out how the storm developed and its aftermath. Encourage students to use graphics in their research, such as a map that shows the path of the storm and photos of the damage it caused. Have students describe the precautions that people took to stay safe from the storm. Display students' research for other students to share and discuss.

Find Out More About Hurricane Preparedness

 Tell students that people cannot stop severe weather, but they can be prepared when it strikes. Ask students to come up with a severe weather plan for their family, including an evacuation plan and a disaster supplies kit if their home loses power, water, gas, and phone services. Encourage students to portray their evacuation plans and disaster kits with colorful posters.

EVALUATE

 Have students record their answers to the Wrap It Up questions in their science notebook.

Wrap It Up!

1. **IDENTIFY** **Name two types of hazardous weather.** (thunderstorms and hurricanes)

2. **EXPLAIN** **Why are hurricanes hazardous?** (They bring high winds that can damage property and heavy rains that can cause flooding.)

3. **INFER** **Look at the large photo. What could this type of weather do to houses built along a beach?** (Students should infer that a storm that is strong enough to cause damage to a pier as shown would also be strong enough to damage or destroy houses built along a beach.)

TEACHING WITH TECHNOLOGY

Describing Weather Hazards

Project the lesson on a whiteboard. Ask one student to circle two weather hazards. (thunderstorms, hurricanes) Ask other students to underline phrases that explain the effects of each weather hazard. Have students draw arrows from each of the effects to connect it with the hazards (hurricanes: cause water to rise in land areas, floods damage property, strong winds; thunderstorms: flooding, lightning can damage property)

READING CONNECTION

Describe the Connection

Describe the logical connection between particular sentences and paragraphs in a text (e.g., comparison, cause/effect, first/second/third in a sequence).

Guide students in describing the cause-and-effect relationships in the text. For example, in the EXPLAIN section as you examine the hazards of thunderstorms and hurricanes, help students understand that the hurricane or thunderstorm is the cause. The damage that results from the storm is the effect. Explain that there can be more than one effect for a given cause. Have students find and describe cause-and-effect relationships in the text, for example: *When hurricanes reach the shore, they can cause water to rise into land areas that are normally dry; trees can bend and break;* and *buildings can be damaged by the force of a hurricane's winds.*

PHYSICAL SCIENCE
Forces and Interactions

LIFE SCIENCE
Structure, Function, and Information Processing

EARTH SCIENCE
Weather and Climate

Reducing the Impact of Flooding

NEXT GENERATION SCIENCE STANDARDS | DISCIPLINARY CORE IDEAS

ESS3.B: Natural Hazards A variety of natural hazards result from natural processes. Humans cannot eliminate natural hazards but can take steps to reduce their impacts. (3-ESS3-1)

Objective Students will be able to:
- Describe how humans can reduce the impact of flooding.

Science Vocabulary
flood, levee, dam

ENGAGE
Tap Prior Knowledge

- Ask students if they remember a time when there was a very heavy rain. Ask: **How did the rain affect the land or your home?** Use students' responses to initiate a discussion about how heavy rains impact their homes. (Some students may say that rainwater leaked into basements or low parts of the home; streams may have overflowed into yards; they may have observed rainwater rushing down streets or in gutters; small plants or other objects may have washed away.)

EXPLORE
Explore the Impact of Flooding

- Have students look at the large photo on pages 138–139. Ask probing questions to encourage exploration. For example, ask: **Without looking at the caption, what would you say happened in the large photo?**

- Have students share their answers. Some students may say that a storm caused water to flood the homes in the pictures. Some students may suggest that a hurricane is responsible for the flooding.

Set a Purpose and Read

- Have students read in order to learn how humans can reduce the impact of flooding.

- Have students read pages 138–139.

EXPLAIN
Describe Events That Cause Floods

- Call students' attention to the word *flood,* and have a student read its definition aloud. Ask: **What are some different events that cause floods to happen?** (short, heavy rains; rains that fall for a long time; and hurricanes) **What are two ways that hurricanes can cause flooding?** (Heavy rains can fall over land, and winds can push ocean water onto land.)

- Explain to students that in 2005, Hurricane Katrina struck several states that lie on the Gulf of Mexico. In New Orleans, Louisiana, the powerful surges from the gulf waters caused several levees to break, resulting in widespread flooding that damaged or destroyed thousands of homes. Ask: **How do you think people might be more prepared for such a storm in the future?** (Possible answer: People can build stronger dams and levees; they can build houses on higher ground.)

Contrast Levees and Dams

- Point out the vocabulary words *levee* and *dam.* Tell students that the word *levee* comes from the French word *lever,* which means "to lift." Ask: **What is the main difference between a levee and a dam?** (A levee is an earthen wall; a dam is a concrete wall built across a river.) **How are levees and dams alike?** (Both are built to control the flow of water.) **Why are sandbags useful for controlling floods?** (They can block the water for a short period of flooding.)

- Point out the photos in the small boxes. Ask: **How might the levee protect the house it surrounds?** (It forms a barrier to keep water from flowing into the house.) **How might an expandable tube protect a home from floods?** (The tube expands and keeps water from entering the house under the door.)

ELABORATE

Find Out More About Levees

 Invite interested students to find out more about how engineers rebuilt the levees in New Orleans, Louisiana, after Hurricane Katrina. Students' research should include a description of the damage caused by the hurricane and why the levees failed. They should conclude their report with information as to what is being done to modify the levees now in New Orleans.

Research Dams

 Step 1: Ask students to research dams in your state, where they are located, and how they are used to control flooding. Tell students that many dams are built along the narrow part of a river and may change the shape of the river they control. Students may also be interested in researching the world's largest dams.

Step 2: If time permits, allow students to present their findings with graphics such as photos, maps, and diagrams.

EVALUATE

 Have students record their answers to the Wrap It Up questions in their science notebook.

Wrap It Up!

1. **CAUSE AND EFFECT** **What causes flooding?** (short, heavy rain; rain for a long time; and hurricanes)

2. **EXPLAIN** **How do people try to reduce the damage caused by flooding?** (People build levees and dams, and construct barriers to keep the floodwaters away.)

PHYSICAL SCIENCE
Forces and Interactions

LIFE SCIENCE
Structure, Function, and Information Processing

EARTH SCIENCE
Weather and Climate

ELL SUPPORT

Floods, Dams, and Levees

Beginning Ask either/or questions to help students compare levees and dams. For example, ask: **Are levees built with concrete or earth materials?** (earth materials)

Intermediate Provide sentence frames to help students compare lesson vocabulary. For example: *Dams are built with (concrete). Levees are built with (earth materials).*

Advanced Have students use sentence stems to write about lesson concepts. For example: *Hurricanes cause flooding because …. Levees reduce the impact of flooding by…. Dams reduce the impact of flooding by….*

READING CONNECTION

Describe the Connection

Describe the logical connection between particular sentences and paragraphs in a text (e.g., comparison, cause/effect, first/second/third in a sequence).

Guide students in describing the cause-and-effect relationships in the text. For example, in the EXPLAIN section as you examine the impact of floods and hurricanes, help students understand that a hurricane's wind or heavy rain is the cause. The damage that results is the effect. Have students find and describe cause-and-effect relationships in the text. For example: *Both the heavy rains and the wind pushing ocean water onto land cause floods during hurricanes.* Point out to students that in this example, more than one cause (heavy rains and wind) can have the same effect (flooding).

Reducing the Impact of Wind

NEXT GENERATION SCIENCE STANDARDS | DISCIPLINARY CORE IDEAS
ESS3.B: Natural Hazards A variety of natural hazards result from natural processes. Humans cannot eliminate natural hazards but can take steps to reduce their impacts. (3-ESS3-1)

Objectives Students will be able to:
- Describe how humans can reduce the impact of wind.

ENGAGE

Tap Prior Knowledge

- Ask students if they remember a time when there was a very strong wind. Ask: **How did the wind affect the land or your home?** Use students' responses to initiate a discussion about how strong winds impact their homes. (Some students may say that a very strong wind blew branches off trees or pieces of tiles or shingles off a roof, blew around small objects such as trash cans and plant containers, or caused fences or other structures to collapse.)

EXPLORE

Explore the Impact of Wind

- Have students look at the large photo on pages 140–141. Ask probing questions to encourage exploration. For example, ask: **Without looking at the caption, what would you say happened in the large photo?**

- Have students share their answers. Some students may say that strong winds from a storm caused the damage to the homes. Some students may suggest that a hurricane or tornado is responsible for the damage.

Set a Purpose and Read

- Have students read in order to learn how humans can reduce the impact of wind.

- Have students read pages 140–141.

EXPLAIN

Compare and Contrast Events That Cause Wind Damage

- Ask students to think about what they learned from the previous lesson about weather hazards that can cause damage. Ask: **Which of these hazards might cause serious damage from winds?** (hurricanes) Ask: **What kind of damage might a hurricane cause?** (Strong winds cause damage to homes and break tree limbs; flood waters damage property.) Remind students that hurricanes are storms that form over the ocean. Ask: **How do you think a hurricane is different from a tornado?** (Accept all reasonable answers.) Explain to students that tornadoes are associated with large thunderstorms. A tornado is a narrow funnel of rotating wind, whereas a hurricane is a circular storm that may extend for hundreds of miles. Hurricanes move relatively slowly, and lose strength when they move over land. Tornadoes, however, move much faster and may cause extensive destruction in a matter of minutes.

Describe How to Reduce the Impact of Wind

- Ask: **How can doors and windows be protected against the strong winds of tornadoes and hurricanes?** (They can be made of special glass that resists breaking.) Ask: **What can people do to protect themselves when a storm is approaching?** (They can close the doors; they can stay in the basement or in a place that has no windows. They can stay in a storm shelter.) Ask: **What can people do to protect their homes from wind?** (They can build roofs that slope on all sides. They can attach their roofs with nails instead of staples.)

PHYSICAL SCIENCE
Forces and Interactions

LIFE SCIENCE
Structure, Function, and Information Processing

EARTH SCIENCE
Weather and Climate

ELABORATE

Find Out More About Tornado-Resistant Homes

 Invite interested students to find out more about ways to make homes in tornado-prone areas safer. Have students use the Internet or other resources to research ways that the walls, roof, windows, and doors of a home can be made to withstand strong winds. Encourage students to illustrate their research with diagrams and photos.

Extend Your Thinking About Tornado Safety

 Step 1: Ask students to think about different situations they might be in as a tornado approaches. Suggest students use various resources and talk to family members about how they can protect themselves in the following situations: 1) if they are in their home; 2) if they are outside in open areas such as a field; 3) if they are in a car; 4) if they are at school.

Step 2: If time permits, have volunteers share and discuss their findings.

EVALUATE

 Have students record their answers to the Wrap It Up questions in their science notebook.

Wrap It Up!

1. **IDENTIFY** **Name two storms with strong winds.** (tornadoes and hurricanes)

2. **EXPLAIN** **Tell how people can protect property from strong winds.** (People can use wind-resistant glass and roof tiles held with nails rather than staples to make safer buildings. They can also build roofs with four sloping sides.)

3. **DESCRIBE** **How can people protect themselves during a storm with strong winds?** (People can go to the basement, to a closet or other small interior room without windows, or to a storm shelter to protect themselves from strong winds.)

DIFFERENTIATED INSTRUCTION

Extra Support Have students make a two-column chart comparing the impact of wind with the impact of water. Guide them in filling out the similarities and differences between the causes and impacts of each.

Challenge Have students write a radio weather report announcing a hurricane or tornado warning. The report should explain to listeners why the weather event is happening, how people can stay safe, and what to expect. Invite students to "broadcast" their reports by reading them aloud.

READING CONNECTION

Ask and Answer Questions to Demonstrate Understanding

Ask and answer questions to demonstrate understanding of a text, referring explicitly to the text as the basis for the answers.

Guide students in asking and answering questions to demonstrate understanding of a text. For example, in the EXPLAIN section as you ask students what people can do to reduce the impact of wind damage, have students point to the text, illustrations, or captions where they found their answers. Ask students if they have any other questions about the dangers of wind or how people can protect themselves from the impact of wind.

141

Reducing the Impact of Lightning

NEXT GENERATION SCIENCE STANDARDS | DISCIPLINARY CORE IDEAS
ESS3.B: Natural Hazards A variety of natural hazards result from natural processes. Humans cannot eliminate natural hazards but can take steps to reduce their impacts. (3-ESS3-1)

Objective **Students will be able to:**
- Describe how humans can reduce the impact of lightning.

ENGAGE

Tap Prior Knowledge

- Ask students to describe any experiences they have had with lightning. Ask: **When are you most likely to see lightning?** (Students may say that they are most likely to see lightning during a thunderstorm, even though lightning and thunder can occur without rain.)

EXPLORE

Explore the Impact of Lightning

- Have students look at the large photo on pages 142–143. Ask probing questions to encourage exploration. For example, ask: **How would you describe the lightning you see on the page?**

- Have students share their answers. Students may suggest that the lightning appears like spidery flashes in the sky. Other students may say that the lightning extends from the sky to the buildings below.

Set a Purpose and Read

- Have students read in order to learn how humans can reduce the impact of lightning.

- Have students read pages 142–143.

EXPLAIN

Describe How Lightning Happens

- After students have read page 142, ask: **What is lightning?** (It is a bright electrical discharge.) **Where does lightning happen?** (It can flash between parts of a cloud, from the ground to a cloud, or from a cloud to the ground.) Point out to students that lightning causes thunder during a thunderstorm, but that it does not necessarily rain when either lightning or thunder occur.

Explain the Impact of Lightning

- Ask: **Why is it important to stay safe from lightning?** (Lightning can cause fires and kill or injure people.) **What is the best way to stay safe from lightning when you are indoors?** (Stay away from windows and water; don't use electronic equipment.) **Why do you think it is important to stay away from electronic equipment?** (Possible answer: Lightning is an electrical discharge. If lightning strikes a house, the electricity could travel through electronic equipment.) **Why is it important to stay away from tall objects such as trees when you are outside during a lightning storm?** (The lightning could strike the tree, causing it to catch on fire; the lightning could travel down the trunk of a tree and injure a person standing under or near the tree.)

Describe How to Reduce the Impact of Lightning

- Ask: **What is one way that people can protect their homes from lightning?** (by using a lightning rod) Call attention to the small photo and captions at the top of page 143. Ask: **How does a lightning rod work?** (The lightning strikes a metal rod, then travels down a wire to the ground. The electricity from the lightning goes into the ground.) **Why do you think that the lightning travels down the metal rod to the wire?** (Possible answer: Metal is a material that conducts electricity—that means that electricity will move through it.)

ELABORATE

Find Out More About Lightning

 Ask students if they are familiar with Benjamin Franklin. Some students may know that Franklin was one of the founding fathers of the United States. Tell students that Franklin's ideas about lightning and electricity led him to invent the lightning rod. Ask students to find out more about Franklin's invention of the lightning rod.

Research Lightning

 Invite interested students to work with a partner to find out interesting facts about lightning. Ask students to present their information in an illustrated booklet.

Extend Your Thinking About Lightning

 Students may have noticed that during a thunderstorm, they often hear thunder a number of seconds after seeing a flash of lightning. Tell students they can calculate the approximate distance of a thunderstorm by counting the seconds between seeing the lightning and hearing the thunder, and then dividing the number of seconds by five. The result is the approximate distance of the thunderstorm in miles. Have students calculate the distance of a thunderstorm if thunder is heard ten seconds after seeing lightning. (2 miles away)

EVALUATE

 Have students record their answers to the Wrap It Up questions in their science notebook.

Wrap It Up!

1. **DESCRIBE Why is lightning dangerous?** (Lightning can cause fires and harm people.)

2. **EXPLAIN What should you do if you are caught outdoors during a thunderstorm?** (Stay away from water and from tall objects in the area.)

3. **INFER Many people unplug their electronic equipment when a thunderstorm is predicted. Why do you think this is so?** (Answers will vary. Possible answer: I know that electricity travels through wires. If a home were hit by lightning, it might travel through the electric wires and harm the electronic equipment.)

An additional interactive assessment activity can be found in the Exploring Science Digital Book.

SCIENCE BACKGROUND

Lightning

Thunderstorm clouds are turbulent masses of air, water, and ice moved around by powerful winds. Ice crystals are smashed against one another, generating charges of static electricity. The top of such a cloud and the ground can become positively charged, and the bottom can become negatively charged. Lightning is electricity jumping between negatively and positively charged areas. The air around the lightning bolt is heated to temperatures that reach about 33,000°C, many times hotter than the surface of the sun. This ionizes the air and causes it to glow brightly. The sudden surge of heat also results in rapid expansion of air, creating a shock wave that results in the sounds heard as thunder.

READING CONNECTION

Describe the Connection

Describe the logical connection between particular sentences and paragraphs in a text (e.g., comparison, cause/effect, first/second/third in a sequence).

Guide students in describing a sequence in the text. For example, in the EXPLAIN section as you examine how a lightning rod works, have students describe the sequence using words such as *first, next,* and *last.* You might also ask students to reread the first paragraph on page 142 and describe the various sequences lightning can follow as it flashes. (between parts of a cloud, from the ground to a cloud, or from a cloud to the ground)

PHYSICAL SCIENCE
Forces and Interactions

LIFE SCIENCE
Structure, Function, and Information Processing

EARTH SCIENCE
Weather and Climate

Make a Claim

NEXT GENERATION SCIENCE STANDARDS | PERFORMANCE EXPECTATION

3-ESS3-1: Make a claim about the merit of a design solution that reduces the impacts of a weather-related event. [Clarification Statement: Examples of design solutions to weather-related hazards could include barriers to prevent flooding, wind resistant roofs, and lightning rods.]

Objectives Students will be able to:
- Conceptualize a house design that reduces the impacts of a weather-related event.
- Identify the merits of the design solution.

CLASSROOM MANAGEMENT

Materials *For groups of 4:* poster board; drawing materials; ruler

Time 20 minutes for planning; 20 minutes to draw designs; 15 minutes to present designs and solutions; 20 minutes to evaluate feedback: 20 minutes to make revised designs and solutions

Advance Preparation Find several photos of homes that have been damaged by hurricanes, such as Hurricane Katrina, Hurricane Andrew, and Hurricane Sandy. Post the photos on a bulletin board, or project them on a whiteboard. Photos should show various types of damage. Before and after images of structures are particularly useful for identifying elements of structures that fail in extreme conditions.

Teaching Tips Students should generate the details of their designs by themselves. Coach students through the planning process without instructing them about specific details to include. In order to meet the performance expectation, students must articulate the merit of the design solution themselves, so their designs must be detailed enough to support their claims.

What to Expect Students will design a house that has solutions for protecting it from hurricane damage. They will explain why their solutions are good ones. They will rebut any challenges to their claim using scientific facts they have learned in this series of lessons, as well as additional information they find during their research.

ENGAGE

Set the scene.

- Ask students to recall what they have learned about the impact different weather events can have on people. Say: **Describe some severe weather events and the effects they have on people.** (Possible answers: Flooding from storms such as hurricanes can wash away homes; strong winds from storms such as hurricanes and tornadoes can destroy homes and hurt people; lightning can strike and cause fires.) Discuss what students remember about how people can reduce the impact of such weather events. You may wish to direct them to the text on pages 136–143 to skim the text and photos. (Humans can build dams and levees.)

Define the problem.

 Have a volunteer read the introductory paragraph on page 144. Remind students that an engineer is a person who applies scientific principles to solve problems. Ask: **Why are engineers concerned with designing houses that can stand up to the impact of hurricanes?** (People cannot stop hurricanes from happening, but engineers can apply science to design homes to reduce the effects of hurricane winds and flooding. If homes have less damage or no damage, then people won't lose their homes due to a storm.) Have students record the problem statement in their science notebook.

EXPLORE

Find a solution.

- Have students look at the photo spread on pages 144–145 and read the caption. Ask students to describe the details in the picture. Students should note that the house is tipped over and standing in water. Ask: **What do you think happened to the people who lived in**

PHYSICAL SCIENCE
Forces and Interactions

LIFE SCIENCE
Structure, Function, and Information Processing

EARTH SCIENCE
Weather and Climate

this home? (Students may say that the people had to leave, or evacuate, the home before the storm.)

- Display a map of the United States and the surrounding ocean. Have a student locate and point to the Atlantic Ocean and the Gulf of Mexico. Tell students that most hurricanes form over the Atlantic Ocean. Some move toward land and can affect any of the states along the eastern seaboard and surrounding the Gulf of Mexico. Point out that most hurricane damage is a result of flooding and storm surges—the rise of the level of seawater along coastlines. Explain that in this lesson, students will think like an engineer and try to solve the problem of damage to homes that result from hurricanes.

- Ask: **What kinds of materials can be used to build homes that are stronger and can withstand hurricanes?** Allow groups time to discuss and share responses. (Possible answers: Homes can be built with stronger materials, special windows and doors, and specially designed roofs.)

SCIENCE AND ENGINEERING PRACTICES

Engaging in Argument from Evidence

- Remind students that they improved their designs with input from their peers. They based their solutions on evidence about the problem and evidence supporting their solution. Then ask: **What kind of research would you do or evidence would you collect to improve your design even further?** (Possible answers: I would test my design in a real storm. I would like to know what other materials are available to use in my design.)

CROSSCUTTING CONCEPTS

Cause and Effect

- Say: **Engineers know that cause-and-effect relationships are routinely identified, tested, and used to explain change.** Ask: **How did you identify a way to reduce damage caused to homes by a hurricane?** (Answers will vary depending on which problem students tried to solve. Accept reasonable design solution responses supported by evidence from the proposed design.)

- Encourage students to link concepts of cause and effect, as well as weather related hazards, with other disciplines of science. For example, in physical science, the physical properties of different materials can determine how well they stand up to external forces, such as severe storms.

These properties could include strength, flexibility, resistance to water and fire, and density.

Connections to Engineering, Technology, and Applications of Science
Influence of Engineering, Technology, and Science on Society and the Natural World

- Remind students that engineers improve existing technologies or develop new ones to increase their benefits (e.g., better artificial limbs), decrease known risks (e.g., seat belts in cars), and meet societal demands (e.g., cell phones). Ask: **What designs can you think of that meet the increased demands of people?** (Possible answers: Cars are now safer and get better gas mileage than many earlier models. Computers are faster and lighter than the original designs.)

Connections to Nature of Science
Science is a Human Endeavor

- Remind students that science affects everyday life. Ask: **What are some things you do or use in daily life that can be related to advances in science that people have made?** (Possible answers: I use forms of transportation that people developed. I might need medicine developed by scientists. I use computers, phones, and many other devices made possible by people who study science and engineering.)

Make a Claim (continued)

EXPLORE (continued)

- Ask: **How might you use different shapes in designing your homes?** Encourage students to be creative in designing their homes. Remind them that they need to consider different factors in their home designs. Point out that they are solving problems caused by floodwater, storm surges, wind, and flying objects.

- After students have agreed on a design with members of their group, direct them to draw what their house will look like in their science notebook. Have them include labels with materials and design details.

  Example: Our group will design a house that is built on stilts. The stilts will protect the house from floodwater and storm surges. The stilts will be made of steel beams. The doors will have bars to keep them closed during a storm. All of the windows will be made with shatterproof glass. The windows also will have shutters that can be closed and locked when the storm hits. The roof of the house will be made of metal and shaped to protect against the impact of strong winds.

EXPLAIN

Defend your solution.

- After groups have presented their designs to the class, allow time for students to share ideas on how to improve the designs. Encourage students to support their claim that their designs will prevent hurricane damage with evidence. Guide students by asking questions such as:

  - **What problems do your house designs solve? Does the design protect against wind? Floods? Storm surges? Flying objects?**

  - **What kinds of materials did you use in your design?**

- **How does the shape of your home help to protect it against hurricane impact?**

- **In what ways do you think your house design can be improved?**

Refine or change your solution.

- Challenge students to make changes to their designs based on feedback. When groups are satisfied with their solutions, revisit the question from the beginning of the investigation: *How can you design a house to protect it from hurricane damage?* Require students to use evidence from their reading and research to rebut any challenges to their claim that the solution they devised will help protect a house from hurricane damage.

- Have each group use its notes and drawings to present its plan and final design to the class. Encourage them to explain the features of the house and how it will withstand the impact of a hurricane.

- Ask: **How did you think like an engineer while you completed this activity?** (I worked within the constraints and used the criteria to design a possible solution to prevent hurricane damage to homes.)

ELABORATE

My science notebook Extend the investigation by having students revise their plans based on further feedback from the class. Display the designs so students can share and discuss ideas.

- Challenge student groups to use the Internet or other resources to find pictures of hurricane-resistant houses. Student groups should find at least four different examples of houses and display them on a poster. Encourage students to add captions that describe the features of the home that help it withstand the impact of storms. Have students display the posters and compare the houses to their own designs. Ask students to discuss how they might further revise their designs and solutions to improve them.

EVALUATE

 Check to make sure students have recorded solutions and design drawings in their science notebook. Then ask students these questions. Have them record the answers in their science notebook.

1. **SUMMARIZE** **What impacts from hurricanes might cause damage to a house?** (floods, storm surges, wind, flying objects)

2. **EXPLAIN** **How does the design of your house help prevent it from being damaged by hurricanes?** (Students' responses will vary based on their designs and solutions.)

3. **EVALUATE** **Do you think specially designed houses are a good solution for homes that are in your community? Explain why or why not.** (Answers will vary. Students that live in coastal communities along the eastern seaboard or Gulf Coast may say "yes" because they are more likely to be hit by a hurricane; those in more inland communities may not think they are necessary or may suggest that different types of modifications would be more useful to protect against the types of severe weather experienced in your area.)

RUBRICS

Teacher Rubric Use the scale descriptions to guide your assessment of the student's work. Assess each item separately, and then decide on one overall score, using the following scale:

4: Student performs with thorough understanding.

3: Student performs with adequate understanding.

2: Student performs with basic understanding.

1: Student performs with limited understanding.

Rubric	Scale			
The student participated in a group to design a house that could serve as the basis to answer the question.	4	3	2	1
The student drew a picture of the house design in his or her science notebook.	4	3	2	1
The student participated in evaluating the effectiveness of the design and helped revise the design based on student feedback.	4	3	2	1
The student recorded all stages of the design process, from problem to initial designs to refined designs.	4	3	2	1
Overall Score	4	3	2	1

Directions: Have students complete a self-evaluation similar to that shown below.

Rubric	Yes	Not Yet
1. I can work with my group to plan a design for a house.		
2. I can draw a picture of the design in my science notebook.		
3. I can participate with my group in deciding why my design is a good one and make changes based on group discussion.		
4. I can record all stages of the design process.		

PHYSICAL SCIENCE
Forces and Interactions

LIFE SCIENCE
Structure, Function, and Information Processing

EARTH SCIENCE
Weather and Climate

Severe-Storms Researcher

NEXT GENERATION SCIENCE STANDARDS | CONNECTION TO THE NATURE OF SCIENCE
Science is a Human Endeavor Science affects everyday life.

Objective **Students will be able to:**
- Connect the concept of weather with the career of a severe-storms researcher.

ENGAGE

Tap Prior Knowledge

- Ask students if they have seen a movie or film about a tornado such as *The Wizard of Oz*. Then ask them if they think the movie was realistic in terms of the way the storm was shown. Then ask them to consider what it would be like to be close to a storm such as a tornado. Allow time for students to share and discuss their answers. Use students' thoughts as a starting point for guiding them to understand how dangerous it is to be close to such a powerful storm.

EXPLORE

Preview the Lesson

- Call attention to the title of the lesson. Ask: **What do you think a severe-storms researcher does?** (Accept all reasonable answers. You may wish to record students' responses on the board.) Tell students they will learn more about the science career of a severe-storms researcher in this lesson.

Set a Purpose and Read

- Have students read in order to describe the career of a severe-storm researcher.
- Have students read pages 146–147.

EXPLAIN

Describe the Work of a Severe-Storms Researcher

- Write the word *severe* on the board. Ask: **What does *severe* mean?** (Answers will vary.) Tell students that *severe* describes something that is harsh or intense, such as a tornado. Then

ask: **What does a severe-storms researcher like Tim Samaras do?** (study tornadoes to learn more about their winds and air pressure) **How did Tim Samaras study tornadoes?** (He designed special equipment to study tornadoes, and he put the equipment in place to measure the force of the storm winds.)

Connect Science Topics to the Career of a Severe-Storms Researcher

- Direct students' attention to the large photo and caption on page 147. Ask: **Why is it so dangerous to study and research tornadoes?** (Possible answer: A storms researcher needs to be close enough to the storm for his or her equipment to collect readings from the storm. Tornadoes happen very quickly and are unpredictable, making it risky for researchers to get close enough to them for their equipment to be useful.)

- Ask: **What kinds of classes do you think you would need to take to become a severe-storms researcher? Explain.** (Possible answer: Students may say they would need to study earth science, weather patterns, and meteorology. A severe-storms researcher would need to know where tornadoes are likely to occur, how to stay safe from them, and how to operate the equipment used to study them.)

Find Out More

- Ask: **Is this a career you would find interesting? Why or why not?** (Allow students to share their answers. Accept all positive and negative responses.) For students who find this an interesting career, ask: **Why would you like to be a severe-storms researcher?** (Possible answer: I would like to be a severe-storms researcher because it would be interesting to study the winds to find new ways to help protect people from these storms.)

- Call attention to the photo on page 147, and have students read the caption. Ask: **Why did Tim Samaras want to study tornadoes?** (He wanted to help people by understanding storms better in order to find ways to reduce deaths and damage caused by storms.)

- Ask: **Why do you think severe-storms research is important?** (Answers will vary. Students may say that when scientists understand more about tornadoes or other severe storms, they can find ways to help people stay safe from them by building storm-resistant houses or by learning how to better track and predict the storms so people can evacuate the area.)

ELABORATE

Research Other Careers Involving Severe Storms

 Invite groups of students to research more about the career of severe-storms researcher. Students will find that a storm researcher uses equipment that measures the pressure, temperature, humidity, wind speed, and direction of tornadoes as they pass over the instruments. Researchers also use video cameras to provide visuals of the inside of a tornado funnel as it passes overhead. Ask students to find examples of videos and other visuals of tornadoes to share with the class.

Explain How Tornadoes Are Formed

 Tell students that most tornadoes over land begin in a severe thunderstorm called a supercell. Ask students to research how tornadoes are formed. They should include factors required for tornadoes to form, what a tornado looks like, and how the tornado moves over land. Encourage students to present their information using graphics, posters, or a software-generated slide show.

EVALUATE

 Ask students these questions. Have students record their answers in their science notebook.

1. **RECALL** **What is a severe-storms researcher?** (A severe-storms researcher is someone who studies tornadoes to learn more about their winds and air pressure, and to discover ways for people to be better prepared for these storms.)

2. **APPLY** **Why is the job of a severe-storms researcher a dangerous one?** (Students may say that a severe-storm researcher has to get close to a tornado; being in the direct path of a tornado could result in death as in the case of Tim Samaras.)

ELL SUPPORT

Word Study

Beginning Have students complete simple sentence frames such as, *Tim Samaras was a (severe-storms researcher). Tim Samaras wanted to learn about (tornadoes).*

Intermediate Invite students to skim the lesson and make a word web of action verbs they find, for example: *learn, help, prepare, measure, destroy.* Encourage students to draw pictures to show the action of the verbs.

Advanced Challenge pairs of students to make a crossword of nouns mentioned in the lesson, for example: *storm, tornado, wind, air pressure, equipment, researcher.* Students may use a dictionary to find definitions for each term.

READING CONNECTION

Determine the Main Idea and Details

Determine the main idea of a text; recount the key details and explain how they support the main idea.

Guide students in determining the main idea of the text and the key details that support the main idea. For example, in the EXPLAIN section as students discuss the job of a storm researcher, ask them to find one sentence in the text that describes the main idea. Remind students that the main idea is often found at or near the beginning of a paragraph. (*Tim's goal was to answer questions about tornadoes to help people better prepare for these violent storms.*) Then invite students to find key details in the text that support this main idea.

PHYSICAL SCIENCE
Forces and Interactions

LIFE SCIENCE
Structure, Function, and Information Processing

EARTH SCIENCE
Weather and Climate

Disciplinary Core Ideas Review

Next Generation Science Standards
Disciplinary Core Ideas Review

Physical Science
Forces and Interactions

PS2.A: Forces and Motion
PS2.B: Types of Interactions

Life Science
Interdependent Relationships in Ecosystems

LS2.C: Ecosystem Dynamics, Functioning, and Resilience
LS2.D: Social Interactions and Group Behavior
LS4.A: Evidence of Common Ancestry and Diversity
LS4.C: Adaptation
LS4.D: Biodiversity and Humans

Inheritance and Variation of Traits: Life Cycles and Traits

LS1.B: Growth and Development of Organisms
LS3.A: Inheritance of Traits
LS3.B: Variation of Traits
LS4.B: Natural Selection

Earth Science
Weather and Climate

ESS2.D: Weather and Climate
ESS3.B: Natural Hazards

PHYSICAL SCIENCE
Forces and Interactions

LIFE SCIENCE
Structure, Function, and Information Processing

EARTH SCIENCE
Weather and Climate

Review Questions

Physical Science Forces and Interactions

DIRECTIONS: Read each question. Then choose the best answer.

 What is the definition of a force? (PS2.A)

- (A) a push or pull
- (B) a stopped object
- (C) energy you use
- (D) an object in motion

 Which of the following does every force have? (PS2.A)

- (A) a push
- (B) a pull
- (C) strength and direction
- (D) direction and speed

 What force is Willis using to change the direction of motion of the ball? (PS2.A)

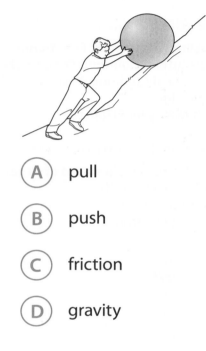

- (A) pull
- (B) push
- (C) friction
- (D) gravity

Name_____ Date _____

Physical Science   Forces and Interactions

 4 Ted pulls Alice in a wagon while Ginger pushes. Evan walks beside them. Which of them is not placing a force on the wagon? (PS2.A)

(A) Ted

(B) Alice

(C) Ginger

(D) Evan

 5 Alicia and Samantha are playing tug-of-war, but neither is moving. What are they demonstrating? (PS2.A)

(A) push and pull

(B) unbalanced pulls

(C) gravity and friction

(D) balanced forces

 6 When Ted, Alice, and Ginger pull Alicia, Samantha, and Juan over in a game of tug-of-war, what are they demonstrating? (PS2.A)

(A) gravity and friction

(B) unbalanced forces

(C) pushes and friction

(D) balanced forces

 7 When a batter swings and hits a pitched ball, how is he or she using a force on the ball? (PS2.A)

(A) to maintain the speed of the ball

(B) to pull the bat to the ball

(C) to change the direction of the ball

(D) to increase the pull of gravity on the ball

Physical Science   Forces and Interactions

8 **Which force can you observe if you ride in a horse-drawn carriage?** (PS2.A)

(A)   The horse pushes the carriage from behind.

(B)   The horse uses a pull.

(C)   Gravity keeps the carriage rolling.

(D)   Balanced forces move the horse.

9 **How does a boy on a playground swing demonstrate regular motion?** (PS2.A)

(A)   The swing moves back and forth in a predictable pattern.

(B)   The boy swings higher when he is pushed.

(C)   Balanced and unbalanced forces cause his movement.

(D)   The boy is using a force to move the swing.

10 **What can you tell by watching a merry-go-round in motion?** (PS2.A)

(A)   Unbalanced forces will cause the ride to instantly stop spinning.

(B)   The direction it is spinning will suddenly change.

(C)   Gravity will make it stop unexpectedly.

(D)   Its next spin will be in the same direction as its last several spins.

11 **Isaac is leaning against a small apple tree. The tree bends slightly when his back pushes it. What force prevents Isaac from falling over backwards?** (PS2.B)

(A)   Gravity will prevent him from falling.

(B)   Magnetic force.

(C)   The force of Isaac pushing the tree is balanced by the tree pushing back on Isaac.

(D)   The tree cannot hold him, and must break soon.

Physical Science Forces and Interactions

12 A pen, a notebook, and a glass of water are sitting on a desk. Which objects are exerting forces? (PS2.B)

- A the pen, the notebook, the glass, the water, and the desk

- B the pen, the notebook, the glass, and the water

- C the pen, the notebook, and the glass

- D the desk

13 When two students arm wrestle, how do they apply forces? (PS2.B)

- A They change gravity.

- B They use attractive forces.

- C They are in contact.

- D They apply forces from a distance.

14 A bike is parked on the sidewalk. The kickstand keeps the bike from falling over. What can you tell about the kickstand? (PS2.B)

- A The sidewalk and the kickstand are not in contact.

- B The sidewalk and the kickstand are exerting forces on each other.

- C The bike is not leaning on the kickstand.

- D The kickstand is pushing harder than gravity is pulling the bike.

15 Which sets of magnetic poles will attract each other? (PS2.B)

- A N, S

- B N, N

- C S, S

- D E, W

Physical Science Forces and Interactions

16 Marcel holds a bar magnet very close to a paper clip. What happens? (PS2.B)

(A) The paper clip is repelled from the magnet.

(B) The paper clip is pushed away from the magnet.

(C) The paper clip is attracted to and moves to the magnet.

(D) The paper clip has balanced forces acting on it when it moves to the magnet.

17 Willa places the same poles of two bar magnets near each other. What will the magnetic force do? (PS2.B)

(A) attract the magnets to each other

(B) repel the magnets from each other

(C) cause the magnets to spin

(D) become an unbalanced net zero force

18 Which of the following can make the magnetic force between two magnets weaker? (PS2.B)

(A) putting electric current through them

(B) shaping them into horseshoe magnets

(C) rubbing them against wool cloth

(D) moving them farther apart

19 How are electromagnets different from other magnets? (PS2.B)

(A) Electromagnets are smaller.

(B) Electromagnets are bigger.

(C) Electromagnets can be turned on and off.

(D) Electromagnets can pick up anything.

Physical Science   Forces and Interactions

 20 Nigel discovered he could stick a balloon to a wall after rubbing it on a wool sweater. What is the most likely reason this is happening? (PS2.B)

- (A) gravity

- (B) static electricity

- (C) magnetic attraction

- (D) The balloon is repelled by the ground.

 21 What can you conclude about two balloons that seem to push away from each other without touching? (PS2.B)

- (A) They both have north poles.

- (B) One has a north pole, and the other has a south pole.

- (C) They have the same charge.

- (D) They have opposite charges.

 22 Which of the following can you demonstrate using a balloon charged with static electricity and pieces of tissue paper? (PS2.B)

- (A) Electric forces between objects do not require that the objects be in contact.

- (B) Electric forces between objects require that the objects be in contact.

- (C) Magnetic forces between objects do not require that the objects be in contact.

- (D) Magnetic forces between objects require that the objects be in contact.

Name_____ Date _____

Review Questions

Life Science Interdependent Relationships in Ecosystems

DIRECTIONS: Read each question. Then choose the best answer.

1 **Which is true about the effect of fire on a forest ecosystem?** (LS2.C)

(A) Everything that is burned dies.

(B) All of the animals in the ecosystem die.

(C) New growth occurs afterward.

(D) Animals are driven away for good.

2 **Which natural physical event might cause animals to move from their environment?** (LS2.C)

(A) drought

(B) average rainfall

(C) building construction

(D) normal temperatures

3 **A dormouse becomes inactive in the winter. Its body does not use much energy. What is this called?** (LS2.C)

(A) feeding

(B) reproduction

(C) hibernation

(D) survival

4 **How does the construction of buildings affect the ecosystem for animals living there?** (LS2.C)

(A) It increases the food available to the animals.

(B) It increases the space available to the animals.

(C) It decreases the space and food available to the animals.

(D) It does not change the ecosystem.

Name _____   Date _____

Life Science Interdependent Relationships in Ecosystems

5 Which population might increase because of a beaver dam? (LS2.C)

(A) trees

(B) wildebeests

(C) fish

(D) bees

6 Why do animals migrate? (LS2.C)

(A) to find food

(B) to cope with changing temperatures

(C) to find water

(D) all of the above

7 What can people in a city do to improve the ecosystem for some of the wildlife? (LS2.C)

(A) clear more land

(B) plant rooftop gardens

(C) pave more parking lots

(D) put plants inside buildings

8 In what way does a fish ladder at a dam help salmon populations? (LS2.C)

(A) It provides water.

(B) It gives them access to food.

(C) It helps with migration.

(D) It gives them a way to avoid pollution.

Life Science Interdependent Relationships in Ecosystems

9 How do wolves in a pack help one another? (LS2.D)

A They hunt large prey together

B They help each other catch small prey

C They act together to relocate their nest.

D They hide together from predators.

10 What kind of group do fish form for protection? (LS2.D)

A pack

B prey

C school

D swarm

11 What kind of change do bees cope with by swarming? (LS2.D)

A hunting for food

B finding other bees for mates

C finding water on dry days

D finding a less crowded place for a new hive

12 What can living in groups help animals do? (LS2.D)

A get food

B defend themselves

C care for young

D all of the above

Life Science Interdependent Relationships in Ecosystems

 Why are some plants and animals no longer living anywhere on Earth? (LS4.A)

(A) They decided not to reproduce.

(B) Their environment changed and could no longer support them.

(C) They migrated to other places.

(D) They went undiscovered and disappeared.

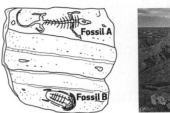 

14 **The drawing shows evidence of organisms that once lived at the location shown in the photo. Fossil A lived on land in a very dry environment. Fossil B lived in water. How has the environment changed over time in this area?** (LS4.A)

(A) The area changed from a dry environment to a water environment.

(B) The area changed from a water environment to a dry environment.

(C) The area changed from a forest to an ocean.

(D) The area changed from a desert to a wetland.

Life Science Interdependent Relationships in Ecosystems

 15 **What are fossils?** (LS4.A)

Ⓐ   types of plants and animals

Ⓑ   the actual skin and bones of organisms that lived long ago.

Ⓒ   traces of organisms that lived long ago

Ⓓ   environmental changes that took place long ago

16 **What can you infer about fossils found in two layers of rock in the same area?** (LS4.A)

Ⓐ   The fossil in the bottom layer is older.

Ⓑ   The fossil in the top layer is older.

Ⓒ   The fossil in the bottom layer is younger.

Ⓓ   Both organisms lived in the same conditions.

17 **Fish fossils are found in some deserts, and fern fossils have been found in Antarctica. What evidence does this provide?** (LS4.A)

Ⓐ   that these plants and animals became extinct

Ⓑ   that other kinds of organisms may have lived there, too

Ⓒ   that plants and animals lived in all places on Earth

Ⓓ   that areas on Earth have changed a lot over time

 18 **How are polar bears able to survive in a cold environment?** (LS4.C)

Ⓐ   Their thick fur and body fat keep them warm.

Ⓑ   They stay in the cold for only a short time during the year.

Ⓒ   Their bodies do not produce heat so they do not get cold.

Ⓓ   They avoid walking in snow or on ice.

Name _____ Date _____

Life Science Interdependent Relationships in Ecosystems

19 **Why would a leopard frog not survive in a dry place?** (LS4.C)

Ⓐ It needs water to swim for exercise.

Ⓑ It needs water to lay its eggs and keep its skin moist.

Ⓒ Dry soil rubs away the frog's skin.

Ⓓ It eats only food that it catches in water.

20 **How does the angler fish use light in the deep ocean?** (LS4.C)

Ⓐ It follows sunlight to the surface for food.

Ⓑ It feeds only when daylight reaches the deep water.

Ⓒ It produces its own light to attract prey.

Ⓓ It does not need light at all.

21 **What makes up an ecosystem?** (LS4.D)

Ⓐ soil and water

Ⓑ living things and trees

Ⓒ living and nonliving things

Ⓓ rocks and nonliving things

22 **What is an organism's habitat?** (LS4.D)

Ⓐ the place where it gets everything it needs to survive

Ⓑ the shelter it builds when the seasons change

Ⓒ the set of behaviors it uses to get food

Ⓓ the ways it changes its ecosystem

Life Science Interdependent Relationships in Ecosystems

 23 **How can a decreased amount of rain affect a grassland habitat?** (LS4.D)

(A) Wildflowers take the place of grasses.

(B) Too much moisture can kill grasses.

(C) Dried up grass leads animals to migrate to find food.

(D) Trees grow larger and block the sunlight from the grasses.

 24 **What is a population?** (LS4.D)

(A) all the plants and animals living together in an ecosystem

(B) a group of the same kind of living thing living in an area

(C) one family grouping of a particular type of animal

(D) the plants that provide food for animals in an area

 25 **What do some animals do in winter to survive?** (LS4.D)

(A) migrate to colder places

(B) lose weight

(C) die off

(D) migrate to warmer places

 26 **What can you infer about plants that live in a desert habitat?** (LS4.D)

(A) They require less sunlight than forest plants.

(B) They produce no food for animals that live there.

(C) They require a great deal of water to survive.

(D) They do not require much water to survive.

Name_____ Date _____

Review Questions

DIRECTIONS: Read each question. Then choose the best answer.

1 What does reproduction do for plants and animals? (LS1.B)

    Ⓐ It helps each kind of plant and animal find food.

    Ⓑ It helps each kind of plant and animal find water.

    Ⓒ It lets each kind of plant and animal continue to live on Earth.

    Ⓓ It helps each kind of plant and animal find shelter.

2 Which of the following is a correct example of a life cycle? (LS1.B)

    Ⓐ egg ⟹ tadpole ⟹ young frog ⟹ adult

    Ⓑ egg ⟹ young frog ⟹ tadpole ⟹ adult

    Ⓒ egg ⟹ young frog ⟹ adult ⟹ tadpole

    Ⓓ egg ⟹ adult ⟹ young frog ⟹ tadpole

3 How are the life cycles of a ladybug and a pepper plant similar? (LS1.B)

    Ⓐ Both have a seed stage.

    Ⓑ Both have an egg stage.

    Ⓒ Both reproduce before they reach the adult stage.

    Ⓓ Both reproduce after they reach the adult stage.

4 Which of the following is the correct life cycle of a salamander? (LS1.B)

    Ⓐ egg ⟹ larva ⟹ young salamander ⟹ adult

    Ⓑ larva ⟹ egg ⟹ adult ⟹ young salamander

    Ⓒ egg ⟹ young salamander ⟹ adult ⟹ larva

    Ⓓ adult ⟹ young salamander ⟹ egg ⟹ larva

Life Science Inheritance and Variation of Traits: Life Cycles and Traits

 Which of these is a trait? (LS3.A)

(A) height

(B) body shape

(C) hair color

(D) all of the above

 What are inherited traits? (LS3.A)

(A) the habits an animal learns from the environment

(B) characteristics offspring get from the environment

(C) characteristics passed down from parents to offspring

(D) what parents teach offspring to do

 What can you infer about the parents of a bird with a curved beak? (LS3.B)

(A) The parents also have curved beaks.

(B) The parents did not feed their young enough.

(C) The parents groomed the young until its beak curved.

(D) The parents taught the bird how to shape its beak.

Life Science Inheritance and Variation of Traits: Life Cycles and Traits

8 **What acquired trait do flamingos get from their environment?** (LS3.A)

(A) curved bills

(B) long legs

(C) coloring

(D) grouping

9 **On a trip to the seashore, Tony noticed that many of the trees growing along the sand dunes had branches growing away from the ocean. What may have caused this growth?** (LS3.A)

(A) inherited trait to bend

(B) acquired trait from strong winds

(C) growing trait passed on from parent trees

(D) not enough sunlight

10 **What trait is NOT passed down from parent to offspring?** (LS3.A)

(A) acquired trait

(B) inherited trait

(C) shape of a bird's beak

(D) coloring

11 **An animal changes its behavior based on interactions with its environment. What is this change in behavior called?** (LS3.A)

(A) inherited trait

(B) function

(C) grouping

(D) learning

Life Science Inheritance and Variation of Traits: Life Cycles and Traits

 12 Why do plants and animals of the same type look somewhat different? (LS3.B)

    (A) learning

    (B) different life cycles

    (C) they have identical inherited traits.

    (D) they have some different inherited traits

 13 What can you conclude about the different shapes of the bills of ducks and flamingos? (LS3.B)

    (A) The birds choose their bill shape based on what they want to eat.

    (B) The birds' bill shapes change depending on where the birds live.

    (C) Because their bills are shaped differently, they also function differently.

    (D) Duck bills work better than flamingo bills.

 14 Which of the following explains why all of the puppies in one litter do not look exactly alike? (LS3.B)

    (A) The mother cares for only puppies that look like her.

    (B) The puppies inherited different information from their parents.

    (C) The males will look like the father, and the females will look like the mother.

    (D) The mother will decide after the puppies are born what they will look like.

Life Science   Inheritance and Variation of Traits: Life Cycles and Traits

 What can you infer about an environment where the flamingos are almost all white? (LS3.B)

 A The flamingos do not have any pink parents.

B A certain kind of food is missing from their diet.

C They have learned a behavior of cleaning their feathers.

D They eat only white food.

16 **A type of grass grows tall and green when it is healthy. What can you infer about an environment where that same type of grass is short and brown?** (LS3.B)

A The environment has everything the grass needs.

B The environment does not have what the grass needs.

C the plant has too much space

D the grass is healthy.

Life Science Inheritance and Variation of Traits: Life Cycles and Traits

17 Students placed a potted plant near a window. They observed that the plant bent toward the window. Infer what environmental factor affected the plant's growth. (LS3.B)

  (A) The plant bent away from the light coming in through the window.

  (B) The plant bent toward the light coming in through the window.

  (C) Watering the plant caused it to bend toward the window.

  (D) Constant winds made the plant bend toward the window.

18 What do you call differences in traits between individuals of the same type of plant or animal? (LS4.B)

  (A) traits

  (B) acquired traits

  (C) new traits

  (D) variations

19 Some traits in certain kinds of living things continue. Other traits in these kinds of living things stop appearing. Why does this happen? (LS4.B)

  (A) Only the traits of individuals that survive get passed on.

  (B) Only acquired traits get passed on.

  (C) All inherited traits get passed on.

  (D) Animals can decide not to pass on some traits.

Life Science Inheritance and Variation of Traits: Life Cycles and Traits

20 A male frigatebird fills the bright red pouch on his throat so that it swell like a red balloon. He opens his wings wide and shakes his head. How do these behaviors help the male frigatebird? (LS4.B)

A It helps the male bird scare away predators.

B It helps the male bird attract a mate.

C It helps the male bird teach its offspring how to dance.

D It helps the male bird find food.

21 The arctic fox's coat turns white in winter. How does a fox that has a very white coat in the winter have an advantage in surviving? (LS4.B)

A The whiter coat keeps it cooler.

B The whiter coat makes it stand out to warn off predators.

C The whiter coat helps it hide while hunting food.

D The whiter coat helps it find a mate.

Review Questions

Earth Science **Weather and Climate**

DIRECTIONS: Read each question. Then choose the best answer.

1 Which of these is NOT true about weather? (ESS2.D)

- (A) Weather describes the conditions in the air outside.

- (B) Weather can change from day to day.

- (C) Weather can change from season to season.

- (D) Scientists always know what the weather will be.

2 What instrument measures air pressure? (ESS2.D)

- (A) thermometer

- (B) wind vane

- (C) barometer

- (D) rain gauge

3 A front is moving toward Denver, Colorado. What will the weather in Denver probably be like as the front passes through? (ESS2.D)

- (A) warmer and dry

- (B) colder and dry

- (C) colder with rain

- (D) warmer with snow

Earth Science Weather and Climate

4 Wind speed is measured with which instrument? (ESS2.D)

    (A) thermometer

    (B) anemometer

    (C) wind vane

    (D) rain gauge

5 Why do scientists measure changes in weather? (ESS2.D)

    (A) So that they will be able to change the weather

    (B) to know exactly how much precipitation there will be tomorrow

    (C) to determine when summer will start

    (D) to predict what kind of weather might happen next

6 What are weather maps used for? (ESS2.D)

    (A) to predict weather

    (B) to change weather

    (C) to collect weather data

    (D) to measure weather data

7 What are seasons? (ESS2.D)

    (A) a pattern of increasing temperature

    (B) changes in the weather from one week to another

    (C) rainy and warm periods that occur in different locations

    (D) a pattern of weather changes throughout a year

Earth Science   Weather and Climate

8 **What is the difference between weather and climate?** (ESS2.D)

(A)   Weather describes the conditions in the air outside at a certain time and place. Climate is the general pattern of weather in an area over a long period of time.

(B)   Weather is the general pattern of weather in an area over a long period of time. Climate describes the conditions in the air outside at a certain time and place.

(C)   Weather describes changes with the seasons. Climate is the conditions in the air outside at a certain time and place.

(D)   Climate describes the seasons of a certain place. Weather is the pattern of conditions in an area over a long period of time.

9 **Study the graph of average seasonal precipitation data for Charlottesville, Virginia. Which of the following is a correct interpretation of the data?** (ESS2.D)

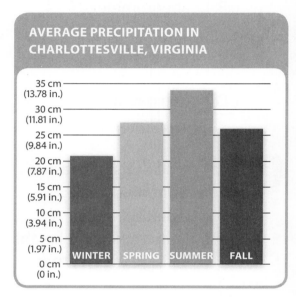

AVERAGE PRECIPITATION IN CHARLOTTESVILLE, VIRGINIA

(A)   Spring and summer are the wettest seasons.

(B)   Winter and fall are the wettest seasons.

(C)   Fall is wetter than summer.

(D)   Spring brings the most rain.

Earth Science   Weather and Climate

 10 Juanita took the following temperature readings outside her classroom one day. What could she predict from her data? (ESS2.D)

Time	Temperature
9:00 AM	9 °C
10:00 AM	11 °C
11:00 AM	13 °C
12:00 PM	16 °C

Ⓐ The falling temperature will likely bring rain.

Ⓑ The afternoon will likely be warmer, and she might not need her jacket.

Ⓒ The air temperature will likely rise by 16°C throughout the day.

Ⓓ The afternoon will likely be cooler, and she will likely need a jacket.

 11 Ted's hometown received 90 cm of snowfall last winter. What can you conclude from that data? (ESS2.D)

Ⓐ Next year it is unlikely to snow as much there.

Ⓑ A lot of rain probably fell in the spring.

Ⓒ His town is located in a climate with cold winters.

Ⓓ The climate in his town is getting colder and wetter.

 12 How are thunderstorms and hurricanes hazardous? (ESS3.B)

Ⓐ They can cause flooding.

Ⓑ Strong winds can damage trees and buildings.

Ⓒ They can produce lightning.

Ⓓ all of the above

Earth Science Weather and Climate

13 What part of a hurricane produces the most hazardous impact? (ESS3.B)

(A) high temperatures

(B) low temperatures

(C) flooding

(D) lightning

14 Which of the following does NOT reduce the impact of flooding? (ESS3.B)

(A) storm shelter

(B) levee

(C) dam

(D) bags of sand

15 How does a levee work? (ESS3.B)

(A) It protects people from the strong winds of a hurricane.

(B) It slows or stops water from flowing into an area.

(C) It soaks up water faster than the water can flood an area.

(D) It gives people a high place to go in case of a flood.

16 Which of these is hardest to prepare for to reduce its impact? (ESS3.B)

(A) flood

(B) lightning

(C) hurricane

(D) tornado

Earth Science Weather and Climate

 17 How does a lightning rod help to prevent fire and other damage?
(ESS3.B)

(A) It stops the flow of electricity.

(B) It directs electricity safely to the ground.

(C) It uses the electricity to power electronics.

(D) It bounces the electricity back to the cloud.

18 Sam heard thunder from lightning while he was in the pool. What should he do? (ESS3.B)

(A) Go get an umbrella and wait beside the pool.

(B) Stand next to a taller object until the storm passes.

(C) Go indoors and stay away from windows, water, and electronic equipment.

(D) Stay in the water until after the storm has passed.

Preguntas de repaso

Ciencias físicas Fuerzas e interacciones

INSTRUCCIONES: Lee cada pregunta. Luego, elige la mejor respuesta.

1 ¿Cuál es la definición de fuerza? (PS2.A)

(A) empujar o jalar

(B) un objeto quieto

(C) la energía que usas

(D) un objeto en movimiento

2 ¿Cuál de las siguientes opciones tienen todas las fuerzas? (PS2.A)

(A) empujar

(B) jalar

(C) potencia y dirección

(D) dirección y velocidad

3 ¿Qué fuerza usa Waldo para cambiar la dirección de movimiento de la pelota? (PS2.A)

(A) jalar

(B) empujar

(C) fricción

(D) gravedad

Ciencias físicas   Fuerzas e interacciones

 **4** Tom jala del vagón en que va Alicia mientras Gina lo empuja. Emilio camina junto a ellos. ¿Quién no está ejerciendo fuerza sobre el vagón? (PS2.A)

A Tom

B Alicia

C Gina

D Emilio

5 Alicia y Samantha juegan a jalar de la cuerda, pero ninguna de las dos se mueve. ¿Qué demuestran? (PS2.A)

A empujar y jalar

B jalones desequilibrados

C gravedad y fricción

D fuerzas equilibradas

 6 Tom, Alicia y Gina jalan de Andrea, Samantha y Juan cuando juegan a jalar de la cuerda, ¿qué demuestran? (PS2.A)

A gravedad y fricción

B fuerzas desequilibradas

C empujes y fricción

D fuerzas equilibradas

 7 Cuando un bateador mueve el bate y golpea una pelota, ¿cómo usa una fuerza sobre la pelota? (PS2.A)

A para mantener la velocidad de la pelota

B para jalar el bate hacia la pelota

C para cambiar la dirección de la pelota

D para aumentar la atracción de la gravedad sobre la pelota

Ciencias físicas Fuerzas e interacciones

8 ¿Qué fuerza puedes observar si viajas en un carruaje jalado por caballos? (PS2.A)

(A) El caballo empuja el carruaje por detrás.

(B) El caballo jala.

(C) La gravedad hace que el carruaje ruede.

(D) Las fuerzas equilibradas mueven el caballo.

9 ¿De qué manera un niño en un columpio en un patio de juegos demuestra un movimiento habitual? (PS2.A)

(A) El columpio se mueve hacia atrás y hacia adelante en un patrón predecible.

(B) El niño se columpia más alto cuando lo empujan.

(C) Las fuerzas equilibradas y desequilibradas causan este movimiento.

(D) El niño usa una fuerza para mover el columpio.

10 ¿Qué notas cuando observas un carrusel en movimiento? (PS2.A)

(A) Las fuerzas desequilibradas harán que deje de girar instantáneamente.

(B) La dirección en que gira cambiará de repente.

(C) La gravedad hará que se detenga inesperadamente.

(D) La próxima vuelta será en la misma dirección que las últimas vueltas.

11 Isaac está apoyado contra un manzano pequeño. El árbol se dobla un poco cuando su espalda lo empuja. ¿Qué fuerza evita que Isaac se caiga de espaldas? (PS2.B)

(A) La gravedad evitará que se caiga.

(B) La fuerza magnética.

(C) La fuerza de Isaac que empuja el árbol se equilibra con el árbol que empuja a su vez a Isaac.

(D) El árbol no lo puede sostener, y se romperá pronto.

Ciencias físicas Fuerzas e interacciones

 12 En un escritorio hay un bolígrafo, un cuaderno y un vaso de agua. ¿Qué objetos están ejerciendo fuerza? (PS2.B)

Ⓐ el bolígrafo, el cuaderno, el vaso, el agua y el escritorio

Ⓑ el bolígrafo, el cuaderno, el vaso y el agua

Ⓒ el bolígrafo, el cuaderno y el vaso

Ⓓ el escritorio

 13 ¿Cómo aplican las fuerzas dos estudiantes que juegan a las vencidas? (PS2.B)

Ⓐ Cambian la gravedad.

Ⓑ Usan fuerzas atrayentes.

Ⓒ Están en contacto.

Ⓓ Aplican fuerzas a la distancia.

14 Una bicicleta está estacionada en la acera. El soporte evita que se caiga. ¿Qué puedes saber sobre el soporte? (PS2.B)

Ⓐ La acera y el soporte no están en contacto.

Ⓑ La acera y el soporte ejercen fuerzas entre sí.

Ⓒ La bicicleta no está apoyada en el soporte.

Ⓓ El soporte empuja más fuerte que lo que la gravedad jala la bicicleta.

 15 ¿Qué par de polos magnéticos se atraerán entre sí? (PS2.B)

Ⓐ N, S

Ⓑ N, N

Ⓒ S, S

Ⓓ E, O

Ciencias físicas Fuerzas e interacciones

 16 **Marcel sostiene un imán de barra muy cerca de un clip. ¿Qué sucede?** (PS2.B)

(A) El imán repele el clip.

(B) El clip se aleja del imán.

(C) El imán atrae el clip y lo mueve hacia él.

(D) Las fuerzas equilibradas actúan sobre el clip cuando este se mueve hacia el imán.

17 **Vanesa acerca los polos iguales de dos imanes de barra. ¿Qué hará la fuerza magnética?** (PS2.B)

(A) Hará que los imanes se atraigan.

(B) Hará que los imanes se alejen.

(C) Hará que los imanes giren.

(D) Se convertirá en cero fuerza neta desequilibrada.

 18 **¿Cuál opción puede hacer que la fuerza magnética entre los imanes sea menor?** (PS2.B)

(A) ponerles corriente eléctrica

(B) darles forma de herradura

(C) frotarlos con un paño de lana

(D) alejarlos

19 **¿En qué se diferencian los electroimanes de otros imanes?** (PS2.B)

(A) Los electroimanes son más pequeños.

(B) Los electroimanes son más grandes.

(C) Los electroimanes pueden encenderse y apagarse.

(D) Los electroimanes pueden recoger cualquier cosa.

Ciencias físicas Fuerzas e interacciones

 20 **Nina descubrió que podía pegar un globo a la pared después de frotarlo con un suéter de lana. ¿Cuál es la razón más probable por la que sucede esto?** (PS2.B)

Ⓐ la gravedad

Ⓑ la electricidad estática

Ⓒ la atracción magnética

Ⓓ El suelo repele el globo.

 21 **¿Qué conclusión puedes sacar sobre dos globos que parecen alejarse sin tocarse?** (PS2.B)

Ⓐ Ambos tienen polos norte.

Ⓑ Uno tiene un polo norte y el otro tiene un polo sur.

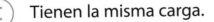

Ⓒ Tienen la misma carga.

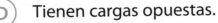

Ⓓ Tienen cargas opuestas.

22 **¿Cuál opción puedes demostrar usando un globo cargado con electricidad estática y papel de seda?** (PS2.B)

Ⓐ Las fuerzas eléctricas entre los objetos no exigen que los objetos estén en contacto.

Ⓑ Las fuerzas eléctricas entre los objetos exigen que los objetos estén en contacto.

Ⓒ Las fuerzas magnéticas entre los objetos no exigen que los objetos estén en contacto.

Ⓓ Las fuerzas magnéticas entre los objetos exigen que los objetos estén en contacto.

Preguntas de repaso

INSTRUCCIONES: Lee cada pregunta. Luego, elige la mejor respuesta.

1 ¿Cuál opción es verdadera sobre el efecto de un incendio en un ecosistema forestal? (LS2.C)

(A) Todo lo que está quemado muere.

(B) Todos los animales del ecosistema mueren.

(C) Se produce un nuevo crecimiento más adelante.

(D) Los animales se alejan para siempre.

2 ¿Qué acontecimiento físico natural podría causar que los animales abandonaran su medio ambiente? (LS2.C)

(A) sequía

(B) precipitación promedio

(C) construcción de edificios

(D) temperaturas normales

3 Un lirón está inactivo en el invierno. Su cuerpo no usa mucha energía. ¿Cómo se llama esto? (LS2.C)

(A) alimentación

(B) reproducción

(C) hibernación

(D) supervivencia

4 ¿Cómo afecta la construcción de edificios el ecosistema para los animales que viven allí? (LS2.C)

(A) Aumenta el alimento disponible para los animales.

(B) Aumenta el espacio disponible para los animales.

(C) Disminuye el espacio y el alimento disponible para los animales.

(D) No cambia el ecosistema.

Ciencias de la vida   Relaciones interdependientes en los ecosistemas

5 ¿Cuál población podría aumentar debido a un dique de castores?
(LS2.C)

(A) los árboles

(B) los ñus

(C) los peces

(D) las abejas

6 ¿Por qué migran los animales? (LS2.C)

(A) para hallar alimento

(B) para hacer frente a un cambio de temperatura

(C) para hallar agua

(D) todas las anteriores

7 ¿Qué pueden hacen las personas en una ciudad para mejorar el ecosistema para la vida silvestre?
(LS2.C)

(A) despejar más terrenos

(B) plantar jardines en las azoteas

(C) pavimentar más estacionamientos

(D) poner plantas dentro de los edificios

8 ¿Cómo ayudan a las poblaciones de salmones las escaleras para peces que se ponen en un dique?
(LS2.C)

(A) Brindan agua.

(B) Les dan acceso a alimento.

(C) Ayudan con la migración.

(D) Brindan una manera de evitar la contaminación.

Ciencias de la vida Relaciones
interdependientes en los ecosistemas

 ¿Cómo colaboran entre sí los lobos de una manada? (LS2.D)

(A) Juntos cazan una presa grande.

(B) Juntos cazan una presa pequeña.

(C) Juntos reubican sus madrigueras.

(D) Juntos se ocultan de los predadores.

 ¿Qué tipo de grupo forman los peces para protegerse? (LS2.D)

(A) una manada

(B) una presa

(C) un cardumen

(D) un enjambre

11 **¿Qué tipo de cambio logran enfrentar las abejas cuando forman un enjambre?** (LS2.D)

(A) cazar para tener alimento

(B) hallar otras abejas para reproducirse

(C) hallar agua en días secos

(D) hallar un lugar menos poblado para una colmena nueva

12 **¿Cómo ayuda a los animales el vivir en grupo?** (LS2.D)

(A) obtienen alimento

(B) se defienden

(C) cuidan a sus crías

(D) todas las anteriores

Ciencias de la vida Relaciones
interdependientes en los ecosistemas

13 **¿Por qué algunas plantas y animales ya no viven en ninguna parte de la Tierra?** (LS4.A)

(A) Deciden no reproducirse.

(B) Su medio ambiente cambió y ya no podía sustentarlos.

(C) Migraron a otros lugares.

(D) Nadie los descubrió y desaparecieron.

14 **El dibujo muestra evidencia de organismos que alguna vez vivieron en la ubicación que muestra la fotografía. El Fósil A vivía en tierra, en un medio ambiente muy seco. El Fósil B vivía en el agua. ¿Cómo ha cambiado el medio ambiente con el tiempo en esta área?** (LS4.A)

(A) El área cambió de un medio ambiente seco a un medio ambiente acuático.

(B) El área cambió de un medio ambiente acuático a un medio ambiente seco.

(C) El área cambió de un bosque a un océano.

(D) El área cambió de un desierto a un humedal.

Ciencias de la vida Relaciones
interdependientes en los ecosistemas

 ¿Qué son los fósiles? (LS4.A)

(A) tipos de plantas y animales

(B) la piel y los huesos de organismos que vivieron hace mucho

(C) rastros de organismos que vivieron hace mucho tiempo

(D) cambios ambientales que ocurrieron hace mucho tiempo

16 ¿Qué puedes inferir sobre los fósiles hallados en dos capas de roca en la misma área? (LS4.A)

(A) El fósil en la capa inferior es más antiguo.

(B) El fósil en la capa superior es más antiguo.

(C) El fósil en la capa inferior es más reciente.

(D) Ambos organismos vivieron en las mismas condiciones.

17 Se hallaron fósiles de peces en desiertos y fósiles de helechos en la Antártica. ¿Qué evidencia nos da esto? (LS4.A)

(A) que estas plantas y animales se han extinguido

(B) que otros tipos de organismos también pueden haber vivido allí

(C) que las plantas y animales vivieron por toda la Tierra

(D) que las áreas de la Tierra cambiaron mucho con el tiempo

 ¿Cómo sobreviven los osos polares en un medio ambiente frío? (LS4.C)

(A) El pelaje grueso y la grasa corporal mantienen su calor.

(B) Están en el frío por un período breve del año.

(C) Sus organismos no producen calor, entonces no sienten frío.

(D) Evitan caminar en la nieve o en el hielo.

Ciencias de la vida Relaciones interdependientes en los ecosistemas

19 ¿Por qué una rana leopardo no sobrevive en un lugar seco? (LS4.C)

(A) Necesita agua para nadar y hacer ejercicio.

(B) Necesita agua para poner sus huevos y mantener la piel húmeda.

(C) El suelo seco raspa la piel de la rana.

(D) Sólo come el alimento que atrapa en el agua.

20 ¿Cómo usa la luz el pez rape en el océano profundo? (LS4.C)

(A) Sigue la luz solar hasta la superficie para tener alimento.

(B) Sólo se alimenta cuando la luz solar llega al agua profunda.

(C) Produce su propia luz para atraer a la presa.

(D) No necesita luz.

21 ¿Qué forma un ecosistema? (LS4.D)

(A) el suelo y el agua

(B) los seres vivos y los árboles

(C) los seres vivos e inertes

(D) las rocas y los seres inertes

22 ¿Cuál es el hábitat de un organismo? (LS4.D)

(A) el lugar donde obtiene todo lo que necesita para sobrevivir

(B) el refugio que construye cuando cambian las estaciones

(C) el conjunto de comportamientos que usa para obtener alimento

(D) las maneras en que cambia su ecosistema

Ciencias de la vida Relaciones
interdependientes en los ecosistemas

 23 **¿Cómo la disminución de las precipitaciones puede afectar un hábitat de pastizal?** (LS4.D)

(A) Las flores silvestres ocupan el lugar de las hierbas.

(B) El exceso de humedad puede acabar con las hierbas.

(C) Las hierbas secas hacen que los animales migren para hallar alimento.

(D) Los árboles crecen y bloquean la luz solar de los pastos.

 24 **¿Qué es una población?** (LS4.D)

(A) todas las plantas y animales que viven juntos en un ecosistema

(B) un grupo de la misma clase de seres vivos que viven en un área

(C) un grupo familiar de un tipo específico de animales

(D) las plantas que dan alimento a los animales de un área

 25 **¿Qué hacen algunos animales en invierno para sobrevivir?** (LS4.D)

(A) migran a lugares más fríos

(B) pierden peso

(C) mueren

(D) migran a lugares más cálidos

26 **¿Qué puedes inferir sobre las plantas que viven en un hábitat de desierto?** (LS4.D)

(A) Necesitan menos luz solar que las plantas de los bosques.

(B) No producen alimento para los animales que viven allí.

(C) Necesitan mucha agua para sobrevivir.

(D) No necesitan mucha agua para sobrevivir.

Preguntas de repaso

Ciencias de la vida Herencia y variación de características: Ciclos de vida y características

INSTRUCCIONES: Lee cada pregunta. Luego, elige la mejor respuesta.

 1 **¿Qué hace la reproducción para las plantas y animales?** (LS1.B)

(A) Ayuda a todas las plantas y animales a hallar alimento.

(B) Ayuda a todas las plantas y animales a hallar agua.

(C) Permite que todas las plantas y animales sigan viviendo en la Tierra.

(D) Ayuda a todas las plantas y animales a hallar refugio.

2 **¿Cuál opción es el ejemplo correcto de un ciclo de vida?** (LS1.B)

(A) huevo ⇒ renacuajo ⇒ rana joven ⇒ adulta

(B) huevo ⇒ rana joven ⇒ renacuajo ⇒ adulta

(C) huevo ⇒ rana joven ⇒ adulta ⇒ renacuajo

(D) huevo ⇒ adulta ⇒ rana joven ⇒ renacuajo

3 **¿En qué se parecen los ciclos de vida de una catarina y una planta de pimiento?** (LS1.B)

(A) Ambos tienen una etapa de semilla.

(B) Ambos tienen una etapa de huevo.

(C) Ambos se reproducen antes de llegar a la edad adulta.

(D) Ambos se reproducen después de llegar a la edad adulta.

4 **¿Cuál opción es el ciclo de vida correcto de una salamandra?** (LS1.B)

(A) huevo ⇒ larva ⇒ salamandra joven ⇒ adulta

(B) larva ⇒ huevo ⇒ adulta ⇒ salamandra joven

(C) huevo ⇒ salamandra joven ⇒ adulta ⇒ larva

(D) adulta ⇒ salamandra joven ⇒ huevo ⇒ larva

Ciencias de la vida Herencia y variación de características: Ciclos de vida y características

 5 ¿Cuál opción es una característica? (LS3.A)

(A) la altura

(B) la forma del cuerpo

(C) el color del cabello

(D) todas las anteriores

 6 ¿Qué son las características heredadas? (LS3.A)

(A) los hábitos que un animal aprende de su medio ambiente

(B) las características que las crías obtienen de su medio ambiente

(C) las características que los padres les transmiten a las crías

(D) lo que los padres les enseñan a hacer a las crías

 7 ¿Qué puedes inferir sobre los padres de un ave con un pico curvo? (LS1.B)

(A) Los padres también tienen un pico curvo.

(B) Los padres no alimentaron a su cría lo suficiente.

(C) Los padres lamieron a la cría hasta que su pico se dobló.

(D) Los padres enseñaron al ave a darle forma a su pico.

Ciencias de la vida Herencia y variación de características: Ciclos de vida y características

 8 ¿Qué característica adquirida obtienen los flamencos de su medio ambiente? (LS3.A)

(A) picos curvos

(B) patas largas

(C) color

(D) agrupación

9 En un viaje a la costa, Tony notó que muchos de los árboles que crecen en las dunas de arena tenían ramas que crecían en dirección opuesta al océano. ¿Qué puede haber causado este crecimiento? (LS3.A)

(A) una característica heredada para doblarse

(B) una característica adquirida por los vientos fuertes

(C) una característica de crecimiento transmitida por los árboles madre

(D) la falta de luz solar

10 ¿Qué característica NO se transmite de los padres a las crías? (LS3.A)

(A) las características adquiridas

(B) las características heredadas

(C) la forma del pico de un ave

(D) el color

11 Un animal cambia su comportamiento según las interacciones con su medio ambiente. ¿Cómo se llama este cambio? (LS3.A)

(A) característica heredada

(B) función

(C) agrupación

(D) aprendizaje

Nombre _____ Fecha _____

Ciencias de la vida Herencia y variación de características: Ciclos de vida y características

12 ¿Por qué las plantas y los animales del mismo tipo se ven un poco diferentes? (LS3.B)

- Ⓐ aprendizaje
- Ⓑ diferentes ciclos de vida
- Ⓒ tienen características heredadas idénticas
- Ⓓ tienen algunas características heredadas diferentes

13 ¿Qué conclusión puedes sacar sobre las diferentes formas de los picos de los patos y los flamencos? (LS3.B)

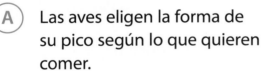

- Ⓐ Las aves eligen la forma de su pico según lo que quieren comer.
- Ⓑ La forma de los picos de las aves cambia según dónde viven.
- Ⓒ Como sus picos tienen distintas formas, también funcionan diferente.
- Ⓓ Los picos de los patos funcionan mejor que los picos de los flamencos.

14 ¿Cuál opción explica por qué todos los cachorros de una camada no lucen exactamente iguales? (LS3.B)

- Ⓐ La madre sólo cuida a los cachorros que lucen como ella.
- Ⓑ Los cachorros heredaron diferente información de sus padres.
- Ⓒ Los cachorros machos lucirán como el padre y las hembras lucirán como la madre.
- Ⓓ La madre decidirá cómo lucirán los cachorros después de que nazcan.

Ciencias de la vida Herencia y variación de características: Ciclos de vida y características

15 ¿Qué puedes inferir sobre un medio ambiente en que los flamencos son casi todos blancos? (LS3.B)

A) Los flamencos no tienen padres de color rosado.

B) A su dieta le falta cierto tipo de alimento.

C) Han aprendido un comportamiento para limpiar sus plumas.

D) Sólo comen alimentos blancos.

16 Un tipo de hierba crece alta y verde cuando está sana. ¿Qué puedes inferir sobre un medio ambiente en que el mismo tipo de hierba es baja y marrón? (LS3.B)

A) El medio ambiente tiene todo lo que la hierba necesita.

B) El medio ambiente no tiene todo lo que la hierba necesita.

C) La planta tiene mucho espacio.

D) La hierba está saludable.

Ciencias de la vida Herencia y variación de características: Ciclos de vida y características

17 Los estudiantes colocaron una planta cerca de una ventana. Notaron que la planta se dobló hacia la ventana. Infiere qué factor ambiental afectó el crecimiento de la planta. (LS3.B)

(A) La planta se dobló alejándose de la luz que entraba por la ventana.

(B) La planta se dobló hacia la luz que entraba por la ventana.

(C) Regar la planta hizo que se doblara hacia la ventana.

(D) Los vientos constantes hicieron que la planta se doblara hacia la ventana.

18 ¿Cómo se llaman las diferencias en las características entre individuos de la misma clase de planta o animal? (LS4.B)

(A) características

(B) características adquiridas

(C) características nuevas

(D) variaciones

19 Algunas características de ciertas clases de seres vivos perduran en el tiempo. Otras características dejan de aparecer. ¿Por qué sucede esto? (LS4.B)

(A) Sólo se transmiten las características de los individuos que sobreviven.

(B) Sólo se transmiten las características adquiridas.

(C) Se transmiten todas las características heredadas.

(D) Los animales pueden decidir no transmitir algunas características.

Ciencias de la vida   Herencia y variación de características: Ciclos de vida y características

20 Un rabihorcado macho hincha la bolsa roja brillante de su garganta como un globo rojo. Despliega las alas y sacude la cabeza. ¿A qué le ayudan estos comportamientos? (LS4.B)

A Le ayudan a ahuyentar a los predadores.

B Le ayudan a atraer a una hembra.

C Le ayudan a enseñar a danzar a su cría.

D Le ayudan a hallar alimento.

21 El pelaje del zorro polar se vuelve blanco en invierno. ¿Por qué es una ventaja para la supervivencia que el zorro tenga este pelaje blanco durante el invierno? (LS4.B)

A El pelaje blanco le ayuda a estar fresco.

B El pelaje blanco hace que sobresalga para ahuyentar a los predadores.

C El pelaje blanco le ayuda a ocultarse cuando caza para alimentarse.

D El pelaje blanco le ayuda a encontrar una hembra con quien reproducirse.

Preguntas de repaso

Ciencias de la Tierra
Estado del tiempo y clima

INSTRUCCIONES: Lee cada pregunta. Luego, elige la mejor respuesta.

1 ¿Cuál opción NO es verdadera sobre el estado del tiempo? (ESS2.D)

(A) El estado del tiempo describe las condiciones del aire exterior.

(B) El estado del tiempo puede cambiar de un día a otro.

(C) El estado del tiempo puede cambiar de una estación a otra.

(D) Los científicos siempre saben cuál será el estado del tiempo.

2 ¿Qué instrumento mide la presión atmosférica? (ESS2.D)

(A) termómetro

(B) veleta

(C) barómetro

(D) pluviómetro

3 Un frente se desplaza hacia Denver, Colorado. ¿Cómo es probable que esté el estado del tiempo en Denver mientras pasa el frente? (ESS2.D)

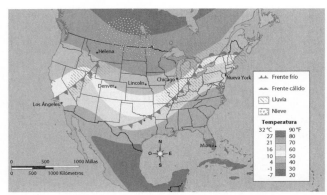

(A) más cálido y seco

(B) más frío y seco

(C) más frío con lluvia

(D) más cálido con nieve

Ciencias de la Tierra Estado del tiempo y clima

4 ¿Con qué instrumento se mide la velocidad del viento? (ESS2.D)

(A) termómetro

(B) anemómetro

(C) veleta

(D) pluviómetro

5 ¿Por qué los científicos miden los cambios del estado del tiempo? (ESS2.D)

(A) para que puedan cambiar el estado del tiempo

(B) para saber exactamente cuánto lloverá mañana

(C) para determinar cuándo comenzará el verano

(D) para predecir qué tipo de estado del tiempo podría haber luego

6 ¿Para qué se usan los mapas del estado del tiempo? (ESS2.D)

(A) para predecir el estado del tiempo

(B) para cambiar el estado del tiempo

(C) para recopilar datos del estado del tiempo

(D) para medir datos del estado del tiempo

7 ¿Qué son las estaciones? (ESS2.D)

(A) un patrón de temperatura que aumenta

(B) cambios en el estado del tiempo de una semana a otra

(C) períodos lluviosos y cálidos que ocurren en diferentes lugares

(D) un patrón de cambios climáticos en un año

Ciencias de la Tierra Estado del tiempo y clima

8 **¿Cuál es la diferencia entre estado del tiempo y clima?** (ESS2.D)

(A) El estado del tiempo describe las condiciones del aire exterior en cierto momento y lugar. El clima es el patrón general del estado del tiempo en un área durante un período de tiempo largo.

(B) El estado del tiempo es el patrón general del tiempo en un área durante un largo período de tiempo. El clima describe las condiciones del aire exterior en cierto momento y lugar.

(C) El estado del tiempo describe los cambios con las estaciones. El clima son las condiciones del aire exterior en cierto momento y lugar.

(D) El clima describe las estaciones en cierto lugar. El estado del tiempo es el patrón de condiciones en un área durante un largo período de tiempo.

9 Estudia la gráfica de los datos de precipitaciones por estación en Charlottesville, Virginia. ¿Cuál opción es una interpretación correcta de los datos? (ESS2.D)

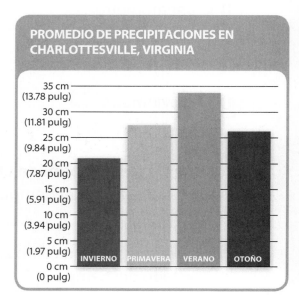

PROMEDIO DE PRECIPITACIONES EN CHARLOTTESVILLE, VIRGINIA

35 cm (13.78 pulg)
30 cm (11.81 pulg)
25 cm (9.84 pulg)
20 cm (7.87 pulg)
15 cm (5.91 pulg)
10 cm (3.94 pulg)
5 cm (1.97 pulg)
0 cm (0 pulg)

INVIERNO PRIMAVERA VERANO OTOÑO

(A) La primavera y el verano son las estaciones más lluviosas.

(B) El invierno y el otoño son las estaciones más lluviosas.

(C) El otoño es más lluvioso que el verano.

(D) La primavera es la más lluviosa.

Ciencias de la Tierra Estado del tiempo y clima

 10 Un día, Juanita tomó los siguientes registros de temperatura fuera de su salón de clases. ¿Qué podría predecir con los datos? (ESS2.D)

Hora	Temperatura
9:00 a.m.	9 °C
10:00 a.m.	11 °C
11:00 a.m.	13 °C
12:00 p.m.	16 °C

Ⓐ Es probable que el descenso de temperaturas traiga lluvia.

Ⓑ Es probable que la tarde sea más cálida y tal vez ella no necesite usar chaqueta.

Ⓒ La temperatura del aire probablemente suba 16 °C durante el día.

Ⓓ Es probable que la tarde sea más fresca y tal vez ella necesite usar chaqueta.

11 En la ciudad de Ted, cayeron 90 cm de nieve el invierno pasado. ¿Qué conclusión puedes sacar de estos datos? (ESS2.D)

Ⓐ Es improbable que el próximo año vuelva a nevar tanto.

Ⓑ Probablemente llovió mucho durante la primavera.

Ⓒ Su ciudad tiene un clima con inviernos fríos.

Ⓓ El clima de su ciudad se está volviendo más frío y lluvioso.

12 ¿Por qué son peligrosos los huracanes y las tormentas eléctricas? (ESS3.B)

Ⓐ Pueden causar inundaciones.

Ⓑ Los vientos fuertes pueden dañar árboles y edificios.

Ⓒ Pueden producir relámpagos.

Ⓓ Todas las anteriores

Ciencias de la Tierra Estado del tiempo y clima

13 **¿Qué parte de un huracán genera el impacto más peligroso?** (ESS3.B)

(A) las altas temperaturas

(B) las bajas temperaturas

(C) las inundaciones

(D) los relámpagos

14 **¿Cuál opción NO reduce el impacto de una inundación?** (ESS2.B)

(A) refugio para tormentas

(B) dique

(C) represa

(D) bolsas de arena

15 **¿Cómo funciona un dique?** (ESS3.B)

(A) Protege a las personas de los vientos fuertes de un huracán.

(B) Desacelera o detiene el agua que podría inundar un área.

(C) Absorbe agua más rápido que la velocidad con que el agua inunda un área.

(D) Da a las personas un lugar alto al que escapar en caso de inundación.

16 **¿Para cuál opción es más difícil prepararse y así reducir su impacto?** (ESS3.B)

(A) inundación

(B) relámpagos

(C) huracán

(D) tornado

Ciencias de la Tierra Estado del tiempo y clima

 ¿De qué manera un pararrayos ayuda a prevenir incendios y otros daños? (ESS3.B)

A Detiene el flujo de electricidad.

B Dirige la electricidad de forma segura al suelo.

C Usa la electricidad para potenciar los artefactos eléctricos.

D Hace que la electricidad rebote y vuelva a la nube.

 Sam oyó el trueno de un relámpago mientras estaba en la piscina. ¿Qué debe hacer? (ESS3.B)

A Ir a buscar un paraguas y esperar al lado de la piscina.

B Pararse al lado de un objeto más alto hasta que pase la tormenta.

C Ir adentro y alejarse de las ventanas, el agua y los aparatos electrónicos.

D Quedarse en el agua hasta que haya pasado la tormenta.

Answers to DCI Review Questions

Physical Science
Forces and Interactions

PS2.A: Forces and Motion

1.	A	5.	D	9.	A
2.	C	6.	B	10.	D
3.	B	7.	C		
4.	D	8.	B		

PS2.B: Types of Interactions

11.	C	15.	A	19.	C
12.	A	16.	C	20.	B
13.	C	17.	B	21.	C
14.	B	18.	D	22.	A

Answers to DCI Review Questions

Life Science
Interdependent Relationships in Ecosystems

LS2.C: Ecosystem Dynamics, Functioning, and Resilience

1. C
2. A
3. C
4. C
5. C
6. D
7. B
8. C

LS2.D: Social Interactions and Group Behavior

9. A
10. C
11. D
12. D

LS4.A: Evidence of Common Ancestry and Diversity

13. B
14. B
15. C
16. A
17. D

LS4.C: Adaptation

18. A
19. B
20. C

LS4.D: Biodiversity and Humans

21. C
22. A
23. C
24. B
25. D
26. D

Answers to DCI Review Questions

Inheritance and Variation of Traits: Life Cycles and Traits

LS1.B: Growth and Development of Organisms

1. C
2. A
3. D
4. A

LS3.A: Inheritance of Traits

5. D
6. C
7. A
8. C
9. B
10. A
11. D

LS3.B: Variation of Traits

12. C
13. C
14. B
15. B
16. B
17. B

LS4.B: Natural Selection

18. D
19. A
20. B
21. C

Answers to DCI Review Questions

Earth Science
Weather and Climate

ESS2.D: Weather and Climate

1.	D	5.	D	9.	A
2.	C	6.	A	10.	B
3.	C	7.	D	11.	C
4.	B	8.	A		

ESS3.B: Natural Hazards

12.	D	16.	D
13.	C	17.	B
14.	A	18.	C
15.	B		

Investigate

Salamander Life Cycle

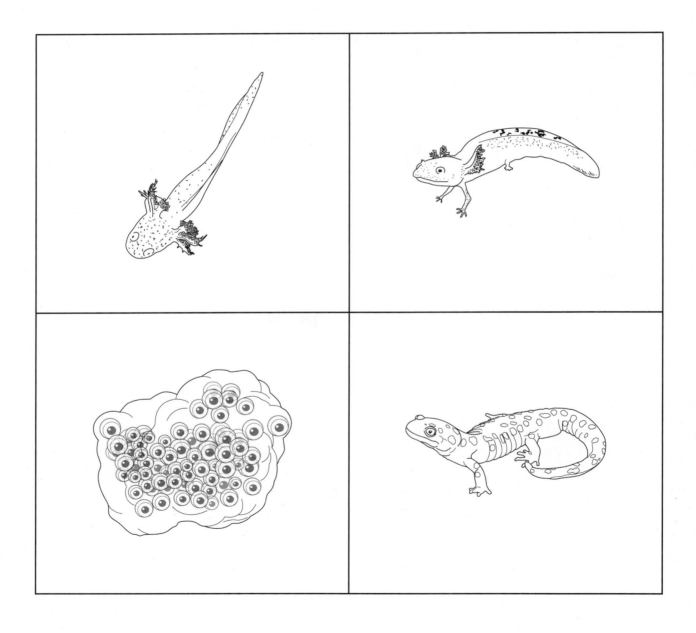

Investigación

Ciclo de vida de la salamandra

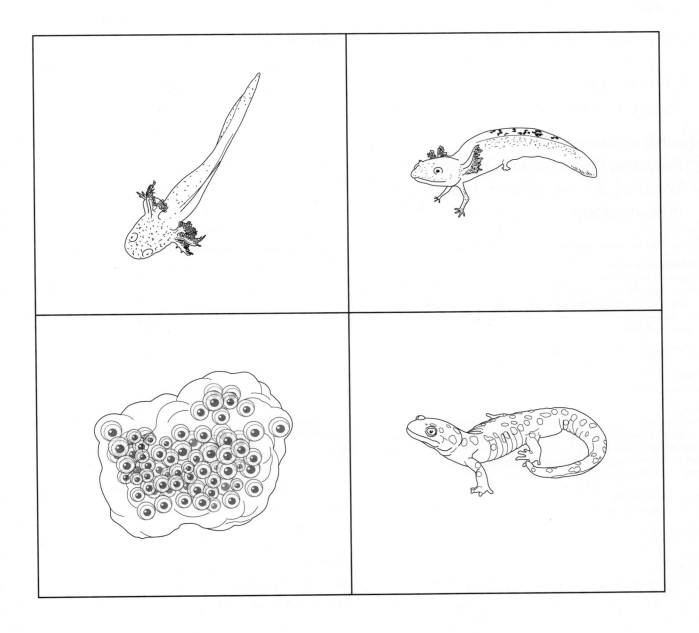

Program Authors

Randy L. Bell, Ph.D.
Associate Dean and Professor of Science Education, College of Education, Oregon State University

Malcolm B. Butler, Ph.D.
Associate Professor of Science Education, School of Teaching, Learning and Leadership, University of Central Florida

Kathy Cabe Trundle, Ph.D.
Department Head and Professor, STEM Education, North Carolina State University

Judith S. Lederman, Ph.D.
Associate Professor and Director of Teacher Education, Illinois Institute of Technology

Program Consultants

Gina Cervetti, Ph.D.
Assistant Professor of Literacy, Language, and Culture, University of Michigan

Nell K. Duke, Ed.D.
Professor of Literacy, Language, and Culture, University of Michigan

Philip E. Molebash, Ph.D.
Executive Director of the Center for Math and Science Teaching and Associate Professor, School of Education, Loyola Marymount University

Acknowledgments
Grateful acknowledgment is given to the authors, artists, photographers, museums, publishers, and agents for permission to reprint copyrighted material. Every effort has been made to secure the appropriate permission. If any omissions have been made or if corrections are required, please contact the Publisher.

NEXT GENERATION **SCIENCE** STANDARDS *For States, By States* is a registered trademark of Achieve. Neither Achieve nor the lead states and partners that developed the Next Generation Science Standards was involved in the production of, and does not endorse, this product.

Credits
150 (tr) ©National Geographic School Publishing. **159** (tl) ©National Geographic School Publishing, **159** (tr) ©Doug Lemke/Shutterstock.com, **169** (tl) ©BMJ/shutterstock.com, **169** (tr) ©DmitryND/iStockphoto.com. **170** (tr) ©Mapping Specialists/National Geographic School Publishing. **172** (tr) ©National Geographic Learning.

Illustration Credits
Unless otherwise indicated, all maps were created by Mapping Specialists.

For permission to use material from this text or product, submit all requests online at www.cengage.com/permissions

Further permissions questions can be emailed to permissionrequest@cengage.com

Visit National Geographic Learning online at NGL.Cengage.com

Visit our corporate website at www.cengage.com

Printed in the USA.

Globus Printing & Packaging, Inc.
Minster, Ohio, USA

ISBN: 978-13050-76938

15 16 17 18 19 20 21 22 23 24

10 9 8 7 6 5 4 3 2 1